THE SECRET EMPIRE BLACKROCK

First edition. October 20, 2024.

Copyright © 2024 Edward Branson.

ISBN: 979 8224105311

Written by Edward Branson.

Table of Contents

The Secret Empire BlackRock

Edward Branson

CHAPTER 1

BlackRock: The Most Powerful Multinational Yet Unknown to the Public

New York, May 2020. Never has the city that never sleeps been so quiet. Just a few weeks earlier, before the city mourned hundreds of victims per day and became the epicenter of the Covid-19 epidemic, planes still thundered over the city every five minutes. Now, the few passersby look up when a solitary plane crosses the sky to reach JFK or LaGuardia airport. Not so long ago, New Yorkers were still complaining about the millions of tourists who, with their heads thrown back, stared at the skyscrapers, thereby blocking the sidewalks. Now, Times Square seems deserted, and the lights of Broadway theaters have dimmed. At the southern tip of Manhattan stands the statue of the "Charging Bull," the bull supposed to represent the indomitable force of capitalism, alone on its central median. The large New York stock exchange, not far away, has been closed since March. At the opening of the stock exchange at 9:30 a.m. local time, only the concierge or the service technician is allowed to take turns on the deserted marble balcony of the trading floor to ring the world's most important bell. Trading continues within the 228-year-old institution, but now exclusively electronically. Banks and investment firms have drastically reduced the occupancy rate of their trading floors, moved a good portion of their traders to emergency sites, or simply sent them home. There, those who are nicknamed the "Masters of the Universe," who normally have at least four screens and sophisticated communication tools, have rigged up makeshift workstations, nicknamed "Rona Rigs," with only extension cords and their improvisational skills, like the trader who set up his laptop on an ironing board or his Texan colleague teleworking who, with his bottles of whiskey and guns, gives the whole setup a local flavor. It's almost hard to remember the time before the crisis.

Wall Street. Once an unavoidable stop for tourists in New York. A guide, already hoarse, led, not long ago, a group of Chinese people in front of the neoclassical facade of the New York Stock Exchange waving an umbrella, where teenagers from the American Midwest gathered, laughing around their annoyed teacher. Spanish, Japanese, German could be heard. Smartphones and iPads were constantly drawn, and selfies immediately posted. Here, presumed the visitors, stood the heart of our financial system, the most powerful institution of capitalism.

They were wrong.

The most powerful institution in our financial system is six kilometers north, five stops on the green subway line. It hides in one of the glass office towers lining the urban canyons of New York by the dozens, soaring into the sky. If you walk down this street in Midtown Manhattan, you will have to look very carefully around you to discover the name displayed above the revolving doors.

BlackRock.

The most powerful multinational in the world.

An institution like the world had never seen before.

BlackRock is an "asset manager." But to say that would be like saying that the Palace of Versailles is a summer residence or the Pyramids are a pile of tombstones. No major bank, no insurance company can match its influence. Goldman Sachs, Deutsche Bank, or Allianz seem insignificant in comparison. No government or central bank has as much information about the economy. But, above all: no one controls as much capital. On the eve of the Covid-19 crisis, the amount of funds managed by BlackRock amounted to 7.4 trillion dollars. 80 million Germans would have to work for two years to generate this sum. And that's not all. Over 20 trillion dollars pass through the company's analysis and trading platforms. That's a number with thirteen zeros: $20,000,000,000,000 (see Appendix 1, p. 405). This means that more than 5% of all global financial instruments – stocks, bonds, currencies, letters of credit, derivatives, and certificates – pass through the systems of a single company: BlackRock.

From its mundane office tower in Midtown, BlackRock weaves its web across the globe. Like an octopus, the company has spread its tentacles into every corner of the world. Americans are active in a hundred countries. BlackRock's network includes offices in Bogota, Brisbane, and Budapest, branches in Munich, Melbourne, Montreal, but also in Cape Town, Kuala Lumpur, and Copenhagen.

Representatives of BlackRock come and go in finance ministries. They advise the US Federal Reserve (Fed) and the European Central Bank (ECB). Among their clients are the Californian CalPERS, the largest US pension fund weighing 300 billion dollars, as well as the Abu Dhabi Investment Authority, the sovereign fund of the glittering oil kingdom of Dubai, and the investment branch of Singapore. BlackRock lobbyists charm regulators in Washington as well as in Brussels. BlackRock is a major shareholder in JPMorgan Chase, Citigroup, and Bank of America – the largest banks in the world. BlackRock is also one of the largest shareholders of oil giants ExxonMobil and Chevron. As well as Apple, McDonald's, and the Swiss group Nestlé. New Yorkers are also the largest owners of the "Deutschland AG". They hold shares in all DAX-listed companies. They are equally involved in the largest German construction group Hochtief, as well as in its smaller rival, Bilfinger. BlackRock holds shares in Airbus, the European aviation and aerospace giant, as well as in Core Civic, the leading manager of penitentiary facilities in the United States. Since February 2020, it has been one of the main shareholders of the Bayer group and its subsidiary Monsanto, acquired in 2016, as well as of the arms giants Raytheon, Lockheed Martin, and General Dynamics, all involved in equipping US drones and missiles.

The company also owns real estate throughout Germany. And while iShares, the provider of popular "Exchange Traded Funds" (ETFs), is well known and appreciated by small investors, few people know that it is also part of the BlackRock empire. In 2019, the capital invested in iShares exceeded 2 trillion dollars. iShares reported net inflows of 185 billion dollars and a global market share of 33%, as stated in one of their press releases. "iShares has thus established itself as the leading provider of ETFs."

On the eve of the declines caused by the 2020 pandemic, the number of countries where BlackRock managed more than 1 billion dollars in assets for its private clients was more than forty.

BlackRock is also involved in currency and commodity markets. When miners extract iron ore in Brazil or work hard in the gold mines of Mali, at the other end of the chain, it is BlackRock that benefits. Descendant of an influential British banking family, Evy Hambro has been responsible for commodity investments at BlackRock for over twenty-two years. He manages, among others, the BlackRock World Mining Trust Fund. In 2019, Australian Olivia Markham became Hambro's co-manager. She began her career at BHP Billiton, an Australian-British mining conglomerate. When Hambro speaks, as reported by the Sydney Morning Herald, CEOs and boards of directors of the world's most powerful commodity companies not only listen, they act accordingly. The fund holds significant stakes in BHP Billiton and its rival Rio Tinto, in gold producer Barrick, and in Anglo American plc, which controls 40% of platinum production. Until at least December 31, 2019, the portfolio also included Vale, the mining company responsible for the dam collapse in Brumadinho, Brazil in January 2019, which resulted in the loss of two hundred and seventy lives. An internal investigation showed that the company had apparently been experiencing problems with the dam for years. In any case, the major mining companies and commodity manufacturers, these giants that supply virtually the entire global economy with raw materials and precious metals, are thus grouped together in BlackRock funds. "In a country where major mining companies are accused of controlling the government, it is interesting to see the influence that Hambro wields," wrote the Sydney Morning Herald in 2013 in a portrait of the BlackRock fund manager. And the Australian journalists wondered: who is pulling the strings behind the scenes?

There is no major conflict in the world that does not affect the interests of the New York firm. Take, for example, Russia's attack on Ukraine in 2014. Curiously, BlackRock's interests suddenly aligned with those of Vladimir Putin. Admittedly, Larry Fink, the CEO of BlackRock, publicly criticized Moscow's strongman. He said in an interview with the London Sunday

Times in March 2014 that Putin could not "play" like this if he wanted Western capital. He also pointed out that the Moscow Stock Exchange had fallen due to capital outflows by foreign investors. "Capital markets have destroyed Russia," he said at the time. This could have been interpreted as a threat that BlackRock would also withdraw from Russia. However, despite the events in Ukraine, BlackRock remained committed to the country. As of March 31, 2020, the ten largest investments of the Emerging Europe Fund (a BlackRock investment fund) included the top two Russian energy companies, Gazprom and Lukoil, as well as Tatneft, founded by the Soviet-era Ministry of Oil. The company extracts oil, among other things, in war-torn Syria. The list of top investments in the fund's portfolio also includes Sberbank, 50% owned by the Russian Central Bank. Until March 2020 – six years after Putin's invasion of Crimea – the Emerging Europe Fund had invested nearly 60% of its investment capital in Russia. BlackRock was also a partner in the Russian Direct Investment Fund (RDIF). This partnership, for example, led to a $50 million investment in a chain of private clinics. In 2015, the RDIF was at the center of a political and financial scandal for lending the handsome sum of $1.75 billion to the petrochemical giant Sibur at rates, according to a Reuters report, lower than the rates generally practiced at the time. Guennadi Timtcheko, one of Sibur's main shareholders at the time, is a close circle of Putin's inner circle, to which the United States has imposed sanctions. Another confidant of Putin's, Kirill Shamalov, whose son-in-law married Putin's youngest daughter in 2013, was also one of the owners of Sibur. According to information from both Western and Russian media, Shamalov Junior is the man who married Vladimir Putin's youngest daughter in 2013.

Or take Saudi Arabia. On October 2, 2018, Jamal Khashoggi entered the Saudi embassy in Istanbul. The Saudi citizen, journalist, and critic of the dynasty, who had been living in exile in the United States for some time, wanted to retrieve documents from the embassy for his imminent marriage to a Turkish citizen. He was brutally murdered by Saudi agents. A UN investigation later concluded that Khashoggi was the victim of "a premeditated extrajudicial execution, for which Saudi Arabia is responsible." Riyadh has denied to this day that the crime was committed by officials, or even by Crown Prince Mohammed bin Salman (known as MBS). Initially, Western multinational leaders said they were deeply shocked, and the investment summit, to which MBS had invited the cream of the international finance and business world, was a flop. BlackRock boss Larry Fink boycotted the meeting.

But barely seven months later, Fink was leading a roundtable with the Saudi finance minister in Riyadh. "The fact that a place is criticized in the press does not mean that I should flee from it," he explained to CNBC journalists who came to interview him. "Often, it is what convinces me that this is where I have to go and invest, because what scares us the most are the things we don't talk about," he added, whatever that may mean. He also praised the "quite impressive" progress the country had allegedly made. The day before, the regime had executed thirty-seven alleged terrorists. Since then, BlackRock has opened a branch in Riyadh. And when Saudi Aramco, the state-owned oil company and main economic pillar of MBS, issued bonds worth $12 billion in April 2019, BlackRock was among the largest investors.

One thing is certain: virtually no major economic transaction takes place without the New York finance lords being at least informed.

Voluntarily Under the Radar

However, only very attentive readers of financial pages know this giant. Larry Fink, founder and CEO of BlackRock, is known to only a few people outside of Wall Street. Despite its enormous size and unprecedented influence, the company has managed to stay well under the public radar. Intentionally.

While the investment bank Goldman Sachs built a palace overlooking the Hudson River by star architect Henry Cobb for $2.1 billion and the Bank of America resides in a fifty-five-story tower with all the modern technological refinements near Times Square in Manhattan, BlackRock has deliberately deprived itself of flashy offices.

Upon entering the firm's headquarters in New York, you will find a Starbucks café and a newsstand in the publicly accessible lobby, which also sells lottery tickets and chewing gum. An artificial waterfall flows discreetly behind bamboo bushes. Men in dark suits, whose falsely discreet appearance immediately betrays their role as security guards, watch with suspicion over the homeless people sitting at the tables next to the café.

On the second floor, there is also no indication of the importance of BlackRock. The reception counter is shared with that of the investment bank Evercore. The only visible luxury is a white orchid in a pot, placed on the BlackRock side. No works of art and marble as in other financial giants trying to impress their visitors.

That said, the people at BlackRock don't need to show off with bling-bling behavior. Wall Street is afraid of them. Because Larry Fink and his men can decide who advances in their career as an investment banker and who must continue their professional life by scratching paper somewhere in the back rooms of finance. Because BlackRock is not only a co-owner of large financial institutions through shares held as an asset manager, but also the number one client of bankers. "If, for some reason, BlackRock no longer wanted to do business with Goldman Sachs, it would be a problem... for Goldman," explains a Wall Street veteran who, like so many others in the industry, only speaks anonymously. Another informant suddenly backs down. He had received a job offer from BlackRock. Therefore, he is not comfortable commenting publicly on their business practices. In fact, he no longer wants to talk about BlackRock at all. When we asked him what position he would have there, the seasoned banker replied, "Whatever Larry offers me, even if I have to scrub the cafeteria floor."

At cocktail parties, investment bankers respond to questions about BlackRock with a look full of innuendo and remark that there would be much to say, but they prefer not to make it public. What they do not say but, I imagine, certainly think: "I have a villa in the suburbs that is not yet paid off, children in private school, and a family with a high standard of living to maintain." Every year, banks and brokerage firms receive hundreds of millions of dollars from BlackRock. Who would want to tarnish their relationship with such a partner?

The Power of BlackRock is Borrowed: It's Our Money

Despite all its power, BlackRock is a newcomer. The history of JPMorgan Chase, the largest American bank, dates back to 1895 and the legend of finance John Pierpont Morgan. The City Bank of New York (now Citigroup) was founded in 1812 and later financed the Panama Canal. The Bank of New York Mellon, one of the world's largest trust banks, can even boast the legacy of founding father Alexander Hamilton, the first Secretary of the Treasury of the young nation and inventor of American capitalism. Fink, on the other hand, built his empire in just over three decades. A start-up, literally founded in the back office of the Blackstone investment fund. In 1988, the founders of the latter, Stephen Schwarzman and Pete Peterson, granted Larry Fink a $5 million line of credit – pocket money, by Wall Street standards – and a phone line. From this fledgling enterprise emerged BlackRock. A success that gives Fink the status of absolute champion among Wall Street's toughest bosses. And that's apparently how he sees himself too. When CNBC journalist Becky Quick asked him in 2010 what his biggest mistake had been, Fink replied that after leaving First Boston, he "didn't have enough confidence to start his own risk management investment firm." Instead, he turned to Schwarzman and Peterson. "They believed more in me than I did. They made the right investment decision, not me." That's it, Dealbreaker, the Wall Street gossip site, quipped, Schwarzman and Peterson made the right decision because they recognized Fink's genius, which he himself hadn't recognized, the "golden god" looking back at him in the mirror.

However, BlackRock's power is borrowed power: it is fueled by our money, the money of small savers, retirees, corporate financial services, insurance premiums, private pension fund contributions, charitable donations, and taxpayer dollars. "OPM": that's what Wall Street prefers to play with. In plain terms: Other People's Money, other people's money. This money pours into ever larger pools. And BlackRock is not the only company benefiting from this. According to a study by the consultancy PricewaterhouseCoopers, by 2025, asset managers will have accumulated over $145 trillion in their accounts worldwide. That's thirty-eight times more than Germany's gross domestic product (GDP) ($3.8 trillion in 2019, according to the IMF) and fifty-three times more than France's ($2.7 trillion in 2019). Money that will mainly come from the United States and Europe, but also increasingly from Asia, Africa, and the Middle East. Larry Fink and his men want to ensure that the majority of these funds end up in their company. In 2014, Fink announced an ambitious goal to his employees: BlackRock would have to grow an additional 5% each year. His company is the absolute leader in the sector with over $7 trillion. Allianz, which is still Germany's largest financial group, is far behind with $2 trillion.

It's our money. Yet, only insiders know where it goes, what it sets in motion, or who it pays. Wall Street people, as cynical and jaded as they may be, distinguish between "smart money" and "dumb money" – the latter too often referring to ordinary investors. There is a reason for these terms. We entrust our savings to BlackRock and its cohorts in exchange for a promise of return and security – without really asking what will happen. Intimidated by a financial system that seems too complicated and perhaps too boring, we, ordinary citizens, do not make the effort to try to understand the processes at play. As for them, they have no reason to inform us.

As a result, almost no one knows precisely what happens to these capital flows. What is even more serious is that no one knows what risks lurk behind such a mountain of capital, not even financial experts from universities or regulatory authorities. And certainly not politicians. Hence Fink's argument: if you can't identify a risk, then there simply isn't one. Yet, history has shown that the truly dangerous risks are those that cannot be foreseen, dangers that cannot even be imagined. "T.B.D.," which stands for "There Be Dragons," a way for risk managers to say that beyond conceivable probabilities lie real dangers.

The story of BlackRock is the story of a power shift on Wall Street. It is the story of a brilliant chess player. The story of a humiliated man who erected the greatest colossus in the history of finance.

It's a story in which we all involuntarily participate. At least, up to now.

CHAPTER 2

The New Owner of Deutschland AG

The Hessian country estate where we find ourselves has met the same fate as many homes once owned by the nobility: it has become a hotel and conference center. Groups in business suits gather in wood-paneled galleries. They sip espressos and "telecommute." Signs announce the day's events, covering topics such as "Europe, More Than the Sum of Its Parts" or "Investing in a Low-Interest Environment." The majority of the audience consists of representatives from small and medium-sized banks and savings banks from all over Germany. University professors' presentations give the event the appropriate solemnity. It's the equivalent of a public fair for carpet sellers for funders. The goal: to promote their activity and products. The BlackRock representative is British. He doesn't hide the fact that he feels provincial. "The first thing you'll notice is that I speak English," he says to greet a stunned participant. "There is no safe return," he warns his listeners. Therefore, he implies, it is all the more important to partner with a strong international partner. BlackRock is known to be the largest asset manager. The Londoner explains to the assembly the superiority of "multi-asset managers," those asset managers who are not fixed on stocks or bonds but who place their investors' money in various securities, depending on what they find attractive. The BlackRock man is also one of those finance jack-of-all-trades. He is experienced. The fact that the representatives of banks and savings banks present do not ask him any questions does not seem to bother him. His message is clear: the world is complex, very risky. BlackRock is big and efficient. When he is done, all the participants thank him politely.

Later, in the evening, between a glass of Grauburgunder and small hake pastries – in an exclusive atmosphere – one of the German investment advisors expresses his dissatisfaction. BlackRock has almost taken over the whole of Germany. "Look, if BlackRock withdraws from the DAX, from the MDAX, it goes phew," he says, tracing a steep downward curve with his hand. Wherever you look in the country, BlackRock is everywhere.

Without this being publicly known, the most important firms in Germany now have a new major owner. DAX companies have long been in the hands of foreign investors. These now represent 85% of the float, according to a 2019 study by DIRK (Deutscher Investor Relation Verband) in collaboration with American researchers from IHS Markit – a figure that has remained stable for several years. Nearly a third of this is held by North American funds. German investors – both private and institutional – only hold 15% of it. In principle, we are pleased with the interest of foreign investors in German heavyweights, assures Norbert Kuhn of the Deutsches Aktieninstitut, the interest group for companies focused on the capital market, before regretting one thing: "German shareholders have largely missed out on the success of our DAX companies in recent years."

BlackRock is the largest investor in the DAX, the stock index of the thirty largest German listed companies. The firm's stake, through various funds, in DAX companies amounts to $66 billion. BlackRock is clearly number one.

A Silent Partner in the Daily Lives of Germans

Let's take an ordinary day in the life of an average consumer family. At breakfast, the parents prepare Nespresso, a coffee brand owned by the Swiss multinational Nestlé, of which BlackRock is one of the major shareholders. The father spreads Sana margarine on his bread, produced by Walter Rau. The former family-owned business in the Teutoburg Forest was taken over by the American multinational Bunge. With over 4% in February 2020, BlackRock is one of the top ten shareholders of Bunge. Meanwhile, the son eats his Kellogg's cornflakes – BlackRock's stake in the American cereal producer was at least 7% as of December 31, 2019. The daughter styles her hair with Elnett Satin Extra Strong hairspray, a product of the French group L'Oréal. According to their own figures, the world's leading cosmetic company sells around fifty products per second worldwide – and BlackRock benefits from this, being one of the top ten shareholders. Under the table, the cat chews on its portion of Hills Pet food. The pet food manufacturer is part of the Colgate-Palmolive group, a multinational consumer goods company of which BlackRock is also a major shareholder. The game can go on endlessly. In the bathroom, for example: Nivea cream and Tempo tissues? New Yorkers are just as involved in Beiersdorf, the manufacturer, as they are in the Dutch group Unilever, which produces, among other things, Rexona and Axe deodorants. Got a foot fungus? Lamisil ointment is produced by Novartis, a Swiss pharmaceutical giant in which BlackRock is also a leading investor. The father's Hugo Boss suit? According to a January 2020 report, BlackRock holds 3.23% of the fashion designer. The BMW 3 Series he drives to work? The Bavarian car manufacturer is held by BlackRock at around 3%. The red traffic light he stops at is made by Siemens. BlackRock is also present there, with over 5% (as of January 2020). And the Smart car his wife drives is made by the competition in Stuttgart. BlackRock is also one of the top shareholders of Daimler (4.5%). When the kids play sports, they wear Adidas sneakers – of which BlackRock is a 6% shareholder (as of January

2020). When they turn on the television after doing their homework (or instead of doing it), they watch the ProSieben channel, and BlackRock is in the background, at least as a shareholder (3.57% as of January 2020).

Present in the media, chemistry, energy, banking, or insurance, there are only a few branches in Europe where BlackRock does not have a stake. Sometimes it goes through a subsidiary, like BlackRock Holdco, based in Wilmington, the American epicenter of shell companies in the state of Delaware, or via BR Jersey International Holding LP, based in Saint Helier, on the island of Jersey, known as a tax haven. Such constructions, devised by savvy tax lawyers, are common in international finance and are by no means secret. They are now part of normal business practices, so BlackRock's clients would be somewhat surprised if the asset manager refrained from such arrangements. Asked about this, BlackRock explains that companies are indeed located in tax havens because the "local legislation and legal infrastructure [are] well-designed and flexible enough to meet [its] business requirements." In addition, BlackRock pays taxes resulting from its European transactions in each European country concerned, regardless of the intermediary companies involved. In order to make ownership conditions more transparent, the Federal Financial Supervisory Authority – a German state institution known by the acronym BaFin – stipulates that large investors whose voting rights exceed certain thresholds must publicly declare them. However, this is only a snapshot, and among insiders, it is an open secret that investors often hold much larger stakes. "For example, the investor declares an exceedance of the 5% threshold, but can then buy up to an additional 10%," reports a specialist from a data provider analyzing such data. It is only when this additional 10% threshold is exceeded that the investor must report it to BaFin. However, BlackRock had to face BaFin due to mandatory disclosures. The regulations are hardly comprehensible, even for professionals. Many investors have gone bankrupt because of the voting rights regime, admits even a official from the federal authority. However, BlackRock would be "quite unique from a quantitative perspective." This certainly explains why the official review process took more than a year and concluded in spring 2015 with a fine of €3.25 million – the "highest fine imposed to date," as indicated in BaFin's press release. In the fall of 2014, BlackRock publicly announced that it would correct the mandatory reports of forty-eight companies, in coordination with the regulatory authority. These reports provide an overview of BlackRock's involvement in the German economy. In addition to the aforementioned companies, investments are made in energy sector conglomerates RWE and E.ON, Lufthansa, Deutsche Telekom, and Deutsche Post. In Bayer and BASF. In tire manufacturer Continental in Lower Saxony. In software design giant SAP. In Deutsche Bank, Allianz, and reinsurer Munich Re – the remaining core of the German financial industry. BlackRock is also the number one shareholder in Switzerland, as shown by an analysis by the Swiss Ministry of Economic Affairs in 2019. In addition to Nestlé, New Yorkers own shares – typically around 3% – in the Winterthur-based industrial group Sulzer, insurer Swiss Life, major banks UBS and Credit Suisse, as well as chocolate manufacturer Lindt & Sprüngli AG. BlackRock would be the "black rock" in the storm of the Swiss stock index SMI, according to the metaphorical wording of the Swiss daily Neue Zürcher Zeitung.

The number of shares held by BlackRock varies – sometimes daily. Just on December 3, 2019, four companies – Morphosys, Wirecard, Munich Re, and Daimler – announced a change in the number of voting rights held by BlackRock. In the case of Morphosys, a German biotechnology company, Wirecard, a financial technology provider that went bankrupt in 2020, and Munich Re, it is an increase of 1%. At Daimler, the stake decreased, but by less than one point, according to dgap.de. This is very rarely a strategy because BlackRock acts as an intermediary: as an asset manager, the company collects money from investors and invests it for them. If so-called "active" fund managers decide which stocks they want to invest the entrusted money in, the majority of BlackRock's investment funds follow stock indices, such as the DAX. Such a "passive" fund therefore necessarily contains stocks of the thirty companies in the German stock index. In this case, no fund manager decides for or against a stock. And if BlackRock's clients sell their shares, the shares BlackRock holds in the DAX will also decrease. Conversely, BlackRock's investment increases when investors put new capital into index funds. In most large index funds such as the DAX, the stocks usually remain quite stable.

However, the fact that BlackRock cannot control the inflows does not mean that the fund manager has no influence on the companies. On the contrary. It is precisely because BlackRock is obliged to hold shares in the company due to its link with the index that the New Yorkers are among its long-term shareholders. Shareholders whose board of directors therefore take more into account the interests and whom they would do well not to antagonize. At first glance, the shares held by BlackRock, from 3 to 5%, do not seem high. What do 61,365,875 voting rights out of a total of 1,069,837,447 issued shares giving a right to vote represent? A lot, as most other shareholders receive much fewer votes. Take, for example, a start-up manufacturing plastic bath ducks. Ownership is divided into twenty shares. They belong to seventeen shareholders. Sixteen of them own only one share, the remaining four are held by a certain BR. Even if BR does not have the majority with four shares, not even a quarter of the total, he still owns more shares than each of the others. Imagine that BR prefers the ducks to be black rather than yellow. There is every reason to believe that the founder of the start-up will consider changing the color.

The king of the German housing market...

BlackRock has not only invested in German companies and stocks. Its portfolio also includes real estate. In a way, BlackRock has become one of the largest property owners in Germany, even if this has been done indirectly. Most of the 20 million rental apartments in Germany counted by the Federal Statistical Office (equivalent to INSEE) in 2014 are still owned by small private owners, at the local level. For a long time, this made it difficult for large investors to invest in German real estate: the operation would have been too costly and too fragmented. This changed under the government of Helmut Kohl, who, in the early 1990s, abolished the non-profit status of municipal apartments, as well as cooperative and corporate apartments. Until then, non-profit housing companies were exempt from corporate, trade, and property taxes. After the abolition of this tax advantage in the early 2000s, municipalities, states, and companies began to sell their real estate holdings. Kohl's successor, Gerhard Schröder, strengthened the trend by abolishing the capital gains tax (we will come back to this). American and British private equity firms (dubbed "locusts" in Germany) were only too happy to buy them on a large scale. The housing stock of the former trade union group Neue Heimat, involved in scandals, later became Baubecon, and the GSW real estate company in Berlin were merged by Blackstone under the name Deutsche Wohnen AG. The German real estate company Deutsche Annington built the London-based private equity firm Terra Firma, among others, from former railway and German energy company housing, E.ON and RWE. Fortress, the New York competitor, used the Federal Office for Employee Insurance (BfA) housing stock, the municipal housing company Nileg in Hanover, and the Dresden-based real estate company Woba, which it merged to form the Gagfah group. At the end of 2014, Gagfah and Deutsche Annington merged to form a giant: the new company owns four hundred thousand apartments in more than four hundred locations. Over a million tenants live under its roofs. There has never been an owner of this size in Germany. This housing giant is also present in Sweden and Austria.

But the concept of private housing groups quickly acquired a bad reputation. New owners such as Fortress, Terra, and Blackstone "polished the balance sheets and let the houses deteriorate," as summarized by the German weekly business magazine Wirtschaftswoche. After the change of ownership, the number of tenant complaints increased. In 2012, tenants of apartments owned by Gagfah in the Wilhelmsburg district of Hamburg submitted a long list of failures to the then city development senator, Jutta Blankau, complaining of poorly insulated windows, walls, and roofs, deteriorating staircases, non-functioning elevators, dilapidated balconies, and run-down outdoor facilities. Apparently, this is not an exception. "The staircases are rotting, repairs are neglected," complains a tenant of the Goldstein settlement in Frankfurt, once an annex for postal workers. Another resident reports that the heating does not work properly and the elevator has been out of order for weeks. The journalist points out that the insults of a snack bar owner against the real estate company, which was then called Annington, could not be quoted. The company rejected the criticism. With 14 euros per square meter of living space invested in renovation in 2011 alone, it is stated in the article that it would be above the German average. In a report by the German radio WDR about a settlement owned by Annington in Bonn, there is talk of mold, opaque service bills, and rent increases. The red-green coalition government of the state of North Rhine-Westphalia even emphasized that housing for Hartz IV beneficiaries was deliberately neglected - under the pretext that the employment agencies would pay anyway, regardless of their condition. A maneuver that the state government did not hesitate to describe as a "Hartz IV economic model". When asked by WDR radio, the real estate company, however, stated that "the company advocates a sustainable, long-term strategy that prioritizes both customer care and real estate management." Its mission would be to "step by step correct the mistakes of the past," it further stated through its CEO Rolf Buch, in an interview tinged with self-criticism. The Gagfah company also solemnly promised improvements and announced investments as well as renovations.

This may not have been entirely voluntary. Referring to internal documents from 2013 proving that the company had accumulated a backlog in its "maintenance order book" amounting to 161 million euros, risking "harming its reputation." Such an amount would be needed to tackle embarrassing cases of mold, repair roofs, and heating systems. According to Stern magazine, Annington's board of directors was concerned about the "transition from local media coverage to national media coverage." In other words: there were too many critical headlines for the managers' taste. The company told Stern journalists that the "board of directors itself increased the maintenance budget without the approval of the supervisory board."

In 2015, Deutsche Annington changed its name. A name without history, but with a ring: Vonovia. "The brand positioning is based on our new design and corporate vision. By deliberately choosing a single word as a logo and dispensing with additional elements, we want to express what we want to focus on: our customers," explained Rolf Buch, CEO of Vonovia. But complaints remained. In March 2019, the Frankfurter Rundschau newspaper reported on the high costs of winter maintenance in Vonovia properties. For example, the newspaper reported that the large owner charged 519 euros in 2016 just for the winter maintenance of a 54-square-meter apartment in Kronberg. That's a cost of 80 cents per square meter per month. In Frankfurt, there are only 4 cents per square meter per month, according to Rolf Janßen, president of the local tenants' protection association. He described Vonovia's approach as "cheeky," and Vonovia had little to say to the newspaper. They would only have charged for services that could be verified and negotiated usual prices for their customers. In a contentious discussion with a tenants' association in East Westphalia at the beginning of February 2020, Vonovia's representative was defensive. The tenants' association described a renovation that resulted in a monthly surcharge of over 90 euros for the tenant - on top of a rent of 355 euros. Accused by one of the discussion participants of only seeking profits for the shareholders, the housing manager retorted, "We are not bandits driving bulldozers." In other words, the company would be aware of its social responsibility.

It is no coincidence that the managers of the housing giant are concerned about their reputation and publicly promise improvement. Something has changed: the "locusts" have harvested and flown away. Terra Firma took Deutsche Annington public as early as 2013. That same year, the investment company Blackstone did the same for Deutsche Wohnen AG. Fortress had cashed out its investment in the stock market much earlier: Gagfah had been listed since 2006 when it was taken over by Annington. While the private equity firms packed up, major international investors entered the newly hatched public companies. In addition to the Norwegian pension fund Norges Bank Investment Management, these include the American fund provider Fidelity and its Boston competitor, Massachusetts Financial Services MFS, but also - last but not least - BlackRock. According to the company, the New Yorkers held more than 7% of Vonovia, over 10% of Deutsche Wohnen, and 7.5% of the real estate company LEG, which bought the real estate portfolio of the state of North Rhine-Westphalia during its privatization, in February 2020.

For the new owners, the investment is only profitable if the share price and dividend increase sustainably. This by no means implies that they do not pay attention to profitability. Mergers in the industry have led to significant staff reductions and organizational changes. At the beginning of 2014, Deutsche Wohnen acquired the Berlin-based real estate company GSW, whose real estate portfolio at the time included sixty thousand apartments, in which nearly one hundred twenty thousand people lived. After the takeover, the new owner laid off nearly half of the three hundred twenty employees. The takeover was paying off for the real estate company, the German business daily Handelsblatt estimated in May 2014. The profit from rentals, which is crucial for real estate companies, had almost doubled in the first quarter to 59.1 million euros. Rent increases of 4.2% contributed to this significant profit increase, among other things. In November 2019, the Berliner Morgenpost announced that rental income continued to grow. In the first nine months, Deutsche Wohnen's operating profit increased by 12.8% compared to the previous year, reaching 416.3 million euros. "The competitor of Vonovia [Deutsche Wohnen], LEG Immobilien and TAG Immobilien have confirmed these outlooks for 2019," the Morgenpost informs us. BlackRock also holds a 6% stake in TAG Immobilien, whose motto is, according to its English website: We make room for profitability.

It is unlikely that BlackRock regrets entering the housing market. For tenants, this profit-increasing method is certainly less joyful. The protest movement Deutsche Wohnen & Co. enteignen ("Expropriate Deutsche Wohnen and company") shows how great the distress is on the housing market. Just a few years ago, its demand to expropriate real estate groups would not have been taken seriously, considered leftist. But during the summer of 2019, activists collected more than 77,000 supporting signatures. They demand that the law against rent increases, introduced in 2015 already, be not only extended until 2025 but also strengthened. Where this law applies, a landlord is generally only allowed to charge 10% more than the standard local rent. This measure helps to slow down the increase in rents, especially in urban areas.

The misery in the housing market has also shed light on the investor behind the major landlords, but not in a positive way. "Real estate developers buy cheap, let tenants pay for renovations, use tax havens, and all sorts of imaginable dirty tricks," critic Werner Rügemer lashes out in the pages of the weekly Der Freitag. He holds "capital organizers" like BlackRock partly responsible. Fans of the 1. FC Union Berlin football club were upset when they learned in 2019, after the team's promotion to the Bundesliga, that the new main sponsor was the Luxembourg-based real estate company Aroundtown SA. Besides commercial real estate, this firm is also involved in residential real estate through its stake in the company Grand City Properties SA, which owns nearly eighty-four thousand apartments throughout Germany, including seven thousand five hundred in Berlin. About a third of these are located in the Treptow-Köpenick district, near the FC Union Berlin football club, according to the German channel RBB. And "the second-largest shareholder of Aroundtown is the controversial asset manager BlackRock." In an interview with the Tagesspiegel, Christian Beeck, a former sports director, stated that this was a problem for a club that fundamentally espouses the anti-commercial values of amateur football. "1. FC Union Berlin is trying to establish itself in professional football. And that's not just done by selling beer and sausages," responded the club's spokesman to the criticism. So, BlackRock also plays a role in the world's most popular sport.

... but also in commercial real estate with the lion's share of the pie

The city of Freising in Bavaria was once a ducal palace, then a center for scholars and the seat of a diocese. Emperor Otto III granted it mercantile rights in 996. It is the "oldest city between Regensburg and Bolzano," as claimed by the city's website for its 46,000 inhabitants. It was severely damaged during the war. In recent years, it has struggled to revive its historic center. Its official motto: "The city center is the heart and soul of a city. Urban planners, politicians, and citizens work hand in hand." But urban planners have rather fought with the owners of one of the largest plots in the center. The "best part of the pie" in the area, according to a report from January 2014 in the Süddeutsche Zeitung. The building on Angerbadergasse street had formerly belonged to Aldi. The discount supermarket chain sold it to an investor, along with other properties. In early 2014, as reported by the Süddeutsche Zeitung, the building was vacant. The city of Freising had wanted to buy the property from the chain and believed it had a right of first refusal. But despite several attempts – including, ultimately, in court – Freising failed. The building became the property of a new investor: BlackRock. Asked what they were going to do with this "gem," the company remained silent at first. The building remained unused for over two years. And so the city's plans remained uncertain. Later, the New Yorkers sold it to the Munich-based real estate investor GIG, who in turn sold it in 2016. In the summer of 2019 – five years after Aldi closed – an Edeka supermarket finally opened on Angerbadergasse street.

In the Bamlerstraße shopping center in the city of Essen, BlackRock was quicker. The bulldozers arrived there in mid-2014. They demolished an Aldi supermarket. The shopping center, ideally located on the A4 towards Bottrop, had been out of fashion for years. The new owner had plans for a complete renovation. In this case, it was BlackRock that sent the bulldozers, as the Kaufpark Bamlerstraße was also part of the giant's real estate portfolio. In February 2017, BlackRock sold the Bamlerstraße shopping center to the Hahn Group for 36 million euros.

These are just two examples of BlackRock's involvement in commercial real estate. In 2013, the New Yorkers acquired a portfolio of a hundred properties throughout Germany by acquiring a company named MGPA. This company was previously the real estate subsidiary of the Australian investment bank Macquarie. MGPA was attractive to BlackRock because it had been one of the most active real estate buyers in Europe and Asia in the previous years. Before its acquisition, MGPA had acquired a portfolio of over $23 billion. Germany, too, was increasingly in its sights in recent years. In 2010, MGPA pulled off a coup: it took over subsidiaries, plots, and a logistics center from Aldi, totaling about a hundred and forty real estate properties. The parties agreed not to disclose the purchase price. In 2012, MGPA did it again by acquiring three neighborhood centers, a commercial park, a hypermarket, and six specialty stores. Among the tenants were the who's who of German supermarkets: Edeka, Rewe, Penny, and Aldi. After the transaction, MGPA's portfolio in Germany included a hundred and seventy-five real estate properties with a total rental area of 340,000 square meters. One of the properties was the Kaufpark Bamlerstraße. A few months later, MGPA itself was taken over: BlackRock bought the real estate specialist for an undisclosed price.

And BlackRock's interest in commercial real estate does not seem to have waned. In April 2018, BlackRock launched the Eurozone Core Property Fund. The fund aims for "high-quality, profit-oriented investments in the eurozone and countries with currencies pegged to the euro," according to the press release. This includes office spaces in Paris, Munich, and Hamburg, as well as commercial properties in Copenhagen. "The primary goal of our investment approach is to ensure stable returns for investors, combined with long-term potential," said fund manager Ian Williamson.

A ghost wanders among us: the invisible super-investor

Despite all the investments and commitments that BlackRock now holds in Germany and the rest of Europe and the world, and the $120 billion that the New Yorkers claim to have raised in their funds from large and small investors in Germany, they have managed to stay under the public's radar for a long time. At the beginning of the investigation, the head of the German subsidiary had agreed to an interview in BlackRock's offices, located in the iconic Opera Tower in the banking district of Frankfurt. The interview revolved around the strategy in Germany and the firm's business objectives. However, BlackRock ultimately refused to allow excerpts from the discussion to be used for the first edition of this book in 2015. The New Yorkers still made headlines in 2018 when Friedrich Merz, who had been chairman of the German subsidiary since 2016, entered the race for the chancellorship. Merz resigned from his position at BlackRock in March 2020.

It seems that the new strategy in Frankfurt is now more about seduction. While his predecessors limited their contacts with journalists to the strict minimum and to the trade press, Dirk Schmitz, the current head of the German subsidiary, is striving to give a friendly and almost harmless face to the black rock. A "forty-something who listens, who responds with good humor to all questions, even the most cheeky ones," as described by journalists from the radio station Deutschlandfunk. The former investment banker whom BlackRock recruited from the struggling Deutsche Bank is portrayed by the weekly Stern, wearing a light blue wool sweater while his dreamy gaze wanders over the skyline of Manhattan on the other side of the Rhine. On this occasion, he says things like: "It is not the position of power that matters to us, it is not our goal. It is the consequence of the services we offer," he assures that "there is no hostile takeover by the Deutschland AG," and finally, that "one should not be afraid of us."

Experienced, Schmitz responds to Deutschlandfunk journalists who ask him if he understands why reports on BlackRock often have titles like "The Worrying Power" or "The Dangerous Giant": "Well, I think it often comes from the fact that we are not known well enough; we are a completely normal fund manager, acting globally and offering completely normal investments to our clients and investors. Obviously, we are of a certain size, which often leads to wanting to tell a certain type of story about us, but these stories have little to do with reality. There is no secret plan, no worrying power, all these things that are often told in these stories do not exist."

So, "a completely normal fund manager," then? About whom only nonsense would be told? Even Schmitz's New York boss would find that a bit too modest.

So here comes Larry Fink into the picture.

CHAPTER 3

The Man Behind the Colossus: Larry Fink, a Wall Street Loser

Even if you've never seen the movie, the image of a finance mogul is often imagined as Michael Douglas, convincingly playing Gordon Gekko in the Hollywood blockbuster Wall Street, with his wide suspenders, pinstripe pants, and slicked-back hair. Fink is nothing like that. At first glance, the most influential man in the finance world looks more like his own accountant. He has what is called a "high forehead," grey temples, rimless glasses. In front of the cameras, he cultivates the demeanor of an Elder Statesman, a man who, thanks to his experience and knowledge, rises above earthly matters.

He carries the gravity expected of a leader of fourteen thousand employees, a CEO of a large company with a market capitalization of $70 billion (as of February 2020). "I am always a student," he replies when consulting firm McKinsey asks him about his leadership style on the theme of "Leadership in the 21st century" – before then giving his interlocutor a lecture on globalization, motivation in management, and the weakness of political leadership around the world. Press access to Fink is meticulously controlled. In recent years, he has rarely given interviews. Today, he is seen more often, but in his messages, he strictly adheres to the image of a well-intentioned administrator towards his clients and investors. "It is a company that is almost paranoid about what might leak outside," explains a public relations officer who worked with Fink's team. It is not surprising that journalists react enthusiastically when allowed to interview the big shot. Carol Loomis – financial journalist and ghostwriter for investment legend Warren Buffett – was allowed to watch over Fink's shoulder as he worked. In her article for Fortune magazine, she describes his daily life as a court chronicler would depict the king in an absolutist monarchy. According to Loomis, Fink's day starts at 5:15 a.m. in his apartment in the chic Upper East Side neighborhood of Manhattan. At 5:45 a.m., a limousine picks him up and drops him off at BlackRock's headquarters. He brings three newspapers with him, the New York Times, the Financial Times, and the Wall Street Journal. For an hour, Fink reflects. Or he video conferences with one of his managers – who has every interest in being at his desk. For breakfast, he eats blueberry and banana cereal. And between all his appointments, according to Loomis, he always finds a moment to call his wife Lori, whom he met at the age of 17 and has been married to for over forty years. At 6:30 p.m., Fink leaves the office and goes home or to an evening appointment. At 10:30 p.m., he turns off the light. The press service prominently placed Loomis' article on the company's website. For readers, it is clear that Fink is working hard for BlackRock and, therefore, for its clients.

Fink never fails to mention at every opportunity that he is aware of his social responsibility. "Our clients are firefighters and teachers," he likes to say, reminding that BlackRock manages the pension funds of American public employees. However, this did not prevent BlackRock from leading a consortium of its top clients into a deal that led to the largest real estate bankruptcies in recent history. It was the New York residential complex Peter Stuyvesant, which BlackRock and the consortium acquired for over $5 billion in 2006, at the height of the real estate bubble. By early 2010, the bubble burst, and BlackRock withdrew. Among the clients advised by BlackRock to participate were CalPERS, the largest public pension fund in the United States. It is responsible for the retirement pensions of 1.6 million California officials. At that time, CalPERS was already severely affected by the crisis and lost an additional $500 million due to Stuyvesant's bankruptcy. "Disappointing their clients" still weighed on him, Fink told Bloomberg Businessweek in December 2010.

The firm's PR battalion promotes the image of a servant dedicated to a higher cause. On CNBC's stock channel, the host introduced him as the "voice and conscience of Wall Street." At the "Buttonwoods Gathering," a conference of the British economic magazine The Economist, the editor-in-chief of the journal announced him as the "star guest" of the event – the appearance of the BlackRock boss was comparable to that of the Rolling Stones. Fink, who almost always wears a light-colored shirt and a delicate purple silk tie, speaks calmly and with a slightly monotonous voice about his concern for the political situation in general and – his favorite subject – the risk of poverty among the elderly.

If you don't know who is on the screen, you could easily mistake Fink for one of the many talking heads, those "experts" who appear on TV shows. But he is not one of those who can capture the attention of the viewer flipping through the different programs of the evening. However, if you are close to him, you feel something else – a latent agitation, a spring still tense within him. Fink keeps an eye on his surroundings. If a journalist's request for a report is too critical, he replies in a way that shows he is used to having the last word. In his personal relationships, he is "intense" and "direct," as insiders like to describe him.

"Larry is and remains a trader," says Larry Doyle, who started at Fink's as a young operator in the 1980s.

Market operators, better known as traders, are constantly on the lookout for profit opportunities and the risk of loss. It's in their skin and in their blood. "No experience marks you as much as when you lose several million," says Doyle. Successful traders are fascinated by numbers, especially those followed by the dollar sign. They are eager and impatient: those who stay in a position too long do not circulate money, and when money does not circulate, it is not earned. At worst, you even lose a bit, because the market turns against you. The market: traders speak of it with the same respect as sailors speak of the sea. Like a natural force, it can turn against those who depend on it for their livelihood. Just as sailors watch the wind, the waves, and the clouds, traders observe the ups and downs of stock prices, interest rates, and order entries. When, as a non-initiate, you listen to traders, you are confirmed in your worst prejudices. When, after the Lehman bankruptcy, criticism of Wall Street reached its peak, an email circulated in the industry. The author condensed his defense speech into these words. "It is our job to make money. Whether it's commodities, stocks, bonds, or any hypothetical piece of paper invented. If we could make a profit with baseball cards, we would do it." Profits would be justified: "We eat what we kill."

Robert Shiller, winner of the Nobel Prize in Economics in 2013 who had warned of the internet bubble and correctly predicted the real estate bubble, looked at the role of finance and its benefits for society. He concludes that our modern economy would not be possible without the financial industry. However, it offers shelter to a certain social group, which would otherwise have difficulty integrating. 3% of the population have sociopathic traits, estimates the economist. "It's better that we place them where they can be useful to our society." Indeed, not everyone is capable of making decisions that can cost millions – and that in a matter of minutes, or even seconds. Or consider risks without taking into account the moral or emotional factors involved.

Trader one day, trader forever, they say on Wall Street.

Fink doesn't like to hear such statements. He does everything possible to distance himself from the people of Wall Street, who have been viewed unfavorably since the financial crisis. "We are not Wall Street," he told a Bloomberg journalist in an interview in 2013. He would even dislike having his headquarters in New York. BlackRock's business model would be 100% different from that of Wall Street. "We are in New York, so we are classified in a category, even if we are not part of it." Fink insists, not only to journalists but also on the fact that he has absolutely nothing to do with Wall Street. For BlackRock's business, the image of the independent outsider is important. Many investors – pension funds, investment funds, foundations – for whom BlackRock manages billions, are wary of Wall Street companies. They too often feel cheated by bankers. It is therefore crucial for Fink to put distance between his business and the usual suspects. But perhaps even more crucial is that regulators do not confuse them in any way with banks and brokerages, or even insurance companies. And so far, Fink has managed to navigate his empire, almost without a hitch, among the hundreds of new rules and directives adopted by legislators and financial regulators since the 2008 debacle.

The Swift Rise of Larry Fink in the Bond Empire

A career on Wall Street was far from a predetermined path for Laurence D. Fink. Unlike most Wall Streeters, Fink is a West Coast guy. He grew up in Van Nuys, a suburb of Los Angeles. His mother was a teacher at the local school, and his father owned a shoe store. Larry, as everyone calls him today, first studied political science at the University of California. He then earned his MBA from the Anderson School of Management, also part of the University of California, specializing in real estate finance. In 1976, at just 23 years old, armed with his degree, Fink headed to New York, to Wall Street. It wasn't an unusual career choice. "Only Hollywood was hotter than Wall Street at the time," recalls a veteran of the industry. However, Larry's origins made him an outsider. Until today, most recruits at major banks come from elite East Coast universities like Harvard, Yale, and Princeton. He was just a kid from L.A., arriving with "turquoise jewelry and long hair," as he himself told journalists. A former colleague still smiles when he remembers Fink's quirk of reminding everyone after the morning meeting: "And don't forget to have fun!" East Coast bankers were still impressed by the intellect of the Californian - even during his studies, Fink stood out as a brilliant mind. He accepted an offer from the investment bank First Boston, where he was placed in the bond department. Unlike today, when commercial departments are thinning out and only gray-haired individuals shuffle paper, bond trading was where it was at in the 1980s. Traders sat in trading floors as vast as gymnasiums, in front of rows of screens, amidst the cacophony of hundreds of phone conversations. Almost none of them were over 35 years old. They thought of themselves as the "Masters of the Universe." Their arrogance and excesses were immortalized by Tom Wolfe in his novel The Bonfire of the Vanities. The 1980s were also a heyday for First Boston, a time when the bank played in the big leagues of investment banks. Its fiercest competitor was Salomon Brothers. Anyone with experience as a trader at Salomon Brothers on their CV enjoyed a kind of distinction that impressed

Wall Street insiders. Salomon's traders were both renowned and infamous for their ruthlessness and knack for pushing the envelope. Taking risks, pushing the limits. Salomon made mortgage trading a lucrative business. The driving force behind it all was a certain Lew Ranieri, whom Michael Lewis immortalized in his book Liar's Poker. Fink became Ranieri's main rival. Not only did he manage to catch up with Salomon - thanks to his department, First Boston dominated mortgage trading in the mid-1980s - but his ingenuity also reportedly brought his employer near-fairy-tale profits: he allegedly made nearly $1 billion for the bank with his department. But Larry Fink didn't just settle for being one of the young wolves of Wall Street in the 1980s. He was more than that: one of the pioneers in the invention of securitized mortgage loans. These same loans that triggered the fall of Lehman Brothers and the Great Recession.

The CMO: Miraculous Debt Instruments from Pandora's Box

Before mortgage debts became the centerpiece of the most devastating speculative bubble since the 17th-century tulip frenzy, they were considered one of the smartest innovations in modern financial affairs. And Larry Fink was one of its inventors in the early 1980s. To appreciate this pioneering work, one must look back. Unlike in Germany, where mortgages - i.e., loans secured by real estate - have been transferred to investors as mortgage bonds since the time of Frederick II, there was nothing comparable in the American market for a long time. The transaction usually went like this: Joe Sixpack, an average American consumer, buys a house. He gets a loan from the local bank, Lake Woebegun Savings & Loan. The bank records the loan, Joe Sixpack pays the interest and repayments over fifteen or thirty years. The end. The money available for aspiring homebuyers was limited by the financial strength of the local bank. Things got complicated when hundreds of regional and local institutions went bust at the end of the 1980s during a major credit crisis, the savings and loan crisis - the US savings banks. This was due to interest rate speculation and simple accounting fraud. The savings and loan crisis could have served as a warning, but the world's memory in general, and Wall Street's in particular, seems to be short.

On one side were mortgage buyers eager for loans, and on the other were large investors such as pension funds and insurance companies seeking safe and profitable investments. This literally required a solution on Wall Street. How about, the financial tinkerers there proposed, if we pooled mortgages and then issued certificates on these pools, which would grant investors the right to a portion of the interest payments on the loans? Consequently, the credit from the balance sheet of the local bank Lake Woebegun Savings & Loan migrated to a fund, jointly owned by investors. This process transformed the mortgage loan into a much easier-to-trade and invest mortgage debt. But this wasn't enough to make mortgages attractive to investors. For them, mortgages had a huge drawback: if Joe Sixpack sold his house or refinanced his debt - for example, to get a loan at a lower interest rate - he could repay his loan before the scheduled date. This would ruin the investors' calculations. Instead of regularly receiving interest payments calculated over ten years, the loan was repaid overnight - future interest payments to investors thus declined, leaving an unfortunate hole in their yield calculation. This was the prepayment risk that investors feared, as it was difficult to calculate. A headache for pension funds and insurers, dependent on continuous inflows.

Fink and his rival Lew Ranieri, from Salomon Brothers, are considered the brains behind finding a solution to this problem: Collateralized Mortgage Obligations, or CMOs. The mortgage pool is divided into different tranches. First, all repayments go to investors holding the first tranche. If a homeowner repays their loan early, it first affects the investors in that tranche. They bear the brunt of the loss of interest income that results. Only when investors in the first tranche have fully recovered their share of the loan amount will those in the second tranche be serviced, and finally, at the end of the process, investors in the third tranche. This last tranche presents the lowest risk of suffering interest losses due to early loan repayments. Subdivision into mortgage pools can also be done according to other criteria - such as default risk. The safest tranches consist of loans to borrowers with the best creditworthiness, while the riskiest tranches contain loans to less creditworthy candidates. The advantage of this risky tranche: interest rates for homeowners with low creditworthiness are higher. The subdivision suddenly made investing in mortgages more predictable for investors - they could choose tranches with desired interest rates and risks according to their needs. Insurers and pension funds loved CMOs. Foreign investors saw them as a way to secure a share of the US real estate market. German regional banks, for example, were among the enthusiastic clients, as were some funds from Asia and Europe. Securitized mortgage debts - variants of CMOs - became a bestseller. In a few years, major investors poured billions into the market. In 1983, Fink presented his first CMO pool to the government-sponsored mortgage buyer Freddie Mac. By the early 1990s, the volume of CMOs had already reached $250 billion. All major US banks and many foreign institutions such as Deutsche Bank entered the market. Former mobile phone sellers and used car dealers turned into mortgage dealers almost overnight - and became rich.

"When I saw Ferraris and Porsches in the parking lot, I knew we had a problem," recalls a banker who frequented local credit institutions in the country. But no one wanted to see the danger; money had too sweet a taste. Originally a quiet niche in the American financial market, mortgage activity grew to become the main activity of the financial sector. 2007 was the golden year for Wall Street: never before had bankers and brokers pocketed so much money. Mortgages were granted in abundance, packaged into tranches, certificates issued, and distributed worldwide. But the ever-increasing demand for mortgages led to skyrocketing property prices to unsustainable levels, making borrowers increasingly fragile. Many factors fueled the final implosion. But the fact is, without CMOs, such a rush to mortgages would never have been conceivable. Like many ideas that make sense in themselves and have a understandable purpose, Wall Street's guys' CMOs led to such madness that they ended up going astray.

Still, Larry Fink continued to stand by his CMOs. "We helped reduce the cost of homeownership," he told Vanity Fair in April 2010. At the time, it must have been thrilling to go to Washington to present the new financial instruments called CMOs with mortgage institutions Fannie Mae and Freddie Mac. "I was only in my twenties, but I was aware of the magnitude of it and its usefulness." The fact is, mortgage instruments provided hundreds of billions of dollars to homeowners almost overnight - and many Americans, who had never before had this opportunity, were able to realize their dream of owning their own home. The fact is also that Wall Street seized this opportunity to push the boundaries ever further to maximize its profits, eventually turning these positive effects into their opposite: hundreds of thousands of Americans lost their homes in the largest real estate crisis in modern financial history.

It is also true that for CMO pioneer Fink and for BlackRock, the debacle that followed the mortgage frenzy ultimately laid the foundation for their empire.

Larry Fink's Fatal Error and Fall

With his mortgage bonds, Fink had positioned himself in pole position for the ascent to the top. "We dominated the market, First Boston was the 800-pound gorilla of the mortgage niche," recalls a colleague. Fink made money for the company and was considered a strong head in his field. Just a few more moves like this, and he could have crossed the finish line to the top leadership position. The California kid had made it clear to the East Coast guys. And then, in the second quarter of 1986, disaster struck. Fink's department lost. Not just a little, not just what you lose on a bad day, a bad month... or even a bad quarter. No, Fink lost $100 million. "That wouldn't be much money today, but at the time...", remembers Doyle, Fink's former junior trader. Upstairs in Boston's management, the alarm sounded loudly. Fink and his men had misjudged interest rate movements. The US Federal Reserve had surprised with a rate cut in March and again in April of the same year. Given this cut, it was expected that American homeowners would soon replace their high-interest-rate mortgages one after the other with new low-interest-rate mortgages. The dreaded risk of early repayment of mortgage bonds exploded almost overnight. And Fink's department was sitting on a mountain of papers that no one wanted anymore, and they could only get rid of them with massive losses. In a few hours, Fink went from being Boston's darling to being untouchable. He wasn't fired. At least, not directly. Even today, there are more subtle ways to get rid of someone on Wall Street. Suddenly, you're not in the right meetings, important information passes you by. Your number is on the blacklist. No one wants to be seen with you, not even in the elevator. Your past successes, the profits you made for the house: forgotten. You're a pariah.

At the time of his "voluntary" resignation, the Wall Street Journal reported that he had not had the opportunity to stay in his position. His employers hadn't even used the famous phrase "new professional horizons" that normally awaits those who get fired. They had pulled a dirty trick on him. The Wall Street Journal's announcement fell on his promising young career like a tombstone. Larry had become Larry the loser. The scar is still sensitive today. When journalists from the upscale magazine Vanity Fair asked him about it in 2010 - more than twenty years after the fact - he visibly looked affected. He had held onto his chair so tightly that his joints had become white and protruding.

After all, Larry Fink has since been satisfied: First Boston sank shortly after his forced departure. The firm's debt is an episode that has gone down in Wall Street history, known as the "burning bed". The term comes from a movie in which actress Farrah Fawcett plays an abused wife who eventually sets fire to her husband's bed. The movie's title, The Burning Bed, became the mocking nickname on Wall Street for First Boston's last big deal. The bank - caught up in the buying fever - had pre-financed the takeover of mattress maker Sealy through a private equity company, one of the corporate hunters, at a dream price of $1.8 billion. The loan granted by First Boston was to be repaid to investors through the issuance of junk bonds.

These corporate bonds are called junk bonds because they are extremely risky. And this was brutally confirmed in the Sealy transaction: the junk bond bubble of the 1980s burst at the exact moment when Sealy's bonds found no takers, and First Boston - an institution dating back to 1932 - suddenly found itself with a billion-dollar hole. Credit Suisse, already a partner of the bank, intervened and took over the ailing business. The combined bank chose to call itself, somewhat awkwardly, Credit Suisse First Boston. When the firm renamed itself Credit Suisse in 2006, there was not even the name of Fink's first employer left on Wall Street.

Blackstone and the Beginnings in the Back Office

After his spectacular fall, Fink remained in the shadows at First Boston for nearly two years. Then he got a second chance. In February 1988, a company named Blackstone contacted him. Behind it were an unlikely couple: Steve Schwarzman and Pete Peterson. Schwarzman was a dealmaker, a mergers and acquisitions specialist who had worked for investment bank Lehman Brothers at a young age and therefore seemed self-assured. Schwarzman had met Peterson at Lehman. Peterson had a political profile, having long worked in Washington, temporarily serving as Secretary of Commerce under Nixon, before coming to Wall Street. From his previous position, Peterson had brought back a "golden address book." When Lehman Brothers, the bank whose collapse had almost brought the world down, had at the time already flirted with bankruptcy, Schwarzman and Peterson had joined forces and created their own investment firm. They saw an opportunity in the still young sector of "locusts" (private equity), companies specializing in the low-cost acquisition - mostly with those so-called junk bonds - of companies or parts of companies. The companies were then to be restructured and above all refinanced to be resold at a profit or taken public. With his golden address book, Peterson had connections, access to the top floors of major American companies, and to the boards of pension funds that were to invest in the new private equity firm. Schwarzman knew how to arrange the financial part so that there was enough left for the partners. To find a name for their young company, the two founders presumably started with their own names: Schwarzman provided the black, "Black". And Peterson freely translated his name from ancient Greek: petros, the stone. Thus Blackstone was baptized.

Schwarzman and Peterson wanted to expand their investment firm to include other business areas, including a fixed income division that would invest in stocks and pension securities. Fink, recommended by a colleague, seemed to be the ideal candidate, despite the bloodbath that had cost him his career. Blackstone's bosses accepted his explanation blaming a computer error and poor data collection. So they proposed to Fink to set up a joint venture named Blackstone Financial Management (BFM). 50% of the new company belonged to Blackstone, and 50% to Larry Fink and his team, which he had brought with him.

Blackstone provided $5 million as a credit line for the launch - peanuts on Wall Street - and Fink's team started. At first, they didn't even have their own offices; they were subtenants in the trading room of investment bank Bear Stearns (the first victim of the great crisis of 2008).

But Schwarzman and Fink were anything but ideal partners. Schwarzman was an investment banker. He viewed traders with suspicion. Losses made him nervous. And Schwarzman's ego has always been legendary, still today. Even on Wall Street, he has always stood out for his thirst for money and recognition. "More rumors circulate about his parties than about his deals," the New York Times once mocked. For his sixtieth birthday, he had reserved the Park Avenue Armory, a former 19th-century barracks transformed into an events venue, in the upscale neighborhood of the Upper East Side. Rod Stewart serenaded him there for the modest sum of $1 million. There was a line of luxury black limousines outside the building from which the heads of major banks such as Jamie Dimon of JPMorgan Chase and Lloyd Blankfein of Goldman Sachs emerged, as well as real estate mogul and reality TV star at the time Donald Trump, with his third wife Melania on his arm. No one suspected he would one day become president. Edward Egan, then cardinal of New York, also honored him with his presence, as did Sir Howard Stringer, chairman of the board of Sony at the time. According to gossip, Schwarzman simply booked the Park Avenue Armory because it was a more intimate setting than his $30 million apartment a few blocks away. Schwarzman and his wife reportedly had it decorated exactly like their summer palace in St. Tropez... The stories about the tastes and dislikes of the king of deals reported by the Wall Street Journal amuse the gallery on Wall Street: he reportedly has fresh Florida stone crabs delivered by plane for $400 apiece and allegedly scolded his butler because the crepe soles of his shoes squeaked too loudly and disturbed him as he tried to relax by the pool of his 1,000-square-meter villa on the wealthy island of Palm Beach, Florida. Furthermore, the butler was not wearing the required black shoes.

Fink and Schwarzman did not take long to clash. By 1992, their joint venture had raised $8 billion in investor capital and generated $13 million in profits. Fink wanted to continue to grow. Blackstone had to give up getting new shares of the company. Fink wanted to use these shares to attract more talent to BFM and lure new partners. But Schwarzman dug in his heels. At that time, he was in the midst of a divorce battle with his wife Ellen, according to his biographers David Carey and John Morris. According to his colleagues, this context would have made him uncompromising towards Fink.

Fink wanted a divorce too. He found an investor, PNC Bank in Pittsburgh, which offered $240 million. Fink then demanded that Blackstone sell its shares in the joint venture to the bank. Schwarzman eventually relented. In June 1994, BFM, which had meanwhile been renamed BlackRock, was sold to PNC. Schwarzman received $25 million. Enough to cover his divorce from Ellen, which, according to Businessweek, cost him nearly $20 million. But Schwarzman later admitted that he still regretted the sale, even today. With it, more than $1 billion would have slipped through his fingers - which did not make him a poor man: when Blackstone went public in 2007, he eventually received nearly $700 million, and he now has a fortune of over $15 billion. But someone like Schwarzman never forgives himself for letting a good deal slip through his fingers. A matter of honor on Wall Street. No one, not even Fink, could have foreseen the spectacular rise of the company that was originally just a modest subsidiary of Blackstone. But knowing that did not console the "king" of private equity.

And the "Black Rock" Started Rolling

So, Larry now had his own business on Wall Street. It's less impressive than it sounds because it's quite common; many bankers and traders eventually become independent. "Hanging up your own shingle," as they say in the business. Lew Ranieri, for example, Fink's old rival from Salomon Brothers, also has his own business. He was fired from Salomon in 1987. His name is still known in certain circles, but he is considered a has-been. "He still lives off his legend at Salomon - and that was almost thirty years ago," says a veteran of the mortgage industry who has worked there for almost as long.

But Fink fundamentally stands out from the Wall Street crowd. He hasn't forgotten his mistakes. He learned from them. The painful episode at First Boston even gave him the inspiration that would transform his business into a global giant and fundamentally change Wall Street.

Fink himself cultivates the legend of the error that turned Larry the loser into a golden Fink. For this, he does not hesitate to be hard on himself. His fault was not only losing $100 million but making hundreds of millions in profit beforehand. Because with his team, he actually did not understand how these gains were realized. They did not perceive the risk they were taking with their trades. The computer programs at the time were not sophisticated enough to calculate what would happen if major variables, such as interest rates, changed. That's why they were overwhelmed by the losses. "We didn't know why we made so much money. We didn't have the tools to understand the risk we were taking," he admitted in an interview, years later. His conclusion: he never wants to be in a situation again where he cannot assess the risks. Never again. With his team, they set out to build a system capable of addressing Fink's obsession with taking them all into account.

BlackRock bid farewell to trader instincts and instead tried to replace them with computer models, fueled increasingly by data. Long before the term big data existed, Fink and his team had already considered the possibilities that this accumulation opened up. They were almost "paranoid about risk," BlackRock representatives like to say, with a superior smile, well aware of what they are saying. The founder's risk paranoia, cited repeatedly, became a system at BlackRock, a creed that today seduces its clients.

The risk obsession is part of the key to Fink's success. But as a former employee denounces, it's not as if BlackRock was the only investment house capable of recognizing risks or having implemented appropriate systems. "They like to blow hot air around them," he says about his former employer. But he admits that Fink remains an exception in the business. What sets him apart from others is that he has crossed one of the inherent boundaries of the financial sector, which remains barely visible to outsiders. Wall Street is like a coral reef: there are zebra fish, clown fish, anemones, and barracudas, there are sharks and cleaner fish, squid, sea urchins, snails, and jellyfish. Just as every living being has its place in the underwater ecosystem, there is a variety of different jobs on Wall Street. And just as in the reef, some live in symbiosis while others are prey. There are investment bankers, stockbrokers, bond traders, analysts, and economists, hedge fund managers, and gamblers (high-frequency trading), private equity tycoons, stock market regulators, and rating agencies.

But there is a gap, which had rarely been bridged before Fink, separating the sell side and the buy side. In essence, a gap between those who offer or negotiate investments and those who must invest money. All types of investors are found on the buy side: hedge funds, investment funds, pension funds, foundations, insurance companies, and small investors. On the sell side are investment bankers, offering companies' shares or bonds to investors, and analysts, offering them research reports and stock price forecasts. There are trading departments responsible for buying and selling stocks or bonds on behalf of buyers.

Until Fink came on the scene, buy-side buyers - apart from hedge funds - relied on sell-side providers for information and offers. It must be imagined like this: a company, like Walt Disney or McDonald's for example, is advised by a bank on its capital structure: how much equity should it have, how many shares should it issue, how much debt should it take on to remain as profitable as possible? Then, the bankers accordingly organize new shares or bonds and offer these securities to buy-side investors.

However, as a provider, the sell side always has an advantage in terms of knowledge, since ultimately it is their representatives who concoct the deals and transactions. Those who work on the sell side are above all good at marketing, whether of their products or services but, above all, of themselves.

Also important: whatever is offered to the client, there must be enough left for their own business, their own bonus, or commission. For the buy side, there remains an eternal and unfortunate information imbalance. And no matter how many billions are controlled each time by buy-side asset managers, no fund can organize a system comparable to that of a bank. This is why rating agencies play such an important role with their evaluations - the buy side saw, at least until the 2008 crisis, a neutral arbitrator between the two parties. However, financial ratings were not enough to compensate for the information imbalance between the sell and buy side - especially since for many buy-side investors, the mortgage crisis had raised doubts about the neutrality of financial ratings: too many mortgage securities rated AAA by rating agencies turned out to be duds in investment portfolios. In January 2015, market leader Standard & Poor's, then suspected of fraudulent practices in mortgage ratings, was investigated by the US Department of Justice and settled out of court by paying $1.37 billion. S&P stated that this settlement did not constitute an admission of guilt. Its rival Moody's was only found liable in early 2017 - nearly a decade after the credit crisis - and had to pay $864 million. Moody's was found to have violated its own evaluation standards, according to a representative of the US Department of Justice.

Fink saw a great opportunity in the existing imbalance between the buy and sell sides: as a pure representative of the sell side, he would make his insider knowledge available to the buy side. He would offer them computer models that could be used to perform calculations and even more efficient systems, like those used by the sell side. With BlackRock, Fink would offer the buy side all the advantages that only the sell side had until then. What may seem mundane to an outsider was a revelation for Wall Street.

You must be eight friends: the founding team

To realize his grand vision, Fink had to have the right people on board at BlackRock. Like Captain America, he assembled his team. In the end, there were eight founding partners, including Ralph Schlossstein, who had been President Carter's economic advisor in the 1970s. Like so many others in Washington, he then went to Wall Street to make money at Lehman Brothers. Schlosstein also brought in Susan Wagner, Sue for short, a specialist in strategic acquisitions at Lehman - an expertise that would be crucial for BlackRock's later expansion. Hugh Frater had worked at Lehman as an investment banker in mortgage finance.

Keith Anderson came from Fink's old stomping ground, the mortgage trading desk at First Boston. Barbara Novick also, after working at the prestigious Morgan Stanley following her economics studies. Bennett Golub also came from First Boston, where he led the financial engineers and came into contact with Fink. With his group, they were responsible for $25 billion in mortgage securitizations at the time. Golub, who holds a Ph.D. from the Massachusetts Institute of Technology (MIT), was tasked with developing BlackRock's initial analytical systems. To do this, Golub bought a Sun Microsystems workstation and set it up in the small kitchen, between the fridge and the coffee machine - an anecdote that is also part of BlackRock's founding legend. With this computer, Golub programmed his first mortgage portfolio analysis models. To help him, the founders hired Charles Hallac, whom Golub knew from his time at First Boston. Hallac, BlackRock's first real employee, later rose through the ranks to become co-president before passing away in 2015. In general, the club of eight remained extremely loyal. Five of the original founders are still with BlackRock. By Wall Street standards, that's an eternity.

And then there was Rob Kapito, another former partner of Fink's at First Boston. Kapito was in Fink's department when he first started with his

CMOs. He had witnessed his rise and fall. "In Fink's place, many bosses would have blamed Kapito: Fink could have done it," says an employee from that time. But Fink decided otherwise. He took Kapito with him, making him a partner in his new venture. The fundamental bond between them is still unbroken today.

While Fink became the public face of BlackRock, Kapito played the role of a gray eminence. He is the man who keeps an eye on the markets, who ensures that BlackRock does not miss any developments. He adjusts the organization internally according to the founders' vision, Fink's vision.

Like Fink, Kapito comes from a modest background. His family ran a garage in Monticello, in the Catskills, the geographically located mountain range about 90 kilometers from Manhattan but socially a distance of Earth to Moon. Kapito's father had a stroke when he was only 13 years old. He still managed to finance his studies, and even an elite - and expensive - degree from the Wharton School at the University of Pennsylvania. (He now sits on the board.) After completing his studies, Kapito also moved to Wall Street to join First Boston. Two years later, he left the bank to earn a Master of Business Administration at Harvard Business School. When he returned to First Boston in 1983, with his degree in hand, he joined the mortgage department where he met Larry Fink. A meeting that, a few decades later, would make him one of the most powerful men in finance.

The decisive mission of General Jack

1994 was a fateful year for BlackRock in several ways. First, there was the separation from Blackstone. Then came the deal that would turn the small back-office firm into a top-tier company. It all started with an unlikely partnership. On one side was the suitor, so to speak, General Electric. The group, whose inventor Thomas Edison is one of the founding fathers (GE still owns Edison's office), is often called "the American economy in a nutshell." This means that the group is involved in almost every sector of the economy. Literally everything: from light bulbs and various power plants, to cancer screening and aircraft parts, to the Internet of Things, it's all in its portfolio. (The company did, however, experience a crisis and had to replenish its cash reserves by selling off some of its divisions.) In the mid-1980s, General Electric also wanted to play a role in finance. So, they bought Kidder Peabody, a venerable Wall Street firm founded by Henry P. Kiffer and the Peabody brothers at the end of the American Civil War in 1865. But, of this old glory, there was not much left, as GE's executives quickly realized. The ink on the sales contract was barely dry when state investigators arrived. The accusation was insider trading. One of the people involved was taken out of his office in handcuffs - an episode that Oliver Stone used in his Hollywood blockbuster. "We wouldn't have touched Kidder Peabody with a ten-foot pole if we had known what kind of skunk was hiding in the company," said Jack Welch, then CEO of GE. Kidder Peabody survived this affair only to be involved in a new scandal in 1994. This time it was phantom trades. Joseph Jett, a bond trader, had manipulated the computer program so that his business generated huge profits - $350 million to be exact. This time, Welch, whom General Electric employees also call "General Jack," finally lost patience. He decided to dismantle Kidder Peabody and sell off its parts. The buyer ultimately was PaineWebber, a bank that was later acquired by the Swiss bank UBS.

PaineWebber politely declined, however, to acquire Kidder Peabody's $10 billion mortgage portfolio, which was made up of CMOs - the financial instruments launched by Fink, and it was difficult to assess what, in this pool of various loans, had real value. GE was about to dump the securities - the main thing being to get rid of the "skunks." It was at this point that BlackRock stepped in with an unusual proposal: instead of a quick but loss-making abandonment, Fink and his team proposed to analyze the portfolio using BlackRock's computer models and develop a plan for General Electric to gradually release the mortgage loans to get a better price. The people at GE were interested. And Fink's team let their computers work. The mission was a great success - and word got out.

"At the time, the Kidder Peabody portfolio was considered one of the most complex investment pools of all time," Rob Goldstein, now head of BlackRock Solutions, the business unit born out of the experience with GE, once said. With the order from the world's largest trust, BlackRock was able to break through. After the job for GE, companies interested in BlackRock were lining up. "It was like the ghostbusters in the Hollywood blockbuster Ghostbusters: if you had an opaque portfolio or dubious assets, you called Larry Fink and company," says an insider.

Grow, grow, grow

Just three years after being acquired by PNC Bank, Fink and his faithful were already so well established that investors had entrusted them with $46 billion. The assets under management had more than doubled since the takeover by PNC, as reported by the specialized magazine Pensions & Investments in 1997. A year later, the parent company PNC – the bankers from Pittsburgh who had helped Fink break away from Blackstone – merged its asset management branch with BlackRock, increasing the amount of capital managed by the company by $108 billion. The bankers at PNC then wanted to see some of the money themselves. They took BlackRock public on October 1, 1999, and sold 14% of their stake. Fink and his partners, on the other hand, kept 16%. With 650 employees and a market capitalization of just under $900 million, BlackRock had become the fifth largest publicly traded asset manager in the United States. Not bad for an investment banker who had been fired. But Larry Fink wasn't about to stop there. Far from it.

Except for its initial public offering, BlackRock was little heard of in the 1990s. The dot-com euphoria had taken over Wall Street and half the world. The internet and its endless possibilities attracted investors big and small. A new economy was born. It was a time when it seemed that only a few hours separated an idea scribbled on a napkin from its debut on the Nasdaq. But not for Fink and his men, who remained faithful to bonds – a corner of the capital markets that seemed dusty during this period. However, well in the shadow of the tech stock market, which was in the spotlight, Fink's company grew and prospered. When the bubble finally burst in the early 2000s, the bond geeks of BlackRock emerged, with their bonds, like prophets to the once enthusiastic but now disappointed investors. By the end of 2000 – while the Nasdaq was falling – Fink could report $200 billion in assets under BlackRock's management. To complement its offerings for clients – pension funds, corporate investment arms, private fortunes – BlackRock bought hedge funds. In 2004, BlackRock acquired SSRM Holdings, the investment arm of the life insurance company MetLife. As a result,

BlackRock managed more than $400 billion in 2005, landing it on the list of the twenty largest asset managers in the world. But Larry Fink wasn't about to stop there. Far from it.

However, there was initially a setback. Or, at least, that's what rumors on Wall Street said. First, there was a real coup that Fink had quietly concocted with Stan O'Neal over breakfast at Three Guys. In this New York diner on Madison Avenue, serving traditional hash browns and scrambled eggs with coffee, no one could have guessed that the two patrons were actually two finance magnates about to strike a deal. O'Neal was the CEO of Merrill Lynch. Mother Merrill, as this institution on Wall Street was affectionately called, was one of the big names. At Merrill, they were proud of their "thundering herd," their raucous band of brokers, capable of selling America the bonds or stocks of their own investment bankers. No one on Wall Street had a trading network as vast. Their logo featured an aggressive bull panting and pawing the ground with its hooves. A few days after breakfast, Merrill Lynch and BlackRock announced that Merrill's asset management activities would merge with BlackRock and, in return, Merrill Lynch would acquire a 49.8% stake in BlackRock. Boom!

The deal was so surprising that a hedge fund manager, who had an interest in betting against the loser in the deal, complained about the difficulty of knowing who had been outfoxed by the other.

Regardless, BlackRock had succeeded in going from a nameless startup to a partner of one of Wall Street's most respected firms. For Stan O'Neal, it was the last good move. Shortly after, it became clear that Mother Merrill had made a bad calculation with the mortgage securities. Merrill was among the banks that had eagerly acquired failing mortgages in their portfolios (others were smarter and quickly sold them... to regional banks across the Atlantic, among others). In 2007, O'Neal was fired. And Fink wanted to succeed him. It's undeniable. He seemed focused on the leadership position at Merrill. Years later, he said in an interview that he had only considered it as an option. And that he had asked for a comprehensive overview of the accounts, which Merrill's board of directors had refused. Then he withdrew from the race. Others have said that the potential conflicts of interest that could have arisen if Fink had led both BlackRock and Merrill were far too dangerous in the eyes of the board.

The fact is that Mother Merrill chose John Thain. It should be noted that Fink and Thain are like fire and water. Thain – who is at least as ambitious as Fink – started his career at Goldman Sachs and, not being able to reach the top position there, settled for the top of the New York Stock Exchange. Only rumors speculate what might annoy Fink about Thain. It is assumed that it is simply because Thain somewhat resembles Superman's alter ego, Clark Kent, with his brown hair and glasses, and thus stayed on the sunny side of Wall Street, unlike Fink. Thain had also gone straight to Wall Street after graduating. But unlike Fink, he climbed the ranks without taking a big fall. A career so meteoric that the specialized magazine Institutional Investor had written an article about him. The title: "The Adventures of Super Thain." Even at Goldman, Thain was seen as icy and smooth. His nickname, "Thain the Humane," was quite ironic. Fink, on the other hand, remains in the shadows. When journalists asked him if it was true that he liked to nickname Thain "John Boy" in a nod to the character from the TV series The Waltons because he was always freshly shaven, the BlackRock boss reportedly smiled knowingly.

With the leadership position at Merrill Lynch, Fink would have done more than redeem his first career mistake at First Boston. He would have become the head bull of the thundering herd. But he found other ways to satisfy his thirst for recognition. Wall Street was soon to become too small for him. In hindsight, he probably even thought it was lucky not to have become the boss of Merrill. Indeed, shortly after this episode in Fink's career, Merrill was caught up in losses from failing mortgages. At the height of the crisis, Thain managed to sell Mother Merrill with a handshake with Ken Lewis, CEO of Bank of America, on a Saturday morning in September 2008, just before the loss of over $15 billion was made public. Blinded by Merrill's reputation, Ken Lewis had taken over the bank without looking closer. Later, he claimed that Ben Bernanke, then chairman of the Federal Reserve, had called him and practically forced him to complete the acquisition, despite the bright red balance sheets. For Lewis, who had turned the originally provincial Bank of America into the second largest financial company in the United States, the Merrill deal was a bitter end to his career. He then returned home to Charlotte and apparently switched to sponsoring the film industry. In Hollywood, however, no one had ever heard of the former banker. Thain lost his job at Bank of America, allegedly because he had spent too much money renovating his office at Merrill during the crisis. Charlie Gasparino, a gossip-loving Wall Street journalist, gleefully reported in the Daily Beast details from internal documents such as chairs for guests costing $87,000 and a commode for $68,000. But it was the $28,000 curtains and the $1,400 waste basket that caused the most sensation. "John Boy" Thain joined the commercial bank CIT, which quickly went bankrupt. And the castrated thundering herd, as part of Bank of America, continued to mourn its independence. But Fink's thunder continued to rumble elsewhere.

CHAPTER 4

The 2008 Crisis: A Windfall for BlackRock

On that Friday in March 2008, the atmosphere on the floor of the New York Stock Exchange was relaxed before the bell rang. Traders were discussing their plans for golfing over the weekend. Then the news came over the tickers: investment bank Bear Stearns is in dire straits! What market participants had feared as a major nuclear accident many times over the past few weeks had just happened! For over a year, deals had been failing here and there, hedge funds were in trouble, and there was talk of mountains of toxic mortgage securities that banks would have to sit on. But now, it was the turn of the fifth largest American investment bank to be in a critical situation.

It was a steep fall for the Bear, as the 85-year-old institution was affectionately called. Many innovations came from the smart guys at Bear Stearns. They were considered the poor children of Wall Street houses. Poor, therefore driven by the rage to become rich. This is how the legendary head of Bear Stearns, Alan Greenberg, known as Ace, wanted his candidates. "Forget the paper clips, bring your own pen and sit on a folding chair," Dealbreaker, the online gossip site about Wall Street, once quipped about Bear's culture. Two Bear Stearns hedge funds had collapsed the previous summer due to misleading speculation on mortgage securities. Their multi-billion-dollar implosion marked the beginning of the global financial crisis. While this crisis was brewing, Bear Stearns CEO Jimmy Cayne lingered over golf or bridge tournaments, as reported by the Wall Street Journal. And even when rumors of serious financial trouble were heard at Bear Stearns in the second week of March 2008, Cayne flew off to the North American bridge championships in Detroit, according to Fortune magazine. Since he didn't have a mobile phone at the time, he was difficult to reach. Even though the stock price had been in free fall for some time, Cayne stayed in Detroit and was slow to join the crisis conference call because he had to attend the bridge tournament first. After being unable to charter a private jet, Cayne waited in Detroit for hours. (Apparently, it didn't occur to him to board a commercial flight.) When he finally arrived in New York in the evening, he was greeted at the office, according to Fortune journalists, with the following message: "We're getting $8 to $12 per share. That's the deal with JPMorgan." (Cayne disputed the version of events reported in the Wall Street Journal and later told Fortune that he had been seriously ill before Bear's collapse.)

The rescue was quickly organized by the Federal Reserve. They wanted to prevent the domino effect that would later be triggered by Lehman Brothers. An acquirer had to be found for the Bear before Monday, when the financial markets would return from the weekend! But Bear Stearns had a "toxic" portfolio of $30 billion that frightened potential suitors. Federal Reserve bankers therefore considered taking over the poisoned portfolio with possibly non-performing mortgage securities themselves. And for the support and resolution of the operation, the president of the Federal Reserve Bank of New York, Timothy Geithner, already had the right contact: Larry Fink.

What makes the mission juicy for BlackRock is that the potential buyer the Federal Reserve is negotiating with regarding Bear is JPMorgan Chase. And Jamie Dimon, CEO of JPMorgan, had also contacted Fink the day before. He also wanted to place BlackRock analysts in Bear Stearns' accounts. They were to give him an assessment of its value. His offer for Bear would be based on this.

BlackRock got both missions. Jamie Dimon offered $2 per share for the Bear. An affront to the people of Bear Stearns. Even when Dimon raised it to $10, many on Wall Street thought it was a ridiculous price. Even today, the former employees grind their teeth and call the takeover a "crime." The deal had also been sweetened for Dimon, as the Federal Reserve had taken over the risky securities from the toxic portfolio, hastening the disappearance of the Bear. The securities now bundled under the name "Maiden Lane" belonged to the Federal Reserve – that is, to the public. And BlackRock took care of the liquidation, as per its mandate.

What is stunning about the Bear Stearns transaction is that no one seemed to care that BlackRock was acting on both sides of the planned transaction, that is, simultaneously for the buyers and the sellers. The Bear Stearns deal would become a model. BlackRock positioned itself as an evaluation professional, and none of the participants openly doubted its neutrality. This model has persisted to this day and has been used by BlackRock in Europe with great success. But in March 2008, this was not yet foreseeable.

The Planet of the Apes: Fink the Survivor

On the evening of September 13, Larry Fink was at the New York airport, about to board a flight to Singapore. Meetings with Asian sovereign wealth funds were scheduled – potentially lucrative contracts for BlackRock on the horizon. But this was one of the longest flight routes in the world, from the East Coast of the United States to Asia, covering nearly half the globe. For Fink, this meant being unreachable for 16 hours. And the situation on Wall Street was more than worrisome. While Fink stood in front of the boarding gate with his luggage, representatives from the Federal Reserve Bank of New York, envoys from the Treasury Department in Washington, and the heads of major investment banks were holed up in Manhattan's financial district. The sense of siege was heightened outside: the sandstone building looked like a fortress, except that you entered it through an underground parking lot, not a drawbridge. Inside, the fates of Lehman, the fourth-largest investment bank, and Merrill Lynch, the largest brokerage house and BlackRock's main owner, were being decided as they teetered under the billions in losses related to toxic mortgage securities. Fink called a BlackRock representative who was present at the Federal Reserve meetings. "Can I take my flight?" he asked. At that moment, it seemed that a buyer would be found for Lehman. "Yes, you can," he was told. And Fink boarded the plane.

That's how he recounted the episode to a Fortune journalist a few weeks later. While BlackRock's CEO was in the air, Wall Street, as it had existed for over half a century, collapsed. When Fink finally disembarked from the plane early Monday morning local time, he was greeted by shocking news: Lehman bankrupt, Merrill Lynch sold to Bank of America, and insurer AIG – with a balance sheet of $1.1 trillion, 74 million policyholders in a hundred thirty countries – was now a staggering giant. "I felt like Charlton Heston in the Planet of the Apes," Fink later recounted. In the Hollywood film, an astronaut played by Heston, who believes he has landed on another planet, suddenly comes across the remains of the Statue of Liberty and realizes that his civilization has disappeared.

But for Fink and his team, it was the beginning of a transformation. From asset managers with a preference for bonds and smart analysts, they became major players behind the scenes of high finance and grand politics. Shortly after the disaster, the Treasury Department and the Federal Reserve contacted Fink. Could BlackRock take care of the toxic securities held by AIG? The largest insurer of the time had miscalculated complex credit derivatives. Someone had to now find out how much these securities were worth and liquidate them gradually. Federal Reserve officials and bankers were simply overwhelmed by such a task.

According to Bear Stearns, BlackRock's "crime experts" were now to tackle AIG's toxic waste. AIG's difficulties did not really surprise Fink's specialists. Robert Willumstad had been hired by the insurer as a reorganizer in June, six months before the collapse. The new CEO had hired BlackRock shortly after because he wanted to discreetly uncover the severity of the problems contained in AIG's portfolios. His predecessor, Maurice Greenberg, known as Hank, had run AIG like a feudal sovereign for decades. Greenberg was always on the lookout for new business sectors. He also wanted to participate in the boom of securitized credits. His favorite, Joe Cassano, whom American journalist Matt Taibbi later dubbed the "patient zero of the global economic crisis," came up with a seemingly brilliant idea: the rating agencies had given AIG the best AAA rating for solvency. Why not make money from this? Thus, AIG would guarantee packages of credits compiled by banks – the famous CMOs and CDOs, now hailed by investors thousands of times over. With AIG's guarantee, the credit packages would also receive the top solvency rating. This was good for the issuers of these credit packages, as they became easier to sell to investors. And it was good for AIG, as the insurer could collect fees for this default guarantee. Cassano assessed the risk as low. Because the credits contained in the packages were largely mortgages on American real estate and there had never been a national real estate crisis, it seemed like an easy deal.

Up to this point, it was smart. AIG quickly became one of the most sought-after partners in the rapidly expanding world of credit derivatives – that's what these transactions are called. European banks in particular loved the securitized credit packages guaranteed by AIG. They could declare them as secured capital contribution to the Central Bank, allowing them to retain less costly equity. The operation seemed profitable for everyone: for the banks, which conducted the securitization, for the insurer AIG, which received premiums on the guarantee, and for the clients, who received what seemed to be a safe and attractive product. But the financial crisis began in 2007: the credit packages that AIG had generously endowed with its own solvency were suddenly considered much riskier than expected. However, in Cassano's contracts, a clause noted in small letters stipulated that AIG had to transfer a sum to the banks as collateral to offset the increased risk of the title in case of such a solvency devaluation. In cash. In plain language, this meant that AIG had to transfer cash to contractual partners such as Goldman Sachs or Deutsche Bank. With each new wave of toxic credits, AIG's partners demanded new, higher levels of security. It became increasingly difficult for AIG managers to find the necessary money. Greenberg's unfortunate successor, Martin Sullivan, a Briton known primarily for being a proud patron of the Manchester United football club, apparently did not understand, for a long time, the quagmire his company was in. With each new doubt about the mortgage loans, the banks invoked AIG's provisioning clause.

Willumstad, who had finally replaced Sullivan in the summer of 2008, asked BlackRock to investigate Cassano's catastrophic derivative products to help stabilize the situation. But it was already too late. The debts owed to the banks had become unpayable. In September 2008, there was nothing but pure panic on Pine Street, in the Downtown Manhattan district, where AIG's Art Deco skyscraper stood. Washington intervened. AIG was nationalized. A measure that was totally unthinkable in the United States, a country considering itself a refuge for free markets. But during this crisis, many things that were previously unimaginable became reality3.

It turned out that Washington's operation did not mean the end of the AIG contract for Fink and his cronies. On the contrary: BlackRock took over the analysis and liquidation of AIG's toxic portfolios for the Federal Reserve.

This is how Maiden Lane II and Maiden Lane III were launched4. The three Maiden Lane funds were now managed by BlackRock.

Moreover, BlackRock was still acting for the Federal Reserve during the financial crisis. In order to protect companies from the credit crisis, the Federal Reserve immediately established several support programs. One of them was called the Term Asset Backed Securities Loan Facility (TALF). Behind this cryptic term was a support action through which investors could obtain discounted loans from the Federal Reserve, provided they invested the money in securities selected by it. The Federal Reserve would also take over all securities purchased under the program whose value had fallen too low. With these subsidies and guarantees, the Federal Reserve sought to reduce risk in the credit market so that market players would dare to do business again. Wall Street's gossipers nicknamed these support actions "cash for trash." BlackRock was hired to analyze securitized credits for TALF. Its rival and sworn enemy PIMCO, a subsidiary of Allianz, was to handle the corresponding evaluations. However, there was a difficult-to-ignore conflict of interest: both BlackRock and PIMCO were also users of TALF. BlackRock's funds, for example, borrowed $2.8 billion under the Federal Reserve program. This made BlackRock one of the top twenty borrowers of TALF.

In short: BlackRock provided securities analyses to the TALF program. At the same time, BlackRock's funds used the TALF to acquire such securities. BlackRock, when asked by Bloomberg, stated that the TALF was used by another department of the firm on behalf of clients. The two departments were strictly separated. According to Bloomberg's report, there would be no possible allegations against BlackRock and PIMCO regarding irregularities in TALF.

The Shadow Finance Minister

Bear, AIG, and TALF were far from the only crisis cases handled by Fink's troupe: in December 2008, the Federal Reserve signed another contract with BlackRock. This time, it involved a portfolio at Citigroup with billions of dollars in losses. Citi had to be supported by the state several times, otherwise toxic mortgage debts would have toppled the world's largest financial group. BlackRock was tasked with testing the portfolio and calculating the potential largest losses.

BlackRock was also in demand in Washington: Fannie Mae and Freddie Mac are mixed-capital public-interest companies, with the legal mandate to support the American mortgage market so that as many citizens as possible can own their homes. The goal is considered politically important: in America, it is assumed that homeowners are much more interested in community affairs than renters because, after all, the value of their real estate depends on it. The two support organizations, Fannie and Freddie, are among the largest buyers of mortgage loans in the world (even more so after the crisis than before). They buy mortgages from banks, which have initially signed them with property owners. However, the two giants bought and securitized too many toxic mortgages and had to be bailed out by the American taxpayer to the tune of almost $190 billion. Fannie and Freddie's experts, too, had apparently been overwhelmed when it came to independently controlling the quality of the mortgage loans acquired in the years leading up to the crisis and which were now in their funds. This analysis mission was entrusted to our old acquaintance from New York: BlackRock.

BlackRock also applied in the fall of 2009 to be one of the managers of another aid program, this time for the U.S. Treasury Department. In this mission, BlackRock was to repurchase damaged securities with its own and public funds, within a program called PPIP (Public-Private Investment Program), from banks, for example, to free their balance sheets from toxic residues. By the end of 2012, BlackRock had wound up the fund and transferred $917 million to the Treasury Department - $528 million was the Treasury's initial public investment and $389 million was the profit for the state's coffers. Robert Kapito, now president of BlackRock, hailed the dissolution of the PPIP fund in a press release. With its commitment, BlackRock would have helped stabilize mortgage markets while generating solid profits. This proves that "a partnership between the state and the private sector can be quite convincing and profitable." The fact that Fink and BlackRock appeared at every nook and cranny of the rescue operation was perceived - at least by some in Washington - as a sign of generous, selfless civic duty. James R. Wilkinson, for example, the right-hand man of George W. Bush's Treasury Secretary Henry Paulson, praised Fink in an interview as a "patriot." Paulson was responsible for crisis management in the early stages of the financial crisis. Before that, however, he had been the head of Goldman Sachs and had already trusted Fink at that time.

BlackRock did not render this service to the country gratuitously. It is difficult to understand in detail what the company received. The Federal Reserve, for example, kept its documents under lock and key for a long time. It was only in 2010 that the financial information group Bloomberg was able to make most of the details public for the first time. To do this, however, it had to file a lawsuit under the Freedom of Information Act, which guarantees American citizens the right to information about public agencies. According to a later report by the US Government Accountability Office, BlackRock received a total of just under $182 million for the Maiden Lane services. For its participation in TALF, the company received the modest sum of $1.25 million. For advisory services for Citigroup, an additional $12 million came from the Federal Reserve Bank of New York. For services in a mortgage purchase program, for which BlackRock supported the New York Fed, the company received $11 million. In a letter to Congress, POGO, a Washington citizen initiative against corruption and abuse of power, raised the alarm: "BlackRock's financial interests are even more confusing than those of other companies, given the large number of contracts and agreements they conclude with the public sector."

At least some elected officials and officials in Washington began to have BlackRock in their sights. The companies involved "have information about when the Federal Reserve wants to sell securities and at what price, and these companies also have financial relationships worldwide," noted Charles Grassley, a combative senator from Iowa, as early as 2009. "The potential for a conflict of interest is large and very difficult to control." It is true that Neil Barofsky, the inspector general responsible for overseeing the bank bailout program on behalf of taxpayers, did not mention BlackRock or PIMCO by name. In his report to Congress in April 2009, however, he describes, according to him, problematic interference in such partnerships. "This lies in the nature and construction of these funds, managed by both public and private entities, that their transactions in the frozen markets in which they operate have a significant impact on the price of the assets involved. In the event of a price increase, everyone who also manages or holds these assets will benefit. This also applies to partner fund managers."

Therefore, Barofsky cites the various ways in which fund managers appointed by the state could benefit from their public mandate: for example, the fund manager could increase the value of certain mortgage securities through purchases. If he holds exactly the same securities in another fund, which he manages for other private clients, then this fund will also increase in value. This, in turn, allows the fund manager to increase the management fees he receives from his private clients. But the fund manager could also enjoy other benefits, according to Barofsky, if, for example, he holds shares in a bank, to which he had bought toxic securities as part of his public contract. The more he values these securities, the better it is for the bank. This would then cause the share price to rise - implying gains for the fund manager holding the bank's shares.

During a congressional hearing in April 2010, Barofsky announced that he wanted to investigate further into BlackRock's role in the financial crisis. No one has heard of this investigation since - at least, publicly. A year later, Barofsky resigned from his position as inspector.

In his book "How Washington Abandoned Main Street while Rescuing Wall Street," written after his resignation, Barofsky describes his struggle with representatives of the Treasury Department in Washington. It was primarily about the necessity of "erecting ethical walls between fund managers, who had received PPIP money, and other departments of their companies, so that they would not game the system and drive up the prices of securities they already held in their portfolios." According to Barofsky, the Treasury refused to make these "ethical walls" mandatory for the PPIP program. He claims that the only thing he ever got from the representative responsible for Timothy Geithner's department was a CD of Pink Floyd's The Wall - a joke. Barofsky now works at a private law firm in New York and represents private companies. His specialty: litigation with government agencies and authorities.

The Bear Stearns transaction had already raised questions among some lawmakers. For example, in April 2008, one month after Bear's fall, Senator Bob Casey, chairman of the economic committee, began investigating how the Federal Reserve ended up engaging BlackRock. The then Federal Reserve chairman, Ben Bernanke, explained that they were "under extreme time constraints." Bernanke did not provide any details but confirmed that, in the rush, no fees had been fixed in advance. Their question was postponed to a later date. Timothy Geithner also responded evasively to the inquiry. During the Bear Stearns rescue operation, Geithner was head of the Federal Reserve Bank of New York and was directly involved in the decisions in 2008. In response to a letter from Grassley, the Iowa senator who also wanted to know the details of the Bear Stearns mission - especially why BlackRock had been appointed manager of Maiden Lane without a tender or other customary, or at least common, process in the public service - Geithner simply replied that the circumstances had made this exception necessary. According to the New York Federal Reserve president, the company was selected for its "technical expertise, operational capabilities, and proven past successes." When the senator wanted a copy of the contract with BlackRock, Geithner replied that the senator had to go to New York to see it, as the document could only be viewed at the Federal Reserve, and in confidence.

Unlike banks such as Goldman Sachs, Morgan Stanley, or Citigroup, BlackRock not only survived the financial crisis but also gained power and capital because of it. What was the difference? BlackRock was better suited to the new world of modern finance that had emerged in the preceding years. Fink's slicing and dicing of mortgages was just a small part of a much larger change. Over the past few decades, money has become increasingly abstract, until today there are flashing figures on screens and entries on spreadsheets. Relationships that once existed between debtor and creditor or between countries can now be expressed in arbitrage equations or interest rates. Even when it comes to cash, it is rarely about a dollar bill or a euro coin. Some of the financial markets moved in this direction very early on: only a few participants in the futures markets in Chicago want to find a bag of wheat, a delivery of pork bellies, or a tank of orange juice at their door at the end of their contract. This was indeed the origin of the modern futures market, when farmers and ranchers in the American Midwest wanted to hedge their corn crop or their cattle against a price drop at the Chicago Board of Trade, established in 1848, and when they wanted to protect meat factories and large bakeries from a rise in raw material prices. Today, these markets are still used by these suppliers and consumers, but there are now many more market participants buying futures contracts on beef halves or corn in Chicago for entirely different reasons. For example, pension funds that fear inflation and therefore invest in commodities. Or hedge funds that simply seek speculative gains. Today, a complex network of financial instruments has formed around the old agricultural markets. Futures markets are just one example. But what leads to making fundamental transactions like this increasingly abstract and globalized threatens to overwhelm the creators of this new financial world - bankers, speculators, investors, and traders. As in 2008.

For Fink and BlackRock, with their computers and computer models, this was, on the contrary, the perfect environment - at least until now. And BlackRock understood better than any other organization how to use it. Especially after the great crisis, when uncertainty and panic gripped all market participants. The name BlackRock appeared in almost every central bank and government rescue operation - more often than any other company. The rise of Fink & Co. is so closely linked to the financial crises in the United States and Europe, and their persistent consequences, that without them, the power and importance of BlackRock would be barely conceivable. But what happened at that time is still not clear today, even to many insiders. Nor is the role played by BlackRock in all of this.

In the circle of power

Timothy Geithner was a key figure on Wall Street, and more importantly, at BlackRock. As head of the New York Federal Reserve, he was effectively the ultimate guardian of the banks there. During the 2008 crisis, he became the ultimate savior. Then he rose even higher: newly elected President Barack Obama appointed him Secretary of the Treasury in early 2009. It was at that time the most important portfolio Obama had to fill. Geithner's career is almost as remarkable as that of the President himself. The fact that Geithner, tall and youthful, was appointed head of the New York Federal Reserve in his mid-forties, was due to his talent and having met the right people at the right time. Geithner was not a banker and had never worked in the finance sector. He was at home in the public sector. While working in Washington as a young Treasury Department official - the same department he would later lead as the ultimate chief - he was noticed by Larry Summers in the early 1990s. Summers made him his assistant. Summers himself was a political protege of Robert Rubin, Secretary of the Treasury under President Clinton. Rubin came from Wall Street. He had led Goldman Sachs before switching to high-ranking government positions. For Goldman's bosses, the move to the Treasury has since become a kind of anointment (as was the case for former Goldman boss Henry Paulson, who took office under George W. Bush). As Treasury Secretary, Rubin maintained friendly relations with his former sector. Above all, as the responsible minister, he was particularly considered a decisive force in preventing regulation of the new derivative products that were being discussed at the time. Derivative products like those that nearly ruined AIG later on. When Rubin resigned from his ministerial position - to return to Wall Street, to lead Citigroup - he gave the position to Summers, his political adoptive son. And Geithner, the third in the line, suddenly became part of the inner circle of power in Washington.

During the Asian economic crisis, and later with the bailout plan for the hedge fund Long Term Capital Management, whose collapse threatened to trigger a global crisis in 1998, Geithner appeared alongside Summers in the negotiations and caught the attention of some big names on Wall Street. Among others, Pete Peterson - the same Peterson from Blackstone who gave Fink a chance after the debacle at First Boston - and who later chaired the oversight committee of the New York Federal Reserve. Anyway, Peterson was looking for a new director for the institution. The New York Federal Reserve Bank is by no means a provincial branch of the Washington headquarters. It performs an important function: while the presidents of the Washington Federal Reserve are responsible for monetary policy, those of the Fed in New York oversee Wall Street.

In fact, the person holding this position must have extensive market experience and a certain status in the industry. Geithner had neither at the time. But his contacts paved the way for him. After a brief stint at the International Monetary Fund, he became head of the Manhattan Federal Reserve. His ability to find the right interlocutor also helped him there: Gerald Corrigan had spent twenty years at the Fed before leaving for Goldman Sachs. He took Geithner under his wing. The latter quickly developed a friendly relationship with Fink's archenemy, "John Boy" Thain, who was still at Goldman at the time, and later became CEO of the New York Stock Exchange. Geithner regularly called him. He also made sure to have dinner with Jamie Dimon, the boss of JPMorgan Chase. Dimon was actually Geithner's superior: JPMorgan's CEO was also a member of the Federal Reserve Bank's board of directors. With Dimon, Geithner also arranged the Bear Stearns transaction, in which BlackRock was also involved. The finance sector unknown who is now president of the Federal Reserve Bank also liked to chat with Fink. Geithner also saw BlackRock's co-founder Ralph Schlosstein and his wife for dinner at Café Boulud or for idea exchanges at home, as shown by Geithner's official calendar. However, it was never about BlackRock's business, but about the general market situation, Schlosstein assured the New York Times. "The talks with Tim were reasonably one-sided. He would call, bombard you with questions, thank you, and then hang up."

The connection with Fink became even closer when Geithner moved to the Treasury Department in Washington. Because at that point, Geithner could no longer be seen with his banker friends. Popular anger over the Great Recession triggered by Wall Street was too great. However, on that day, Fink became the consigliere of the brand-new minister, who was practically overnight faced with the task of saving the American banks and economy. More than any other financial CEO, Geithner consulted with the man from BlackRock. In the period from early 2011 to mid-2012 alone, the two men spoke on the phone nearly fifty times, according to an analysis of Geithner's official journal by the Financial Times. Numbers two and three on the minister's call list: his former political fathers, Robert Rubin and Larry Summers. Fink himself could hardly hide how proud he was of his role in Washington. He would casually mention that he had just received a call from "Tim," recalls a leading financial insider who saw Fink at joint appointments at the time. And Fink left no doubt that he was on familiar terms with the most important minister of the superpower that is America.

On the Emerald Isle: BlackRock's Leap to Europe

Regardless of which of Fink's new friends recommended BlackRock, the Central Bank of Ireland contacted BlackRock in the fall of 2010. The Irish were in a bad situation. For years, their economy had benefited from the boom in the financial sector. The island seemed to have finally found a promising branch. In the end, the banks' balance sheets were so inflated that they amounted to several times the country's GDP. Then the crisis struck, and suddenly banks filled with toxic securities and bad loans threatened to drag the rest of the country into the abyss. A solution had to be found, and quickly. But the rescue operation was beyond the Irish state. Brussels and the International Monetary Fund - the IMF - feared a chain reaction in the rest of Europe. Thus, Dublin received a €85 billion bailout. But the conditions also included a stress test of Irish banks, involving an examination of the accounts and balance sheets of Irish financial institutions to determine how much they were threatened and how much new capital they would need. And who did Patrick Honohan, governor of the Central Bank of Ireland, call? Bingo: BlackRock. The New Yorkers were given this mission alongside the Boston Consulting Group and the British Barclays Bank. In this case as well, as with the U.S. Federal Reserve, BlackRock Solutions was hired without a public tender. The Irish press complained that the contract award had been exempted, arguing that what was "good enough for the Fed should be good enough for Dame Street" - the headquarters of the Central Bank of Ireland is located on Dame Street in Dublin.

The mission would cost nearly $30 million to crisis-stricken Ireland - $6.5 per capita. When asked about this on television, the Central Bank president responded evasively and finally declared that he had to follow the instructions of the EU and the IMF. They had not directly ordered the Irish to choose the Americans, but in the corresponding agreement with Ireland, it is written very clearly: "The diagnostic review shall not be conducted by an accounting firm or consultancy firm that has provided services to any of the banks in the past three years. The Central Bank shall also engage a specialized company with the support of its own staff, to ensure the comprehensibility and integrity of the investigation." If you wish, you can see this as a very clear instruction to hire BlackRock or a similar company. The March 2011 report on the Central Bank of Ireland's procurement states explicitly: "In order to achieve a result for the stress test of credit portfolios that is fully credible on international financial markets, the Central Bank engaged BlackRock Solutions, a leading specialist in the analysis of potential credit losses in crisis conditions."

In the first edition of the book in 2015, Tom McDonnell, an Irish economist, explained to us that the reason Ireland's financial miracle ended in disaster was mainly due to a lack of distance between officials and the financial sector: "It was a known fact that before the crisis, bankers regularly played golf with those from the Central Bank, i.e., the people who were placed at the highest level of bank supervision." McDonnell was not surprised to see familiar names playing a prominent role in the rescue operation. He saw it as the logical continuation of global nepotism: "It's always the same key figures, the Davos clique."

In any case, Fink was delighted with this major mission from Europe. "It's bigger than our intervention with AIG for the Fed and it's even bigger than our action for Bear Stearns: it's a gigantic mission," he enthused to investors, as reported by the financial news agency Bloomberg in January 2011. His joy could only have grown when two more missions followed. And this, despite the fact that BlackRock's calculations proved too optimistic. For the period from 2011 to 2013, they had forecast revenues of at least €1.9 billion for the institutions examined. But they actually only generated a meager €400 million until June 2012, according to the EU Observer, an independent Brussels media outlet.

Nevertheless, there were still questions about potential conflicts of interest. In 2012, BlackRock domiciled more than €160 billion in assets on the Emerald Isle in various investment vehicles such as iShares funds and collective investment schemes (UCITS), and managed more than €5 billion for Irish pension funds and financial institutions. BlackRock evidently decided to immediately use its new contacts on the island: in April 2012, the company opened a branch in Dublin. The Irish Central Bank had just given them a new mission. After the mandates were completed in the fall of 2013, a division of BlackRock then acquired nearly 3% of the Bank of Ireland, one of the banks examined during the stress test by BlackRock analysts. At the time, this stake made BlackRock the fifth largest shareholder in the bank.

Drops in the Aegean Sea

The Dublin mission had paid off for Fink and his troops in many ways, but especially as a ticket into the eurozone. BlackRock's specialty in the European crisis was rummaging through the credit portfolios of affected financial institutions. With this mission, BlackRock intervened in the heart of the crisis: the banks. Their accounts were filled with European government bonds, which were then barely worth more than toxic American mortgages. The banks - driven by cheap money from the ECB - had also lent with a light hand, exposing them to insolvency risk. To avoid the state's bankruptcy, Greece received €240 billion in aid from the European Commission, the ECB, and the International Monetary Fund, the so-called Troika. Capital injection was also planned for the failing banks. But, as in Ireland, the Greeks would discover just how deep their banks were in trouble. What toxic credits were hidden in their accounts? It was now up to BlackRock to find out. In August 2011, the Bank of Greece (the Greek Central Bank) officially entrusted the mission to Fink's team. Why BlackRock? In a word: Ireland. "It was the only company to have already analyzed a banking system during this period," said Charalampos Stamatopoulos, a member of the Bank of Greece, to the New York Times.

Compared to the mission the number crunchers at Fink's received from Greece, Ireland had just allowed them to hone their skills. For a while, it seemed that the financial crisis would mainly wreak havoc in the United States. But the big earthquake then hit the eurozone, in 2010. Gaps suddenly emerged between the southern countries and their northern neighbors. What had been simmering for years under the appearance of a steadily growing and united EU was then loudly revealed by financial market turbulence. Germany in particular suddenly found itself in the unpopular role of guarantor of other countries' mountains of debt. Greece became a sensitive point and a deterrent example. Its colossal debt had long exceeded the country's annual economic output. To be exact, it represented 160% of its GDP. Greece had already employed Wall Street arithmetic before.

When, in 2001, it was a matter of meeting EU budget requirements, the government in Athens turned to various banks. Goldman Sachs eventually got the contract. The idea was to make part of the debt disappear; to this end, the government entered into derivatives transactions with Goldman. In this way, €2.8 billion of outstanding debts disappeared - according to the logic of financial engineers, that is. Greece's bets on the financial markets quickly turned against the country, and the overall deal cost the struggling Greek taxpayer over €5 billion. It was a "sexy story between two fishermen," as Christoforos Sardelis, then in charge of managing the Greek government's debt, put it in an interview. Critics saw it as a high-level accounting makeover. Thanks to these financial shenanigans, the Greeks had managed to rise to the level of Europe.

Operation Solar: A Hot Role in the Heart of the Crisis

For the BlackRock guys, it was a monumental task. Barely less demanding than if the Greeks had asked them to deconstruct and then rebuild the Acropolis from scratch. It was millions of loans from eighteen different banks, credits totaling €255 billion - in Ireland, the operation only concerned four banks. For the loans, the borrowers and guarantees had to be verified, and the corresponding default risk calculated. Unlike Ireland, there was the language barrier. And the duration of the examination was counted in months, not years. But the analysis required more than just powerful computer programs and diligent employees. Tact was decisive. The future of Greece depended on it, as did that of the EU. If BlackRock's auditors defined the capital needs of the banks too optimistically and thus too low, then the institutions would threaten to collapse in case of further defaults, thereby worsening the crisis. But, conversely, if the auditors set capital needs too high, it would then be difficult to find private investors willing to provide funds to the banks. And the more indebted Greek state would have to draw even more from the banks' coffers.

Fink sent a special commando to Athens. In view of the daily reports of street battles, burning tires, and tear gas bombings, the usually stoic Wall Street guys were quite worried: there had never been such protests, with so much discontent, in the United States. The mission, therefore, had to be discreet. Like in a very bad spy thriller, the team gave itself a code name: Project Solar. BlackRock employees were not allowed to transport or wear anything bearing the company logo, as passionately reported by the New York Times. A private security service escorted the American analysts. In the discreet office building in Athens, where the Solar team was housed for months, other tenants must have thought it was a company specializing in solar energy. Years later, Yanis Varoufakis still mocked this disguise. This same Varoufakis, who, as the newly appointed Greek Finance Minister, shocked Merkel, his counterpart Schäuble, and all German viewers with his shaved head, leather jacket, and fiery character, remembered in an interview in 2015 for the first edition: "Even Athens taxi drivers were talking about what the guys from BlackRock were going to do during their mission." Long before the crisis, Varoufakis himself had warned that the banks in his country were simply bankrupt. Because of this revelation, for which he did not need BlackRock's expertise, he became so unpopular in Athens that he received death threats. BlackRock's role was also not to uncover anything, Varoufakis claimed. "With missions like this, advisers know what is expected of them." In this case, they were not to account for the bad loans too high or too low.

For the Greek bankers, it must have been a rather unpleasant moment when the Solar team, sorry, BlackRock, entered and asked to see the documents. But in the end, they had no choice but to respond to the requests of these unwanted guests if they did not want to incur the resentment of their Central Bank and half of Europe. BlackRock's report nonetheless brought nearly €50 billion from the EU to the Greeks to stabilize their banks. Athens' clients were so satisfied with this result from BlackRock that they also commissioned a bank stress test from the New Yorkers two years later. Greece's situation was still miserable. The economy had contracted, the unemployment rate was 30%, and even 50% among young people. In the country, one in three people lived below the poverty line, according to the European statistical agency Eurostat. And bank defaults continued to grow - as BlackRock had predicted. In total, Greek financial institutions held over €70 billion in bad loans, or about a third of the country's GDP. It was time for another intervention. BlackRock's special unit was called upon again. This time as well, much depended on the result, as the country was paralyzed by the austerity measures demanded by the Troika. The Greek government of the time therefore decided to rid itself of the yoke of the Troika. To do this, it wanted to use the BlackRock report. According to Fink's number acrobats, Greek banks were short of about €6 billion. The original bank rescue fund still contained nearly €11 billion. The Greeks' calculation: since the BlackRock report only mentioned a need for €6 billion, the rest of the fund could be used for other relief measures. But the Troika protested. Their team of skinflints had come up with a completely different result than BlackRock's. BlackRock's analysts had been far too optimistic in their calculations. Greek banks were actually short of at least €10 billion according to the ECB. The IMF's computers even arrived at over €20 billion. At least that's what insiders whispered to the Financial Times in March 2014. Others disagreed with this high amount, one not being far from the other. The facts: Athens, Washington, where the IMF is based, and Brussels were arguing over the right amount. The real essence of the dispute: BlackRock's much lower result would give the Greeks the leeway to break away from the Troika. Thus, behind the scenes of the euro crisis, BlackRock tipped the balance with its banking analysis.

Chypre: The Greek Tragedy Continues

The euro crisis turned out to be a lucrative market, not only for BlackRock but also for governments, banks, and central banks desperately seeking external experts. It mainly involved assessments and analyses to calculate and verify assumptions. It also concerned loans granted by banks or complex securities in their portfolios, assets that were not sure if they were real "values." A significant part of the task was also to restore confidence. Just as it is said that in times of war, truth is the first casualty, the first victim of the financial crisis was trust in institutions. If, on the other hand, the central bank president or finance minister could support his assessment with a hundred-page report prepared by a New York company, he could at least hope that his data on the state of banks would be more credible. For the ECB officials and the heads of government of donor countries, it was also practical. They could say: look, dear voters, we have strict guidelines, we are putting governments and banks to work! In addition to BlackRock, the banking advisors of the strategy consulting company Oliver Wyman also rushed into this goldmine. Similarly, the "Big 4" accounting giants - namely Ernst & Young, Deloitte, KPMG, and PricewaterhouseCoopers - as well as companies like Alvarez & Marsal, who among other missions sold Lehman Brothers for the bankruptcy administrator and advised, for a considerable sum, for years, the rusty automobile industry of Detroit - without success, obviously.

Sometimes, these global profiteers of the crisis try to outdo each other, other times they cooperate and share missions. Their fees are always counted in millions, or even tens of millions. However, money is only part of the interest they can derive from these missions: the connections and knowledge they bring are almost more important. The fact that most contacts are made more among public figures than within ministries is not a disadvantage, but rather an advantage. Because they know the ins and outs of public affairs - and generally outlast the governments they serve.

In the fight for missions, the gentlemanly style is not always appropriate. In Cyprus, for example, the rush turned into a real political thriller, full of code names.

The drama unfolding on the Mediterranean island was a sequel to the Greek tragedy. Cypriot financial institutions had fattened themselves by placing the dirty money of Russian oligarchs in Greek state bonds, with high interest rates. In early 2012, the Greek debt restructuring - the largest in history at the time - made these state bonds responsible for significant losses. The largest banks on the island were at risk of collapse. The Cypriots quickly signaled to Brussels. To avoid panic from spreading again in the eurozone, the Troika intervened once again. And there too, its members - the ECB, the European Commission, and the IMF - demanded an analysis of the banks before the arrival of a bailout fund. Panicos Demetriades, then governor of the Central Bank of Cyprus, received offers from PIMCO, BlackRock, Oliver Wyman, and Clayton Euro Risk - well-known companies in the field. Although BlackRock was considered a favorite, it was ultimately its rival PIMCO that was chosen. But it didn't stop there. In late 2012, it became clear that the banks would need the staggering sum of €9 billion. While EU creditors, especially Germany, tired of the many bailouts of indebted banks, welcomed the severity of the requirements, Cypriot bankers protested vehemently and pressured Demetriades. The central bank president did something unexpected: he hired BlackRock analysts, whom he had initially not wanted to give the contract to. They were to provide a second opinion - like a consultation with a specialist doctor. BlackRock was therefore to review the PIMCO report. At PIMCO, they were furious. But they couldn't do much. Like in Greece, the guys from BlackRock tried to keep their activity as much as possible under the public radar. To the point of using pseudonyms for those involved, according to the New York Times, with internal documents to support it. The Cypriot Central Bank had thus been baptized "Claire," PIMCO was now called "Peter," and "Ben" referred to BlackRock.

BlackRock concluded from its analysis that PIMCO had made too pessimistic assumptions: the credit loss forecasts were too high. In short: the financial needs of the banks were, according to them, lower than those set by PIMCO and the Troika. The showdown between Cyprus and the creditors lasted for seven months. In early 2013, the Troika put together the bailout plan - based on PIMCO's figures. The estimate of the financial need was crucial, especially for Cypriots, many of whom had lost their savings. Because their deposits in banks had been used to save them. In contrast to the Greek scenario, this time it was the non-consideration of the BlackRock report that influenced the political fate of the country. The losses suffered by savers had unsurprisingly made the Cypriot government unpopular.

Several hypotheses can explain why the positive BlackRock report was sidelined. Demetriades, who under pressure from Cyprus' new government had been replaced, claims that the report was completed too late. Officially, it was indeed submitted to the Central Bank in May 2013. But people in the know claim that an earlier version had been made available to the Central Bank president as early as January, but he had not informed either the Troika or the new government of these more positive results. Whatever happened on the Mediterranean island, it is clear that BlackRock also played a crucial political role with the report of its analysts.

BlackRock had to pass on Spain. The New Yorkers were on the verge of winning the contract, but Spanish Economy Minister Luis de Guindos backed out at the last minute. He told Bloomberg News: "Don't you think that BlackRock wants to buy assets in Spain? If you're the referee and you're buying the assets at stake, then there's clearly a conflict of interest." Oliver Wyman and Roland Bergen got the contract instead. According to an employee, Fink was furious. He then sought to find out from European officials how such a contract had slipped through their fingers.

Spain was the exception. Like in the United States, Fink's number is among the favorite contacts of central banks, finance ministers, and European leaders. In the summer of 2012, however, Fink pulled off a move that finally allowed BlackRock to establish itself permanently in Europe. But everything in its own time.

On the Magic Mountain

The World Economic Forum in Davos is a conspiracy theorist's dream. Every year in January, in the small Swiss Alps town, the global elite, or rather those considered as such by the organizers and sponsors, gather. In fact, rather than calling it the World Economic Forum, insiders use the abbreviation WEF, pronounced briefly as "weff," almost like a bark. The winter setting is an integral part of the "weff." Once, the American news channel CNN asked the organizers to turn on the snow cannons. The trees had to be as beautifully powdered as possible. The producers did not take into account the objection that this was impossible in case of too high temperatures.

In 2015, the "weff" set new standards. Over two thousand five hundred participants came from one hundred and forty countries. Zurich airport recorded nearly one thousand one hundred additional flights for the period from January 21 to 24, mainly due to private jets.

Between the Swiss banking metropolis of Zurich and the highest town in the Alps (as the community of eleven thousand inhabitants likes to call itself), there were nothing but imposing limousines in the streets. Audi, Mercedes, BMW, SUVs - tinted windows in the back, chauffeur at the wheel. The most impatient ones took the helicopter. The Chinese Prime Minister, on the other hand, is said to have traveled by train. In first class of the Rhaetian Railway, the latest edition of the Financial Times is on every seat: one can therefore assume that these four annual days are not spent skiing or enjoying the fresh Alpine air. The first checkpoints begin about 20 kilometers from Davos. Thousands of Swiss army soldiers are deployed. It is said that water pipes and sources are regularly tested. No one should be able to poison the "weff" visitors. On the roof of the congress hotel, snipers in white camouflage gear are stationed, scanning the area for suspects with their binoculars. The perimeter surrounding the congress center, which looks like an oversized wooden box, is completely sealed off. The police, friendly but determined, only let you pass if you have a special accreditation. You then have to pass through a metal detection arch and through a white plastic tunnel to the next check. Nobel Prize winner Robert Shiller just came out of there. Then the buzz can be heard. Indians, Chinese, Sudanese, Americans, Arabs, Swiss, Italians, Japanese, Egyptians, Ukrainians, Russians, Germans. Here, at the congress center, "power meetings" take place on the lower levels. Conference participants can discuss over coffee at a small table. Journalists are looking for big fish, VIPs from finance and politics. To pass the time, they help themselves freely to cappuccino, latte, tea, and walnut cake at the bars. Everything is free! After all, "weff" time should be used as efficiently as possible and not wasted waiting for change.

Every square meter in the city is used. The hair salon rented its premises to a sponsor who organizes meetings there. The hairdresser then goes to the homes of residents in need of a haircut during the "weff." Credit Suisse rented the furniture store nearby, completely emptied it, and turned it into a meeting place. Microsoft is also represented with a pavilion. Google is said to have paid 30,000 Swiss francs a week for an apartment. Swiss Radio and Reuters have set up in the municipal library. Swiss television SRF, American business channel CNBC, and Fox News have set up their pop-up studios on the roof of the indoor pool, right next to the congress center. Heads of state, economists, and business leaders parade minute by minute, microphone in hand, for live shows and interviews. Nowhere else on the planet can you find as much power as here, in this surprisingly charmless mountain town, with its stacked hotel buildings.

It was not planned for the "weff" to become a kind of global super-organization. That said, founder Klaus Schwab was not lacking in ambition. Born in 1938 in Ravensborg, in southwest Germany, he was involved in the European movement during his youth. He studied mechanical engineering and management, then obtained a master's degree in public administration from Harvard University. He was fascinated by the American approach to intellectual management and business, especially the idea that companies engaged not only the interests of their owners but also those of their employees, customers, and the state. In 1971 - he had by then become a professor at the University of Geneva - he organized a European

Management Forum in Davos. The isolation and the presence of a congress center in the town appealed to him, as did, above all, the intellectual aura that enveloped Davos: Thomas Mann's The Magic Mountain takes place in the alpine resort of Schatzalp, above the town, and sculptor Philipp Modrow wanted to open a women's college there, where teaching would be in Esperanto. That was in 1921. The city council politely refused. When a university was finally opened in 1928, Einstein participated in the inaugural conference. The following spring, Heidegger and Cassirer, the opposing poles of 20th-century philosophy, held their legendary debate there. Whether due to the Alpine air, the ski slopes, or the resonance of great thinkers, Schwab's forum (now called the European Management Forum), which was now held annually, attracted more and more participants and thus became a global phenomenon. In 1987, he renamed it the World Economic Forum.

Around the event has formed a whole conglomerate of research institutes, conferences, and consulting services. The WEF now employs nearly six hundred people at its headquarters in Cologny, near Geneva, one hundred and twenty in New York, eighty in San Francisco, and thirty in Beijing. Schwab's organization is also represented in Tokyo and Mumbai. In 2019, its budget was approximately 344 million Swiss francs. It is funded by membership fees: almost all of the world's largest companies are members. The "weff" is so important to them that they continued to pay, albeit grudgingly, when fees increased by 20% in 2014. The one hundred members representing the most important companies, called "Strategic Partners," who can also have a say in the direction of the program, now pay 600,000 Swiss francs per year. These partners, who according to the "weff" have been selected for their commitment to "improving the state of the world," include companies such as Allianz, SAP, Siemens, Volkswagen, Deutsche Post, Publicis, PepsiCo, the chemical giant Dow Chemical, the pharmaceutical group Novartis, the American infrastructure group Fluor (heavily involved in the reconstruction in Iraq), and the Chinese e-commerce giant Alibaba. Major technology companies are also partners: Facebook, Google, and Cisco. But also obscure participants such as SOCAR, the Azerbaijani national oil company, and Bridgewater Associates. Ray Dalio, the founder of this $160 billion hedge fund, swears by "life and management principles" and demands radical openness from his employees, which is why he records all conversations in the company. And, of course: BlackRock.

Davos visitors all like to count themselves among the global elite. But here, too, there are clear distinctions. The caste to which one belongs is displayed by means of distinct accreditations, which dangle around necks. Thanks to them, one can know who has access to which event rooms. The participants' gaze automatically shifts from the face of the interlocutor to this accreditation. "It was so often the case that I understood for the first time what it must feel like to wear a plunging neckline," once recounted a (male) reporter from The New Yorker.

To access the "real Davos," you need more than the right accreditation. The real conversations do not take place in the congress center or in the surrounding pavilions. Suites are reserved in hotels to organize a proper speed dating between politicians and business leaders. Here, they can meet informally and behind closed doors.

And only those who really are come in and out of the Belvédère hotel: an illustrious circle of central bankers, bankers, group leaders, hedge fund managers, prophets, and heirs of all kinds, astrophysicists, monks, representatives of Silicon Valley, and, generally, Bono. The U2 singer with the pink glasses is now a regular at the "weff" or, less friendly, a jester of Davos. According to Time magazine in 2008, Bono's presence is a good thing. For example, because, during a discussion on poverty, he will mention the absurdity of the situation: the panelists are among the richest in the world. Such self-critical tones are rare.

All "weff" participants are immersed in an atmosphere of shared self satisfaction. Nearly 80% of those present are men, mostly white. "It makes the parties a bit one-sided," regrets a participant who has been attending since 2007. Although everything is much more civilized than at other international meetings, she assures. The New Yorker advises wealthy and institutional investors, and for her, the "weff" is the most important event of the year. There, it's not about direct business, such a crude way of acting is frowned upon. Goodwill is built, opportunities are created, ideas are tested. In short, a foundation is created on which to base more concrete transactions later on. It is said that the North American Free Trade Agreement NAFTA was conceived in Davos. People speak in precise terms, using Davos jargon, as described by the New York insider. "To understand it, you have to have been there several times." And have been able to get in. There is no ticket. No matter if you're a CEO or a guru, you must be invited. This also contributes to the exclusivity of the event.

If you have managed to insert yourself once into the Davos network, then it's settled. "Even if a politician has no chance in his own country anymore, is despised by his compatriots, as long as he remains highly appreciated by the Davos jet set, there are many opportunities available to him today - at the European Commission, at the International Monetary Fund, etc. In fact, contempt from compatriots can even be a plus - after all, it shows that one is willing to do what the international community demands, even if it goes against the interests of the citizens of one's country," argues left-leaning American blogger Matthew Yglesias in his article "The Global Ruling Class."

At first, BlackRock CEO Larry Fink was not very comfortable in this alpine environment. Rumor has it that he was even one of those who considered Davos to be mostly "hot air"... until he himself received an invitation. Yes, Fink, the former "California Kid," is now part of it. He certainly did not dream of this while, as a young boy, he sorted laces and stacked shoe boxes in his father's store. "He's not as smooth as a banker or a politician," observes the New York consultant and Davos veteran. During his meetings in Davos, Fink is still very "transaction-oriented." Apparently, he struggles to forget his Wall Street trading past. In Davos circles, there is some criticism of Fink's tendency to name-drop, and it is also said that he is a bit of a gossip. But, Larry Fink made it. And that's how you find him in January 2015, relaxed, at a cocktail party at the Belvédère, alongside a Russian-Swiss billionaire widow and a former central banker. How did the head of a New York-based investment company, obscure until recently, specializing in the most complex bond products, end up there? And, more importantly: what is he doing there?

The door opener

It was during the summer of 2012 that Fink caught his biggest fish to date. He hired Philipp Hildebrand. "Few executives enjoy such broad recognition for their expertise, judgment, and integrity," BlackRock's boss exclaimed in a press release about his new hire.

Compared to Hildebrand's previous position, however, Fink's offer represented a step back. The man was previously president of the Swiss National Bank - the Swiss central bank. In other words, the lord of Swiss banks. And his departure from this high office was not entirely voluntary. His wife, Kashya Hildebrand, whom he "had known and loved" at his former employer Moore Capital Management, a hedge fund based in New York and London, had caused his downfall, as reported by the Swiss newspaper Tagesanzeiger. According to reports, Hildebrand made a fortune at Moore. He then returned to his alpine homeland to work at Bank Vontobel and at the Union Bancaire Privée in Geneva. At just 40 years old, he became a member of the board of directors of the Swiss National Bank. In 2010, he was appointed president. The couple settled in Zurich, and Kashya opened an art gallery in a side street off Bahnhofstrasse, where upscale shops and private banks line the street. Born in Pakistan, raised in the United States, this "Wall Street gallery owner" specialized in Chinese, Russian, and American artists. Her clientele mainly comes from Asia. But Kashya Hildebrand apparently could not shake off her past. On August 15, 2011, she placed an exchange order for 400,000 Swiss francs against 504,477 dollars - according to Hildebrand's later statements without his knowledge. On September 6, 2011, Hildebrand, in his capacity as president of the central bank, announced that the Swiss franc would now be pegged to the euro, in order to lower the franc's value. His wife's dollar transactions turned out to be very profitable. But this was only known months later when bank employees forwarded the Hildebrand's account documents to Swiss National Councilor Christoph Blocher, a right-wing politician and critic of Hildebrand. Philipp Hildebrand publicly stated that he was not aware of the transaction before making his decision to set a euro floor rate. Various external and internal investigations all concluded that the Hildebrands were not responsible for any violations. But the pressure on Hildebrand was too great. He resigned in January 2012. He had "fought like a lion for the job," he said upon his departure.

Even before his resignation, Hildebrand was a somewhat controversial figure in Switzerland. He began his career - where else? - at the World Economic Forum, as a "baggage handler," as employees responsible for organizing the "weff" are called. Whether he owes it to his time at the "weff" or not, Hildebrand has proven to be a master in the field of networking. He is still considered one of the most well-connected and internationally recognized figures in finance. The Swiss business magazine Bilanz once dubbed him "Der Überbanker." A man who could rival the Britons and Americans dominating the financial markets and who speaks their language. But Hildebrand's familiarity with Wall Street and the City seemed inappropriate for a central banker in the eyes of his Swiss detractors, even before the scandal of the dollar transaction. The multimillionaire not only kept excellent contacts with bankers and hedge fund managers. He was also a leading financial diplomat. Theresa May, the British Prime Minister who had to step down following Brexit, appointed the Swiss to the board of the British Museum - one of the most prestigious titles of the Empire. Hildebrand was a member of the Strategic Committee of the French Treasury Agency, the French institution responsible for debt and asset management. He became Vice Chairman of the Financial Stability Board, the Basel-based international body founded after the 2008 financial crisis to prevent such crises in the future. The president at the time was former Goldman Sachs European branch vice president Mario Draghi, who later became president of the ECB. Hildebrand is also connected to Draghi via the Group of Thirty, whose thirty members are recruited from an exclusive circle of former and current central bankers, academics, and bankers. The goal of this club, founded in the 1970s by the Rockefeller Foundation, is, according to its website, "to deepen understanding of the issues facing international economic and financial markets" and "to examine the opportunities offered by market participants and regulators." Members include former Fed Chair Janet Yellen, abruptly fired by Donald Trump after one term, and former ECB President Jean-Claude Trichet. Former Bundesbank President Axel Weber is also on board, as is Zhou Xiaochuan, governor of the People's Bank of China. Oh, and there's also Larry Summers, who, after serving as Treasury Secretary under Bill Clinton, was president of Harvard University for a while and then became Obama's closest advisor. Hildebrand is as familiar with Summers as he is with Timothy Geithner - Larry Fink's old acquaintance from his New York days - and former President Bill Clinton. Mark Carney, Hildebrand's wedding witness, is a close friend. Carney, a former Goldman Sachs banker, first served as Governor of the Bank of Canada before becoming Governor of the Bank of England from 2013 to 2020.

Hildebrand's marriage to Kashya now belongs to history. It is now Margarita Louis-Dreyfus who is by his side. The French media call her "the Tsarina." Born in Russia, Margarita Bogdanova also experienced an unusual social ascent. After the fall of the Iron Curtain, she married a Swiss. But the marriage did not last long: she met Frenchman Robert Louis-Dreyfus. While he is best known to the public for being the head of Adidas, Robert Louis-Dreyfus was also the heir to an empire: he led the Louis-Dreyfus Company B.V. (abbreviated as LDC), once founded by his great-grandfather, an Alsatian grain trader. LDC is one of the world's giants in the protein sector, along with its American rivals Cargill, Bunge, and ADM, without whom supermarket shelves would be virtually empty: there is practically no food produced without their involvement. Louis-Dreyfus died of leukemia in July 2009. The "blonde Russian with silver eyes," as the Swiss tabloid Blick named his widow, surprised everyone by "taking over the reins of the empire." Hildebrand and the billionaire met in 2013 in Davos - where else? Two years later, they were back - as Larry Fink's escorts at the Belvédère cocktail party.

That the Swiss removed Hildebrand from his position did not prevent him from keeping his friends in high finance and politics. In this world, BlackRock, with its acquired empire, still had the label of the upstart, the newcomer without a family tree. With Hildebrand, doors suddenly opened for Fink that had remained closed to him until then, despite his trillions.

The ECB's Knighthood

Hildebrand's connections likely did not harm BlackRock's most prestigious mission in Europe to date, secured in 2014. The then-President of the ECB, Mario Draghi - well acquainted with former central banker Hildebrand - announced in August that he wanted to implement a program to purchase private securitized credits. BlackRock was to act as a consultant to the ECB. When asked if there had been a tender process, the ECB press office indicated that a "competition-based negotiation process" had taken place. This would align with the ECB's procurement guidelines, as per Article 6.1. Draghi had first publicly mentioned such a program in January 2014 - in Davos, to be precise, at the "weff." Essentially, the program aimed to enable eurozone banks to lend more to individuals and businesses. According to the plan, banks would pool together auto loans, mortgages, and other private loans into pools and then issue securities in the form of tranches. The ECB would then purchase these securities. Because the ECB is a safe buyer, banks would be willing to lend more of this type. The fresh money issued by the banks would then - the idea goes - lead individuals to buy new cars, TVs, and furniture on credit, thus increasing demand. Companies would use borrowed capital to build new factories and create more jobs.

Traditionally, the central bank tries to achieve this goal through interest rate cuts. But the eurozone interest rates were already close to zero at the time. The economies of the Southern countries did not pick up as a result. The purchasing program, for which Draghi's team had commissioned Fink's troupe, was nevertheless important for former Goldman banker Draghi, for political reasons. It was a challenge he threw at his adversary, the President of the German Federal Bank, Jens Weidmann. At the time, the two men clashed behind the scenes. Draghi actually wanted to buy government bonds on a large scale - following the example of the American central bank. The latter had revived the U.S. economy with this method - Quantitative Easing, or QE for short. Despite the apparent success, its real effect remains highly controversial. In any case, Weidmann resisted the QE for a long time. The program for which Draghi commissioned BlackRock is a variant of this. A kind of light QE. Awarding the contract to BlackRock would finally make it clear to Weidmann that QE would indeed happen.

Fundamentally, what Draghi had in mind was nothing more than a desperate attempt to restart the slot machine, which had shattered in 2007 due to toxic mortgages and triggered the crisis. Supporters of buying securitized credits - unsurprisingly, major European banks such as Deutsche Bank and ING were alongside Draghi - argued that the only problem with the slot machine had been the poor quality of the securitized credits. So if one really paid attention to this quality, the slot machine should have the potential to stimulate the European economy.

Such a program also offers banks a good opportunity to get rid of toxic securities to the ECB. And thus, to shift the risk of default onto the taxpayer. A risk that the ECB was apparently willing to take. When announcing the purchase program, Benoît Cœuré, a member of the ECB's board of directors, explained that for the targeted purchase program to fully develop its potential, governments should guarantee at least part of it in case of default: "The securitization market will need much larger public sponsorship," he told Risk magazine. In other words: losses would be borne by the taxpayer. Draghi himself repeated several times that he wanted the conditions for securitization to be relaxed. According to him, the only way to get the market for these securitized credits back on track, a market that had almost dried up after the financial crisis. The combination of state guarantees and relaxed rules: a horror movie scenario for skeptics like Weidmann.

The choice of BlackRock posed enormous problems. Because BlackRock was at the time, at least according to calculations by the Bloomberg economic information group, one of the largest investors in European securitized credits, precisely those that were to be purchased as part of the ECB program. An obvious conflict of interest.

On November 21, 2014, the purchase program was launched under the official name of Asset-Backed Securities Purchase Programme, or ABSPP, as the ECB declared. The ECB wanted BlackRock Solutions, an "independent institution" of BlackRock Inc., to be awarded the mission. BlackRock Solutions would only act as an advisor for the "design and implementation" and would have nothing to do with the ongoing program, according to the statement. The contract between the ECB and BlackRock Solutions included a number of precautions to "largely mitigate conflicts of interest," according to the ECB. Among other things, BlackRock was required to separate employees working on the ABSPP for the ECB from those who would work on securitizations. External auditors would verify this. But the ECB did not want to disclose their names. During the procurement process, BlackRock would have shown "great experience" and "best practices" in managing conflicts of interest, as hailed by the ECB.

In January 2015, when the ECB announced an extension of its purchases, a certain Russ Koesterich, an investment expert, told the Pension Fund Insider website that it was a "positive surprise for investors." While these purchases would certainly not be able to boost growth within the EU, they would support European stock exchanges. Russ Koesterich's employer was none other than BlackRock, a major investor in European stock exchanges. Who else benefited from this purchase program? This is what Positive Money Europe, a non-profit organization seeking to make monetary policies more transparent and democratic, wanted to find out. But when the organization tried to learn more about the securities purchase program - some 290 billion euros nonetheless - in 2017 in the name of freedom of information, the central bank refused to say anything. It was only after a request from the European Parliament that it was revealed that the purchases mainly concerned real estate loans and car purchase credits. In other words, the ECB indirectly subsidizes the French and German real estate and automotive sectors.

BlackRock had not yet had its final say. In 2016, the ECB hired the New Yorkers to advise central bankers during stress tests of European banks. As with each of these exams, explosive information - such as the share of bad loans in bank assets - circulated. Once again, Frankfurt did not seem to fear potential conflicts of interest, even though BlackRock was a major shareholder in the main banks under scrutiny. "The consulting activity is separate from the rest of BlackRock's activities," and "confidentiality is stipulated in the contracts," according to the ECB spokesperson interviewed by Reuters. Were the tests really strict? Banco Popular, for example, Spain's sixth-largest bank, was given the green light by the ECB and collapsed a few months later. Oops. The ECB was apparently satisfied nonetheless. Indeed, BlackRock was hired again two years later for new stress tests.

The Symbiosis with Central Bankers

In 2016, the advisors responsible for stress tests received 8.2 million euros, as revealed by Danièle Nouy, at the time a member of the supervisory board of the central bank, in a letter to German Finance Minister Wolfgang Schäuble. A trifle for BlackRock. But first-rate banks, central banks, are very special clients for the firm. Before the crisis, the "Lords of finance," as Liaquat Ahamed calls them in his eponymous book on the role of central bankers in the 1930s depression, acted in the background. Located somewhere between the state and the financial system, they rarely appeared in public. Since they have been throwing around billions like crazy people throw confetti for Mardi Gras, their names - Janet Yellen and her successor Jay Powell on the Fed side, Mario Draghi and his successor Christine Lagarde on the ECB side - are as well-known as those of heads of state. But, as always, the internal processes of central banks remain difficult to understand, even for economists. Although central banks have now existed for hundreds of years (the Swedish Riksbank, for example, was founded in 1668), these institutions are still surrounded by a certain mystery. Decisions were and still are made behind closed doors. The founding of the Federal Reserve, for example, could have inspired a thriller scenario: the bankers involved in the planning - mostly from Wall Street - traveled in November 1910 by train, under pseudonyms and under the pretext of going duck hunting, to Florida and from there deep into the Deep South, to Georgia, where they finally met on a private island off the coast. The Fed was born from this secret plan three years later. For twenty years, none of the participants revealed a single word about their meeting on the island. They rightly feared opposition from the U.S. Congress, which saw the new institution as a competitor in terms of power and influence. Since then, a crowd of financial sector specialists have done nothing but monitor the Fed or the ECB. Every speech, every appearance of a central banker generates long interpretations spanning several pages. At one of her first press conferences in 2014, Janet Yellen was asked what "for a long time" meant. The Fed had indeed stated in its minutes that it wanted to keep interest rates low "for a long time." Yellen hesitated for a few seconds and then stammered, "Six months or something like that." This answer quickly triggered a collapse in stock and bond markets. With her completely thoughtless statement, the central bank president had suddenly set a concrete date for a rate hike! Alan Greenspan, who was chairman of the Fed from 1987 to 2006, was a grand master in the art of cryptic statements. In order to have the slightest point of reference, Wall Street tried to decipher Greenspan's interest rate decisions in advance by the degree of filling of the briefcase with which the central bank president went to the office on the day of the Fed meeting. (Yes, television was there when Greenspan climbed the stairs of the Fed building on those days!)

If there is anyone who has recognized the political power of the Fed, it is Donald Trump. Not only did he replace the academic Yellen, whom he hated, with former private equity specialist Powell, but, unlike his predecessors, he is not afraid to publicly attack Powell and his Fed committee - that's his way. In his speeches and tweets, he has called the Federal Reserve "pathetic" and "ignorant." Once, he called them "boneheads." Then Trump publicly doubted the mindset of the central bank again: "Fed is going loco." In the summer of 2019, amidst a trade war with the Chinese, the American president even declared that he did not know who was the greatest enemy of the Americans - Fed chief Powell or Chinese President Xi. As bizarre as Trump's tirades against Powell & Co. may seem, they ended up pulling central bankers out of their lofty position and dragging them into the depths of politics.

In Europe as well, central bankers have increasingly come under criticism. In Germany in particular, ECB bankers are seen as money destroyers. German savers would be "secretly expropriated," as famous economist Hans-Werner Sinn stated in the German business magazine Wirtschaftswoche. At a time when old and new rifts are deepening between member states, the ECB has become the key support maintaining the structure. Mario Draghi ultimately defended European unity with the euro. It was therefore logical to choose a politician to succeed him - Christine Lagarde had been Finance Minister in

France before becoming Managing Director of the International Monetary Fund and then President of the ECB.

The importance and role of central bankers have increased over the past decades also because globalization has evolved. In the past, money flows followed those of goods. Today, money fluctuates, seeking investments across the globe. The 2008 crisis disenchanted central bankers but also politicized them. Ben Bernanke, Greenspan's successor, was not afraid to take unprecedented measures to revive the U.S. economy after the 2008 debt debacle. Bernanke allegedly created so many emergency bailout programs like the TALF that a "document containing all the names and their brief descriptions in small print would fill an A4 sheet," as described during the crisis by Neil Irwin, the Fed correspondent for the Washington Post. The Fed de facto pursued and still pursues a countercyclical policy. Republican lawmakers in Congress, especially during Bernanke's tenure, felt that the central bank's actions were an abuse of power. But from Bernanke's point of view, he had no choice but to steer the Fed in this direction. In the end, Congress was paralyzed due to the opposition of the majority of Republicans to the Democratic president. President Obama, newly elected at the time, failed to unlock more money after his initial $800 billion package, which many economists deemed too limited. Thus, the Fed became the only player capable in Washington. Moreover, Bernanke's crisis management served as a model for combating the crisis that erupted in 2020, caused by the Covid-19 pandemic. But we will see more about this later.

Central bankers have thus taken on tasks that politicians cannot or do not want to assume in crisis management. And those who are by their side to help them are BlackRock, PIMCO & Co., responsible for the concrete implementation of measures such as stress tests and bond purchase programs. For BlackRock, for example, central banks are among the most important clients. Fifty central banks have already engaged BlackRock to manage their reserves, among other things. Hildebrand thus told the Central Banking website that his firm's involvement in this area was one of the reasons he accepted the position at Fink's.

Central banks are very interesting clients for financial groups. Both for the prestige and fees as well as the quality of the tasks. But central banks also have valuable information. Especially for market participants. Because no one can control markets like them. Yes, of course, there are the famous "Chinese walls," these organizational precautions through which companies must prevent their employees from learning what they should not know. But when you mention these "Chinese walls" on Wall Street, you generally get a smile and a shrug in return. "Will Joe have a beer with Harry after work? You can bet on it," insiders say. And even if one wanted to, how could one ignore information that one has in one's head? "You can't unknow something" is a common comment on the subject. It's hard to go from knowing to not knowing.

In its statements, BlackRock insists on the existence of "Chinese walls" between its advisors and fund managers. However, the company also communicates about its privileged insider status. Thus, in the 2006 annual report, it is written that "the close links between investment activities and other types of activities remain an important factor in ensuring our long-term success." In the 2013-2014 internal transparency report, the American asset manager defines itself as "a truly international company that combines the advantages of global influence with those of a network of local services." With its twenty-nine primary investment centers, BlackRock is present in all major capital markets, which gives it "greater knowledge of increasingly interconnected financial markets." Finally, "We believe that investment knowledge, acquired locally and disseminated globally, maximizes investment opportunities for our clients." Coddling state institutions would even be an obligation to fund clients, the company stated in a 2016 press release: "It is our duty and job to maintain close and deep relationships with governments around the world, regardless of the party in power." These "close and deep relationships" have aroused suspicion from the Campaign for Accountability, a Washington-based organization that tracks abuses of power and resources. In the summer of 2018, this non-profit organization launched a project dedicated exclusively to BlackRock's practices. Among other questions, the issue of the alleged impermeability of "Chinese walls" raised their suspicions. Lili Forouraghi, for example, moved from the advisory side, where she assisted central bankers and finance ministers, to the investment side, where she advised major institutional investors on their investment strategies. Real estate expert Wayne Fitzgerald, on the other hand, was initially active at BlackRock Solutions before moving to the investment side. Olivier Defaux, a member of the Financial Markets Advisory Team when it was dealing with the Troika and the central banks of Ireland, Greece, and Sweden, before changing departments and advising initially large insurance companies and then being active in the European mortgage investment sector. (He left BlackRock in 2016.)

Politicians have evidently capitulated to the network of central bankers and their right-hand men. When asked if he was not worried about the potential conflicts of interest that BlackRock's mission at the ECB could create, a European parliamentarian known for his critical stance on the finance sector replied: "For such missions, there are only a few experts, so there will always be conflicts of interest." It's not encouraging, but it's reality. A European banker who has long worked in Brussels cannot hide a certain admiration for the guys on Wall Street: "In the end, they created all these complex products and systems, the management and analysis of which are now indispensable."

CHAPTER 5

Shadow Finance Operates in Secret

It could be the lobby of a hotel, accommodation for business travelers enjoying an acceptable expense account. On the windowless walls, a bit dark, there is modern art, neither too provocative nor too tame. Light armchair-sofa sets, side tables with the usual coffee table books and newspapers. However, no one dares to sink into the cushions to comfortably flip through them. Not even the visitors waiting for their BlackRock hosts to come get them. The sofa cushions are embroidered with colors, and if you look closely, you can see a map of the world in the patterns. Perhaps a nod to Larry Fink's penchant for folk art.

This is the headquarters in New York. From here, all the threads unwind across the globe, to Frankfurt, Zurich, London, Shanghai, Tokyo, and Hong Kong. Behind the glass doors of the lobby, the offices are functional, with beige textile wall coverings, and most of the furniture could well have been ordered from the discount store Office Depot. The usual cubicles - the square meter allotted to modern office employees around their work table. A windowless video conference room is dominated by a triptych of screens at human height, and apart from the clock (analog!), there is no decoration on the wall. Nothing is lying around, not even a ballpoint pen. "We are professional, we are efficient, we are focused," says the furnishings. We are far, very far, for example, from the interior of the $2 billion Goldman Sachs tower in Downtown Manhattan, whose sky lobby is the size of a concert hall, with a glass facade offering a panoramic view of the Hudson River, which impresses even the most jaded New Yorkers.

In doing so, Goldman was not a model of discretion. The reputation for being arrogant and brilliant preceded the Goldmans. And representatives of BlackRock strive to convey a similar aura of inaccessibility and infallibility. BlackRock "would like to be Goldman too much," quips a former employee on an online forum.

Before the financial crisis, "Goldman envy," the envious look at Goldman Sachs bankers, was a well-known concept, a widespread malaise on Wall Street and in the City of London. Not just because of the compensation - which was anything but negligible: during its golden period in 2007, Goldman paid out $20 billion to its employees. "Goldman had it factor, the intellectual appeal," enthused Financial Times columnist Gillian Tett. Who wouldn't want to be part of a recognized troupe of financial geniuses who, on the one hand, designed derivative structures capable of making a cybernetician dizzy, and on the other hand, concluded backroom deals that would impress Byzantine diplomats?

Graduates from elite American universities clamored for a chance to join Goldman. And after their careers in world capitals, ministers and heads of administration were happy to join the "government Sachs," as the bank was nicknamed in Wall Street banter. A classic example of this revolving door between Goldman and Washington: Robert Zoellick, a former deputy secretary of state in the George W. Bush administration, who then became CEO at Goldman and finally president of the World Bank. Gary Cohn's passage, number two at Goldman, to Donald Trump's cabinet seems to have been rather hurried. Cohn, who had never managed to take over Lloyd Blankfein's chairmanship of the bank, had probably hoped to make a name for himself in Washington. But, despite being toughened by a long career in one of the most hostile work environments, Cohn lasted only a few months as Trump's advisor. Europe's most eminent revolving door operator was undoubtedly Mario Draghi, once at the World Bank and the Italian Ministry of Finance, then at Goldman Sachs, and finally president of the ECB.

Certainly, Goldman fared better in the financial crisis than most of its competitors, but its reputation for untouchability disappeared. During an interview, Lloyd Blankfein remarked that his bank was doing "God's work." A joke, he later assured, but in vain. There was the Abacus case. A construction of fragile mortgage securities that Goldman put together for hedge fund tycoon John Paulson, and the stroke of genius was that Paulson wanted to bet against it, meaning he was betting that the mortgages would fail. It was not very smart, as later reproached by the SEC, the U.S. securities regulator, to sell Abacus shares to other Goldman clients without telling them about Paulson's bet. According to the SEC, Paulson made $1 billion with his bet, but clients on the other side, like the German bank IKB, lost $150 million. The SEC ordered a $550 million payment to settle the matter, a record amount for a single Wall Street firm, according to the securities authority. An email from a Goldman banker in charge of Abacus, Fabrice Tourre, did not help the investigators much. He stated about the mortgage market: "The whole building is about to collapse. Only Fabulous Fab will survive." By "Fabulous Fab," he was referring to himself, quite modestly. Merciless criticism even came from within their own ranks. Greg Smith, a long-time Goldman manager in London, attached an open letter to The New York Times to his resignation from the bank in early 2012, complaining about Goldman's culture as being "toxic and destructive." There, they liked to denigrate clients by calling them "muppets," among other British slang words for "idiots." Smith's confessions sparked a wave of outrage – but also mockery and sarcasm. The satirical website Funny or Die, for example, published a video sketch, viewed hundreds of thousands of times, in which fictional Goldman managers indulge in cocaine, engage in sexual escapades with Asian interns, and denigrate their clients at a board meeting – until, suddenly, "real" Muppets from The Muppet Show burst in and attack them for "defamation." The fictional Goldman men are unimpressed: "I've got suits made out of bitches like you," says one of the pinstriped men.

Suddenly, the Goldmans were no longer seen as cool and competent but as cunning swindlers. While after the financial crisis Goldman found itself under the harsh glare of the spotlight, BlackRock's secret ascent began. According to Gillian Tett, a Financial Times columnist, "the desire to be like BlackRock replaced the shine of Goldman." Tett takes a scientific look at this development, trained as an anthropologist, she has been observing Wall Street tribes for years rather than Amazonian Indians. On online forums, where university graduates exchange information about career opportunities, alongside the name Goldman, appears the name BlackRock – a name that didn't even exist just over two decades ago. BlackRock is becoming increasingly the destination to aim for after a political career. Tom Donilon, Obama's national security advisor, joined in 2014. Donilon had advised the president for the commando that killed Osama bin Laden and then resigned after the attack on the American embassy in Benghazi, Libya, in which the American ambassador lost his life. Among the most well-connected American recruits was Peter Fisher, Treasury Secretary in the early Bush years before joining the firm, a position he held alongside a non-executive directorship at the UK Financial Services Authority. The BlackRock Transparency Project counted eighty-four former officials from ministries and central banks who joined the asset manager between 2004 and 2018, in the U.S. and elsewhere.

As far as we know, Fink also reportedly tried to recruit Obama's Treasury Secretary, Geithner, after his tenure. But Geithner opted for the private equity firm Warburg Pincus. Perhaps Geithner declined his friend Fink's offer to avoid giving the impression that the job at BlackRock was a thank you for the lucrative public contracts Fink had received during his tenure.

However, the BlackRockers have stayed out of the Manhattan finance scene. They are not bankers. Nor hedge fund managers. They are buy side - intermediaries for small and large investors. But they have little in common with old-school investment firms like Fidelity or American Funds, the traditional buy side. So, they stand apart. And they rarely attract attention.

BlackRockers almost never appear on the notorious pages of Dealbreaker, an online gossip site that gleefully spreads juicy news from the bedrooms and offices of Wall Street. The most spectacular BlackRock scandal to date, as reported on Dealbreaker, had nothing to do with the usual themes – sex & drugs or insider trading. It was about subway fraud. With a lot of style and in a systematic manner, nonetheless.

Jonathan Paul Burrows worked as an investment manager in BlackRock's London office. But, like many of his City colleagues, he preferred to live in one of the green suburbs. He immediately bought several properties for £4 million in East Sussex. But there was the issue of commuting to work. A one-way ticket from his Stonegate station to the City cost £21.50. This investment specialist thought that was too expensive. Being resourceful, he found a loophole: there was no payment barrier at Stonegate, so Burrows could travel to Cannon Station in London. It was only when he exited the subway upon arrival that he validated his electronic transport card, so only the final stations in London were charged, at a cost of £7.20. Burrows apparently practiced this personal fare reduction for more than five years, until a railway employee observed him and uncovered the scheme. The transport company calculated that, in total, the BlackRock man had defrauded them of £67,000. Burrows tried to settle the matter quietly and discreetly by reaching a compromise with the railway company. But transport unionists exposed the arrangement and made his name, along with his employer's, public. Other subway users were enraged, but his cleverness and the fact that he had remained undetected for so long also earned him recognition. In a headline, the Daily Mail even dubbed him "the world's biggest tube fare dodger." The UK financial services authority, however, did not share this admiration and banned him for life from senior roles in the financial industry. Burrows also resigned from his position at BlackRock. His reaction to his banishment was noteworthy: he regretted taking up the time of the financial services authority, which certainly had more serious offenses than his to pursue. Not quite the repentant sinner, it seems. At the New York headquarters, Burrows' fraud elicited some expletives that we won't repeat here. It's not quite the kind of resourcefulness BlackRock wants to be known for.

In any case, the Rice affair was more serious. Daniel Rice III came from a family active in the energy sector. So, it was a good thing that he was the co-manager of various BlackRock funds that also invested in the sector. In 2007, Rice co-founded a company called Rice Energy. A subsidiary of Rice Energy later entered into a joint venture with a coal and gas firm named Alpha Natural Resources. Rice became a director and his three sons took over as CEO, CFO, and chief geologist. By 2011, Alpha was the largest equity position in the BlackRock Energy & Resources fund managed by Rice. Rice's employer, BlackRock, had authorized this sideline activity. Unfortunately, the fund's investors were not informed. Many of them apparently learned about it from The Wall Street Journal. "Fund manager prefers home cooking," the headline read. The SEC did not find the matter amusing. Rice backtracked. And in April 2015, BlackRock settled the matter with a settlement agreement and paid $12 million. "As fiduciary agents of our clients, we take anything that could appear as a conflict of interest very seriously," a BlackRock spokesperson assured The Wall Street Journal. However, he clarified, this settlement was in no way an admission of guilt.

Family ties also caused the downfall of another fund manager. Randy Robertson, with over ten years of experience at BlackRock, was a co-manager of a fund with the unappealing name of BlackRock Multi-Sector Income Trust. According to a presentation prospectus, the fund had "obviously high income and returns" in the past. In 2017, the fund granted a $75 million loan to a film company named Aviron Capital, which represented 10% of the total capital that investors at the time had invested in Multi-Sector Income Trust. Two years later, almost all the money had disappeared. BlackRock sued Aviron's owner for fraud. He admitted to providing documents with a false signature of BlackRock's executives. On top of that, he had a funny story to tell - perhaps not Hollywood-worthy, but it could make a good TV comedy. Aviron had tried to launch the acting career of a certain Rebecca Lee Robertson. Robertson? Yes, like Randy: anything but a coincidence, as she is the daughter of the fund manager. In 2019, Aviron produced the film After: Chapter 1, which tells the story of young student Tessa whose loyalty to her high school sweetheart is tested by Hardin, a young man just as mysterious as he is attractive. "After your first, life is never the same," the movie poster announced. Aviron had managed to get a role for Robertson's daughter in After. Shortly after, the fund managed by Robertson father agreed to contribute $10 million to the financing. "I don't know if he made that decision because his daughter was in the movie," William Sadleir told The Wall Street Journal, "but I can tell you that BlackRock approved this financing after rejecting various other film projects." In its article, The Wall Street Journal sharply pointed out that such a large investment firm should establish standard procedures to "avoid conflicts of interest and prevent fund managers from making risky bets." Ouch... That must have been hard to swallow for Fink & Co. Responding to journalists, BlackRock stated that the company had been a victim of fraud by Aviron and its director. For Randy Robertson, there was certainly no happy ending: he was fired.

As for BlackRock's connection to the major financial scandal CumEx, we will look at that later.

On trading days, an internal briefing is held at BlackRock's headquarters every morning at 8 o'clock. Officially, it's called the "daily global meeting" during which, according to BlackRock's website, colleagues discuss "market news and investment outlooks." Employees from other offices around the globe join the meeting via their screens. Participants identify themselves by their expertise: "US interest rates" or "securitization," instead of their names on the tags. This is how Fortune describes the ritual, which an executive refers to as a "mandatory event." For a former employee, such habits were suspicious. He felt like he was in a "cult." The internal "chichi" and "hype," as he puts it, eventually got on his nerves so much that he resigned. He does not want his name to be mentioned at all. Other former BlackRock employees don't want to say anything, even anonymously, not even something positive. Fink also does not have unanimous support. The boss is said to be temperamental - sometimes he acts like the popular guy and invites people to Starbucks, sometimes he is tough and authoritarian. According to a former executive, colleagues have called him after a meeting with Larry and asked, only half-jokingly, "So, are you still alive?" On Glassdoor, a website where employees can anonymously rate their current or former employers, some complain about "nepotism," scheming, brainwashing - however, the majority of reviews are positive. In a workplace survey conducted by Pensions & Investments, the retirement professionals' magazine, BlackRock still ranked fourth out of sixty-nine asset managers in 2018. "It's the best employer in the industry," "It takes care of us," praised interviewed employees.

Europeans, in particular, seem to struggle with BlackRock's culture. There are complaints that non-Anglo-Saxons are not taken seriously. New York always has the final say.

A former central banker, also from Europe, has an even harsher judgment. He says that people at BlackRock are arrogant, and even "worse than those at Goldman." And he has a disturbing idea to explain why BlackRock has become the new favorite among emerging talents on Wall Street: at Goldman & Co., stricter regulations for banks would reduce their freedom and maneuverability. "What you are no longer allowed to do at Goldman, you can now do at BlackRock." In a way, BlackRock would be the "dark twin of Goldman." One thing is certain: in just a few years, Fink skillfully transformed his former back-office bond shack into a global player, pulling the strings behind the scenes. And that is no coincidence.

The heretic: help, we've shrunk the banks!

The meeting place is the lobby of the Waldorf Astoria. The Art Deco building on Park Avenue was the preferred hotel for American presidents since Herbert Hoover and the birthplace of the eponymous salad. The nearly ninety-year-old building (previously, the hotel was located where the current Empire State Building stands) is a New York icon; Marilyn Monroe stayed there, and Henry Kissinger conducted his diplomatic affairs there. At the time this book was written, the Waldorf resembled those old ladies of New York society whose sparkling diamonds and exuberant reds couldn't hide their gray hair and wrinkled cheeks but who remained the undisputed sovereigns of gala receptions and balls. Today, the chandeliers at the Waldorf glow faintly, the mirrors are slightly tarnished. On the internet, tourists from the provinces complain about blocked bathroom doors, worn-out carpets, and shabby wallpapers. But the Waldorf is still the perfect backdrop for Richard X. Bove. His dark suit is perfectly matched, his tie is neatly tied, his gold cufflinks shine while remaining matte. His white beard is neatly trimmed, his blue eyes flash. "Half badass, half Santa Claus," as Businessweek once described him. When he reaches for his jacket, one is disappointed not to see him pull out a heavy pocket watch but his Samsung cell phone. When you see Bove like this, you could never guess. But this father of seven, grandfather of fourteen, and owner of two pizzerias is a heretic.

To make our financial system safer, banks must be more strongly regulated; the more capital they hold, the more stable credit institutions are; it would be best to break up the big banks: every time Richard X. Bove hears these arguments, he gets angry. Bove is a staunch defender of big banks, financial giants like JPMorgan Chase and Bank of America. He calls them "the guardians of our prosperity." That's also the title of his book, which should be seen less as an essay than as the plea of a pro bono defender in the public opinion courtroom. Bove dismisses attempts to restrict or even dismantle financial behemoths as "nonsense."

Banks have been Bove's bread and butter for over forty years. He is a financial analyst. This means he evaluates the stocks of financial institutions. His judgment helps investors decide whether to buy, hold, or sell bank stocks. Banks and investment firms employ analysts because their clients - big investors - willingly take their studies and recommendations as a service. During the dot-com bubble, analysts working in big banks fell into serious disrepute. If their colleagues in investment banks, for example, took a start-up public, it was because a hot recommendation from these analysts had encouraged them - or at least not dissuaded them from buying. The least glorious example of duplicity was Henry Blodget, who, as a star analyst at Merrill Lynch, publicly praised the merits of web companies while privately calling them crap in emails to employees. The attorney general at the time, Eliot Spitzer, caught wind of this. Spitzer then set out to clean up Wall Street, and his first targets were the analysts. As a result, banks had to pay a combined $1.5 billion fine - a record at the time! - and promise to resolve conflicts of interest. Blodget was banned from the equity sector for life.

Bove has never been one of the analysts at big institutions. Although born in New York, he moved to Tampa, Florida, with his family. His employers have always been what are called "boutiques" on Wall Street: small, independent firms that offer specialized services to clients such as investment funds or hedge funds. Bove made a name for himself as an analyst because he gave his opinion in a "ruthlessly open" way, as the Wall Street Journal somewhat ambiguously noted. When Wachovia, the country's second-largest savings bank, bought California's Golden West for $24 billion in 2006, many analysts hailed the deal as a savvy strategic decision. Bove's opinion: Wachovia had simply brought "nuclear waste" into the house. Because Golden West had specialized in mortgages with rising interest rates, which had subsequently often fallen. Wachovia collapsed two years later due to mortgage losses and was forcibly sold to Wells Fargo by regulators.

Bove is also tough on himself. In August 2005, he warned that banks had created a mortgage bubble with their lending criteria. "This powder keg will explode," the title of his study announced. "When I wrote that, people said I was crazy," explains Bove. "If I had stuck with that, I would have become a hero." But by early 2008, he felt the worst was behind... and recommended buying bank stocks. Lehman collapsed in the fall. His buy recommendation had become a "horror," Bove now says, who dislikes embellishing his major mistakes. His ruthless formulations may be one of the reasons Bove has never worked for a big bank. Bank Atlantic, a regional bank he publicly identified as a fragile candidate in 2008, even sued him for damages. The lawsuit dragged on for years and cost Bove his job and $800,000 in legal fees. In the end, they reached a settlement where Bove didn't have to pay a cent to the bank. The SEC, the U.S. federal regulatory and oversight agency for financial markets, later won a lawsuit against Bank Atlantic because the institution had deceived its investors about the quality of its loans.

But the dispute with Bank Atlantic did not deter Bove in any way.

In the meantime, he has become just as uncompromising in defending the banks as he is relentless in judging their activities. "We are trying to separate ourselves from the financial system - this will end in disaster," he warns grimly. From his point of view, banks were not at all responsible for the crisis. Instead, Bove sees the imbalance in the United States' global trade as the real cause. The United States imports more than it exports, especially with China. Because American buyers pay their international suppliers in dollars, there is an abundance of dollars. "Huge amounts of dollars are overflowing everywhere, looking for a home," Bove regularly explained before the crisis. They eventually found a home in exotic financial vehicles in the U.S. real estate sector. In these famous CDOs, CMOs, and CDSs, of which Larry Fink was once a pioneer. It is clear that banks promoted and accelerated the process. "For dubious or illegal practices, banks should be prosecuted and those responsible should also go to prison," says Bove. But identifying banks as the sole culprits would be wrong. And this false conclusion, which politicians in the United States and Europe, in particular, have popularized, now leads to completely misguided reforms. At the top of his list are higher reserve requirements, which were mainly introduced in the United States and, more hesitantly, in Europe. Even the Volcker Rule, with its strict limits on banks' proprietary trading, finds no favor with Bove. Both measures aim to make banks more stable and thus secure the financial system. But according to him, they have the opposite effect.

When Bove's book, which portrayed banks as Guardians of Prosperity, was published at the end of 2013, he had to take a lot of hits. The book was called "alarmist," as the distinguished New York Times writer Roger Lowenstein put it. And that was a positive evaluation. Less elegantly, a member of an online finance forum described Bove's arguments as "B.S.," which could be translated as "nonsense" to remain polite. But as controversial as Bove's statements may be - it seems difficult to consider stricter rules against excessive penalties for bank customers as a mistake made by regulators - the Wall Street veteran is right on most points. Banks are losing their importance. Their weight on global capital markets is slowly but surely slipping. And the downsizing, praised by bank critics, is showing worrying side effects.

For Bove, the new rules are creating a fundamentally different financial system - a system that harbors new, unknown threats. Transactions and activities are migrating to the realm of shadow banking. "Our hysterical persecution of banks is causing our financial system to increasingly leave the banks, the visible and regulated part, to disappear into the invisible and uncontrolled part," explains Bove. And it is from this darkness, Bove is certain, that our next crisis will come.

What Really Happened?

Shadow banking is not new. According to some definitions, shadow banks have existed longer than regulated banks. Like in Star Wars, there's the Force and the dark side of the Force. The term itself only emerged during the financial crisis. It was coined by Paul McCulley, an economist and veteran at BlackRock's archenemy, PIMCO. At the annual summer meetings between central bankers and certain star economists in the luxurious ski resort of Jackson Hole, Wyoming (the Davos of central bankers), McCulley denounced in 2007 the "little soup of financial vehicles." By then, it was already too late; the first financial vehicles McCulley spoke of - CDOs, CDSs, CMOs, SIVs, and other similar structures - were already showing signs of stress.

The first problem with shadow banks is that everyone wonders who belongs to them. The Financial Stability Board (FSB), the international body established by G20 states after the 2008 disaster, defines shadow banking as "credit intermediation taking place outside the regular banking system." In all countries with a modern financial market, only banks are allowed to accept deposits into a savings account with state deposit insurance. And only banks have direct access to the central bank. Consequently, banks play a special role in the economic fabric and must therefore adhere to specific rules - such as capital requirements, which stipulate the amount of capital a bank must hold for safety. But this by no means implies that banks are the only source of capital. A company, for example, can issue bonds and sell securities to investors - a form of credit shared by many creditors, the bondholders. Hedge funds can allocate credit, as can pawnshops and credit sharks. While the Financial Stability Board defines shadow banking very narrowly, bankers tend to adopt a broader definition: anything a bank does - including trading in securities - but taken up by an institution that is not a bank.

Banks were not the only ones to become giants before the financial crisis. Shadow banks also swelled to unprecedented proportions. In 2007, the

American sector alone reached $24.9 trillion - the combined gross domestic products of the United States and China. While the 2008 crisis did not spare shadow banks, by 2013 they already represented $25.2 trillion in the United States, $5 trillion more than the country's traditional banking sector. Globally, the dark side of finance reached around $116 trillion according to the FSB's 2018 annual report. Banks, on the other hand, lost ground: their share of the financial system dropped from 49% in 2008 to only 40%. The share of shadow banks, on the other hand, increased from 26% to 31% over the same period. A trend that will intensify in the years to come. Banks are considered the main culprits of the 2008 financial crisis. Their dubious, even criminal behavior, must not be glossed over. But it was shadow banks that turned the Lehman crisis into the spark that ignited the global conflagration and ultimately triggered the recession. At the time, money market funds, which were part of shadow banking, played a leading role often overlooked.

It was Wednesday, September 17, 2008, and the world was on the brink. Two days earlier, on September 15, at 1:45 a.m., Lehman Brothers, the investment bank, had to appear before the New York bankruptcy court, in the former customs building at the southern tip of Manhattan, after 158 years of existence. The images of Lehman employees, potted plants, and family photos hastily packed into boxes, went around the world. So far, these two days of September 2008 are considered the climax of the financial crisis. Insiders know all too well.

On the day of the catastrophe, Wednesday, a message suddenly spread through the stock market information channels: the shares of the Reserve Primary Fund, one of the oldest and largest money market funds with $64 billion, had fallen below $1, "breaking the buck," as they say on Wall Street. More than unusual, it was simply not possible. Because money market funds guaranteed their investors a minimum price of $1. You are promised that your share certificates are as hard and strong as cash. What had happened? The profit decline was a direct consequence of Lehman's bankruptcy. Reserve investors fled the fund, fearing that its managers had been sitting on Lehman's debt securities: now that Lehman had filed for bankruptcy, there was a risk of massive losses. Among Reserve's clients - pension funds, insurance companies, small investors - everyone tried to withdraw their capital from the fund as quickly as possible. It was the dreaded "run for the exit" in stock market jargon - the race to find the emergency exit before everyone else, to secure their money without losses. In just twenty-four hours, the Reserve Primary Fund lost two-thirds of its capital. In the end, it even had to be liquidated. A fund that had been around for decades and had $64 billion was swept away! Panic and emergency sales spread to other money market funds. Funds and banks, which normally exchange capital continuously, now distrusted each other: there wasn't even any money to be had from government bonds anymore.

The "run for the exit" eventually spread from the financial sector to businesses. Major corporations such as General Electric, Toyota, telecommunications giant Verizon, and motorcycle manufacturer Harley-Davidson sent distress calls to the central bank and Treasury Secretary Henry Paulson because they had run out of liquidity and could no longer obtain credit in the money market. Never before had we been so close to a complete halt in the capital flows that drive our economy as on that day.

To understand how this happened, we must delve deeper into the heart of Wall Street.

Much has been reported about the reasons for the 2008 crisis. A national economy driven by debt, overheating real estate prices in the United States, securitization of mortgages that allowed credit institutions to resell them almost risk-free, vulgar fraud by borrowers and lenders, bankers' and investors' greed and gullibility, and political control failure. Everything is true, but without a mechanism that could push risky mortgages into the heart of the financial system, we would have had discomfort, not such a cardiac arrest. This mechanism is called the repo market in Wall Street jargon: repurchase agreement, repo contract.

The repo market is reputed to be murky and a bit scary, even on Wall Street. "Bank directors themselves are fierce about repo," says an insider who has been active in this market for years. It's because of its history. The repo used to be part of the "back office," the bank's back office. The bank's activities

- accounting, administration, IT, and the execution of certain securities transactions - are implemented and organized there. The relationship between investment bankers and back-office employees is like that of Hollywood stars with extras. Repo business initially consisted of a kind of securities loan and was dominated by the "Italian guys from Brooklyn when it was still a working-class neighborhood," as one industry veteran puts it. It is precisely the unglamorous business of this gang that has become the nerve center of the modern finance market.

A revolution in the banking sector has indeed taken place, largely unnoticed by the public. In the classic business model, the bank takes money from savers, who are rewarded with interest. The bank must set aside part of the money as security, and the rest is paid out as a loan, for example, to companies or property owners, who in turn pay interest. The bank lives off the difference between the two interest rates. These businesses still exist today, and that's basically how you make your bread in finance. But Wall Street bankers discovered a more lucrative way to keep money and thus move from bread to caviar. Instead of lending money to companies, they became capital brokers. They help companies obtain the financial means they need by issuing stocks and bonds. Instead of interest, they receive fees.

On the other side of the classic model, savers also migrated. They were also lured by investment pools, the so-called money market funds, which promised them higher interest rates and, at the same time, liquidity guarantees such as cash. An interesting combination, especially for large institutions like pension funds, insurers, and the financial services of international groups, which increasingly placed their money there.

For the average employee, money is the sum of the current account balance, the (hopefully) savings, which in case of doubt are also at the bank, and the banknotes and coins in the wallet. For asset managers and international groups, money is something else: the credits they hold, and only that; because they cannot deposit bundles of physical banknotes at the bank. No safe, not even all the Swiss armored cabinets put together, could be enough, not to mention the logistical problems and the risk of theft. And since these sums exceed all deposit guarantees that any state can provide, they represent nothing else, deposited in normal bank accounts, than an uncertain promise of payment (or disbursement) from that bank. With the risk that the bank may not have the money in case of doubt. Professionals must therefore look for alternatives to place their cash as safely as possible. And the path leads straight to shadow banks, which include, among others, money market funds. These essentially constitute the savings account for institutional investors.

Banks adapted. They did business with the new rivals, which seemed to benefit all parties. Banks therefore borrowed money from money market funds and other investors. As collateral, they deposited securities such as government bonds and mortgages they held in their portfolios. Banks were thus able to expand with the money borrowed from money market funds. This exchange between money market funds, which invest their money, and banks, which want to lend it, takes place (still) on the repo market. Wall Street's former back office has become the hub of big money. The hour of the repo guys had struck.

A new kind of bank run

Almost no one perceived the risks inherent in this new model. On the contrary, it seemed even safer than the classic one. While with the classic model savers simply had to trust the bank that their money was securely stored there, with the repo model, they had securities as collateral. But this supposed security was deceptive: it led the world into the Great Recession.

However, at the outset, banks and money market funds seemed to have created an unstoppable money-making machine. The new system was so successful that it was only limited by a lack of securities that banks could use as collateral. So, the banks came up with the idea of boosting mortgage activity. American mortgages were considered ideal for this purpose - practically as safe as US government bonds and with more attractive interest rates. The perfect raw material for securities, it seemed. Banks borrowed money against mortgage securities and used the borrowed funds to finance new mortgages, which they then deposited with creditors to obtain more money, and so on. In order to issue more mortgages, lending institutions lowered credit standards, and borrower solvency requirements quickly became minimal. At the same time, the influx of money drove real estate market prices to unsustainable heights.

However, as central banks and regulatory authorities focused on overseeing traditional banking services, they missed the danger developing in this parallel banking world.

Until it all exploded in 2007: the housing bubble burst and many mortgages with it. Suddenly, fear gripped money market fund operators and other repo creditors: what about their repo deposits? How safe were their guarantees? And if the mortgage securities deposited by banks turned out to be rubbish? Repo creditors demanded more collateral from banks, putting banks in a difficult position again: they had to find funds almost overnight to meet these new security requirements. But they had no reserves for that - there were no such regulations in the shadow world. Banks then frantically sold securities from their portfolios. The prices of these securities then dropped. This triggered a new wave of fear among repo creditors: the general price decline also affected the securities they had received from banks as collateral. Suddenly, their collateral lost value. As a result, they demanded even more collateral, even more guarantees from banks. Until the pressure became too great: in March 2008, Bear Stearns collapsed, and Lehman Brothers filed for bankruptcy six months later. The high finance collateral game had collapsed.

The central bank and regulatory authorities could only watch helplessly as the rapidly deteriorating shadow system paralyzed the official financial system. For financial historian Gary Gorton, the collapse of 2008 is the modern version of a bank run, with the difference that no excited customer stormed the cashiers for their deposits: the rush of repo creditors to banks took place behind the glittering glass facades of Wall Street. Another difference: the enormity of the sums involved. By then, just before the crisis, according to some estimates, up to $10 trillion was liquidated through shadow bank repos. According to Gorton's calculation, banks had to face claims of up to $2 trillion, almost overnight.

The first victims of the repo collapse were money market funds. As an alternative to banks, they had carved out a lucrative niche in this brand new and shiny financial world. They not only replaced the good old savings account or deposits, which large investors had previously held through their bank. They also increasingly acted as lenders to companies. In order to pay their suppliers and employees, corporate CFOs issued short-term debt securities to obtain the cash they needed from money market funds. For years, the operation worked well. Money market funds earned interest, and companies got the money they needed for their daily business. But then Lehman's bankruptcy came, triggering the fall of the Reserve Primary Fund. Money market funds found themselves in a precarious situation: their investors now demanded the capital they had placed there. The funds fought for their survival. They were no longer able to lend to companies: suddenly, an apparently inexhaustible and cheap source of money for the economy dried up, practically overnight! So there was a risk of a domino effect, potentially leading to the insolvency of one company after another.

The then central bank chairman, Ben Bernanke, sounded the alarm. In order to prevent total collapse, he implemented full central bank backing for the faltering money market giants - the equivalent of a safety net on the financial market. The most expensive fishing net in history - cast by the public (taxpayers) for high finance acrobats.

In this regard, it seems almost ironic that banks were reined in by regulatory bodies after the crisis while shadow banks were allowed to proliferate almost unchecked.

The mother of all shadow banks

Before the financial crisis, there were two camps: on one side, investment banks, and on the other, their clients - large investors such as pension funds, foundations, investment funds, and multinational financial services. Sell side and buy side. Banks can be seen as supermarkets, except that the buyers are large investors. The offer does not include vegetables, dairy products, or meat, but rather stocks, bonds, or derivatives. And just as Kellogg's food tinkerers constantly invent new cereals in addition to classic cornflakes, such as Rice Krispies, Honey Pops, and Smacks, financial engineers are constantly developing new products. Instead of a "complete chocolate breakfast experience," the financial laboratory promotes an "interest rate swap operating by arbitrage and entitling to tax deductions." Until the 2008 crisis, it was normal for large investors to shop in bank supermarkets. New rules make it harder for banks to stock their shelves. Because, for most of the "products" they have on their accounts, they must deposit the corresponding equity. Not to mention empty shelves, large investors' confidence in what Wall Street traders offered them in terms of new shiny products was at an all-time low after 2008. It is not surprising that investors sought alternatives.

This was BlackRock's opportunity of the century! The passive role of the buyer, to which many asset managers had resigned, had never really suited Larry Fink and his sell-side-originating co-founders. The banks' slimming cure opened up space... for new masters of Wall Street. And they had a clear vision of the future. Generally, investment bankers advise companies on how to finance themselves: how much equity is needed, how much capital the company needs to borrow? How to finance expansion or acquisition? The bank arranges the issuance of stocks or bonds accordingly, places shares or loans. The bankers then offer them to their investor clients in the financial supermarket.

BlackRock no longer wants to wait that long. When it comes to the company's financial needs, Fink's employees want to be there from the beginning. They do not make a secret of it. This is what Peter Fisher, then head of fixed income securities at BlackRock, explained to Institutional Investor magazine in 2011: "We want to buy and hold investments with the risk-profit profile we want, instead of just having those that are already available on the market." Take the example of the Zayo Group. The company operates fiber optic networks for commercial customers such as data centers and telecommunications companies. Zayo survived the 1990s internet bubble. The Colorado company achieved this mainly by constantly swallowing its rivals, which it did more than thirty times in its history. In the summer of 2012, Zayo struck again. To finance a $1.5 billion acquisition, Zayo wanted to issue bonds. However, the market environment was very bad due to ongoing turbulence in Europe. Investors demanded high interest rates to compensate for the risk. So it seemed to be an expensive deal for Zayo. But then the company received an offer: BlackRock would buy a large part of the bonds, provided it had a say in their terms. An unusual request, considering that these terms, such as interest coupons, maturities, etc., had previously been traditionally agreed in secret in advance by investment bankers with the company. BlackRock was very pleased with the arrangement. "A model that solves problems for all stakeholders," Richard Prager congratulated himself in the pages of Fortune magazine in November 2012. Prager, known as Richie, a former foreign exchange and commodities specialist at Bank of America, joined BlackRock in 2009, where he was tasked with arranging more and more transactions of this type. He was one of the many bankers that Fink and Kapito had poached specifically to develop this department.

According to Prager, it was by no means about pushing investment banks away, as he explained to the Financial Times, which also reported on the new strategy. Nor is it about challenging bankers' banking fees. No, bankers can continue to be quietly involved in deals. BlackRock does not want to overthrow them, as long as one thing remains certain: that the fund manager gains influence. With this new model, BlackRock is not only seeking the best investment opportunities, it is creating them itself. Companies are directly offered a list of gifts from the world's largest investor. "This allows us to sit at the table from the start," Prager bluntly explains. Kapito apparently did not agree with such transparency from his colleagues. He did not see why, as he confided to Institutional Investor magazine, they should publicly talk about a topic that falls under "trade secrets." He would not want to give tips to branch imitators in any case.

However, BlackRock plays an even bigger role in the murky world of debt and private equity.

The alchemy of credit on Wall Street

When the stock market-focused channel CNBC invited two Wall Street heavyweights in front of the cameras in July 2015, it looked like a completely ordinary setup. On one side: Carl Icahn, a billionaire and hedge fund veteran with fifty years of experience. On the other: Larry Fink, also very wealthy, CEO of BlackRock, the world's largest asset manager. But instead of discussing amicably as peers, Icahn and Fink exchanged jabs that bankers and investors on Wall Street still talk about with astonishment years later. BlackRock, Icahn said, is a threat to global financial markets. It's as if his boss, Fink, is driving a bus full of revelers towards a precipice, before they crash onto a "black rock." Then Icahn threw at BlackRock's boss: "Your company is extremely dangerous!" What Icahn was referring to was not the investments in Larry & Co's stocks. The warning from the old finance warhorse was aimed at BlackRock's credit activities, particularly bonds.

When it comes to corporate bonds, no one thinks about the dark side of the financial market. A simple and proven credit instrument: a company borrows money and issues fixed-income securities to creditors. But the market for these routine securities has undergone a transformation in recent years.

Cheap money from central banks has caused disruptions. It turns out that the low interest rates with which they saved the economy after the 2008 credit crisis have since inflated a new credit bubble. This time, it's not homeowners who are indebted, but companies. Industrial bonds are experiencing a historic boom.

The total amount of all loans and bonds owed by companies worldwide was $66 trillion in 2017, according to a McKinsey management consulting study. Corporate debt has almost doubled since the crisis.

This is a global phenomenon. Chinese companies are at the forefront of this credit boom. Relative to the country's economic output, they have the highest level of debt. In Europe, the European Central Bank specifically fueled the trend. Among other things, it bought corporate bonds to accelerate economic growth. Central bankers' demand has lowered the interest rates that companies had to pay. As a result, for many financial department heads, borrowed money has become irresistibly cheap. Volkswagen alone issued €12.5 billion in bonds at the end of 2018: a new record. In 2007, a year before the financial crisis, the total volume of bonds issued by German companies was €33 billion. For 2018, the record year so far, this amount was €123 billion. Investors, in particular, could not get enough of "high-yield bonds," as Wall Street calls junk bonds, with poor solvency. "Investors are crazy about European junk," Business Insider's online newspaper headlined.

One might hope that if companies have borrowed massively, it was to build new factories, hire new employees, or invest in research and development. There is a great need for innovation, for example, to meet the challenges of climate change. But it is clear that companies have found a completely different use for this money: rewarding their shareholders. The magic formula, which turns profits from bonds (i.e., debts) into profits, would have impressed even the alchemist Johann Friedrich Böttger. Once, Augustus the Strong, king of Saxony, gave him the task of finding a formula that could turn iron or other metals into gold. Of course, Böttger did not succeed in turning metal into gold; he did, however, find a formula for producing porcelain. This was the beginning of the Meissen Royal Porcelain Manufactory, a much more enduring achievement than the stock buybacks that constitute the modern formula for making gold, invented by the alchemists of Wall Street.

Companies buy back their own shares on a large scale. By reducing the number of shares outstanding, they drive up the share price for the benefit of their shareholders. Executives, who are largely paid in shares, also benefit. This is an alternative to dividends, which, thanks to the tax advantages it offers, has become increasingly popular. Between 2008 and 2017, U.S. companies spent more than $4 trillion on this, more than half of the profits made during the same period. Given that, in addition, 40% of profits were paid out as dividends, companies, in total, gave more than 90% of their profits to owners. American economist William Lazonick calls this practice, which was prohibited until Ronald Reagan decided otherwise in 1982, "predatory value extraction." A study by his Cologne-based asset manager's think tank on the Boeing 737 Max scandal, which crashed in 2019, concludes that developing an entirely new type of aircraft would have cost Boeing about $7 billion more than the problematic modernization of the 737. According to Lazonick's calculations, this figure corresponded to the amount Boeing had spent on average each year since 2013 on its stock buyback programs - a total of $43 billion. During the same period, the company had also paid out $17 billion in dividends. Shortly after the crash of the Lion Air plane on October 29, 2018, which killed one hundred and eighty-nine people, Boeing announced a 20% increase in dividends and new buybacks of its own shares totaling $20 billion. In early March, the stock reached a record $450. Ten days later, Ethiopian Airlines Flight 302 crashed with one hundred and fifty-seven people on board. No one argues that buybacks caused these tragedies. However, they show the change in priorities of a company's management that, in the past, was a true icon of American industry, proud of its engineers.

In Germany too, share buybacks are on the rise. In 2018, German companies - including Allianz, Siemens, and Munich Re - spent nearly €10 billion buying back their own shares. A figure that may seem modest compared to those in the United States, but nonetheless the highest since the 2008 financial crisis. Companies could invest their money differently, in new products and new jobs. A study by the Flossbach von Storch asset manager's think tank in Cologne asks whether "opportunities are really lacking or whether it is rather a lack of creativity" on the part of companies in a time full of challenges posed by digitization and artificial intelligence.

But if it's a lack of managers' imagination that triggered the wave of credit securities, it's savvy financial engineers who have turned it into a tsunami.

The Queen of "Locusts"

Manhattan, a November morning in 2019. The anticipation is such that the journalists on site don't even pay attention to the view, despite it being spectacular from the Reuters offices in Times Square. Surrounded by skyscrapers, they are located just in front of the Nasdaq facade and its futuristic digital billboards. Impatiently, the journalists await the appearance of the "newsmaker" invited by the news agency. Finally, the long-awaited moment arrives: Steve Schwarzman grants an audience! The co-founder of Blackstone, the company that once gave birth to BlackRock, begins to recount his personal life. As a high school student, Schwarzman participated in an 800-meter relay race, injuring his knee tendon right after the starting block. Well aware that the pain would prevent him from achieving a good time, he ran in a way to hinder his competitors. Despite a significant delay, his team did not give up and eventually won. "It was one of the most important moments of my life because it was not about me, but about my team," he explains to Reuters' editor-in-chief. He mentions one of Blackstone's first acquisitions in the 1980s, Edgcomb Steel, a steel company. The young company went bankrupt when steel prices collapsed. Schwarzman remembers that an investor who lost money on this occasion called him into his office to scold him severely. Another valuable lesson! The financier then swore that it would never happen again. Today, it seems out of the question for anyone to even raise their voice in front of the boss of the nearly $600 billion financial giant. Schwarzman has acquired hundreds of companies. And that's not all: thanks to his millions raised through private equity, his name also appears on the main building of the New York Public Library, whose entrance is guarded by two stone lions named Patience and Fortitude, known to all the city's children. For an institution considered a symbol of the community's social achievements, such a new patron, known primarily for his expertise in accounting, has not been to everyone's liking.

Listening to Schwarzman's stories, one might get the impression that the success of private equity firms is explained by their ability to find companies that can be optimized through better management. A justification that the industry boasts about without blushing, even though it's not even half true. Because what allows private equity firms to make golden profits from companies are often brutal austerity measures combined with financial acrobatics so breathtaking that they have inspired Hollywood films.

In the United States, private equity and hedge fund managers also benefit from a tax privilege. They only pay 20% tax on their income when ordinary taxpayers can be taxed at rates as high as 37%. When President Obama threatened to remove this exception, Schwarzman compared him... to Hitler. He later apologized for this. Donald Trump also promised during his election campaign to end this privilege. "They don't pay, it's incredible, these are guys who move pieces of paper on their desk and take advantage of it," he thundered at a rally in August 2016. "They could commit murder and not be prosecuted!"

However, like his unpopular predecessor, Trump did not change anything about this exceptional regime which, according to New Yorker research, allows Schwarzman to save about $100 million in taxes annually. In the meantime, Schwarzman had become a close confidant of Trump. The president publicly thanked him for his help in achieving the first phase of the trade deal with China when the treaty was signed with great pomp in January 2020. And it was no coincidence that among the guests gathered in the White House Green Room were mostly representatives from the financial sector. They were the ones who had pushed for an agreement to be reached. Because American banks, corporate raiders, and hedge funds currently only make 2 measly billion dollars in the world's second-largest economy. Barely 1.5% of their turnover in Europe. That has to change.

Schwarzman is undoubtedly the most famous, influential, and richest figure in private equity today; but he has only perfected a method that pioneers invented as early as the 1970s.

Jerome Kohlberg, Henry Kravis, and George Roberts met at Bear Stearns, the smallest Wall Street firm at the time, known for compensating for its lack of capital with ingenuity. The scheme they invented: buying a company with borrowed money. So far, not very spectacular. But the trick was that the loan guarantee was subject to a purchase, and the debt was borne by the acquired company, not the buyer. This is called "bootstrapping" in English; it's the financial variant of Baron Munchausen, who managed to extricate himself from quicksand by pulling himself up by his own hair.

In 1976, the three bankers founded their own company, named KKR after their initials. These three letters are also well known in Germany: KKR invested in the Swabian company Württembergische Metallwarenfabrik, known since 1853 for its tableware and cutlery. Two years later, WMF cut hundreds of jobs. Not because business was bad. The Stuttgarter Zeitung reported that the company was doing wonderfully. "The cuts are necessary to make the balance sheet even more wonderful." The pastor of Geislingen, where the company was headquartered, summed up the feelings of the laid-off workers: "There is a lot of anger: some will become very rich immediately while others lose their jobs." In 2016, KKR sold the Swabian company to the French group SEB for 1.59 billion euros. An insider revealed to the Financial News website that KKR had thus achieved, as expected, a return of 40% with WMF. In 2019, KKR bought shares in Axel Springer for 2.9 billion euros, becoming the largest shareholder in the German media group.

In the United States, KKR made history as early as 1988. At the time, Kravis and Roberts—Kohlberg had already left—had their sights set on RJR Nabisco, a producer of cigarettes and biscuits. Originally, Ross Johnson, the head of Nabisco, simply wanted to use the financiers to buy back the company's shares. However, the affair subsequently took a turn that is arguably the most legendary hostile takeover battle in Wall Street history. A competitor of KKR even called the bootstrappers "barbarians at the gate" who needed to be driven away. The phrase even gave its title to a book that Wall Street Journal journalists wrote about the affair. At a price of 25 billion dollars, KKR eventually emerged victorious. However, the mountain of debt affected the group, which had to reduce its workforce. In their book Private Equity at Work, Eileen Appelbaum and Rosemary Batt calculate that the buyout destroyed 45,000 jobs. Leveraged buyouts fell out of favor. But Wall Street fell in love with them.

But without another investment legend, neither KKR nor today's private equity could have existed.

Michael Milken did not invent junk bonds. But it was he, the son of a California accountant and a homemaker, who turned so-called "junk bonds," issued by companies with a poor reputation for solvency, into one of Wall Street's most sought-after investments. A 20-year-old student at the Wharton School, the elite business school at the University of Pennsylvania, he already understood that an investor could profit more from these undesirable securities than from bonds issued by renowned companies with an impressive AAA rating: these bad actors had to compensate for the higher risk of non-repayment with proportionally higher interest rates. But there were only a limited number of these junk bonds at the time. Milken's stroke of genius was to multiply them. He was able to do this when he joined the bank Drexel Burnham Lambert, the heir to a bank founded by the financier John Pierpont Morgan, but now playing in the second division. Milken persuaded his new colleagues to help companies with a poor reputation for solvency issue bonds, which they would then sell to investors promising exceptional returns. A godsend for companies that no bank considered solvent anymore. And for corporate raiders like the KKR trio, it was an endless source of fresh money to finance new takeovers. Milken feasted on it. With earnings of up to $500 million a year, no one on Wall Street at the time could touch him. Driven by excessive ambition, he did not miss any deal, no matter how questionable. In the online journal Business Insider, someone who knew him described him unflatteringly: according to her, Milken was "sort of a Jim Jones [the delusional guru who, in 1978, led his followers to mass suicide] with a billion dollars, a public relations man, and a chic office." In the end, the Securities and Exchange Commission and the US Department of Justice began to take an interest in Milken and the practices of "leveraged buyouts" (LBOs). They sent a young prosecutor who had made a name for himself as a mafia hunter: Rudy Giuliani. Milken's secret was that he used his relationships with the savings and loans (the US savings banks), always eager for new issues of junk bonds. This tangled web, along with investigations into insider trading, eventually brought down the king of junk bonds. In 1990, Milken was sentenced to 10 years in prison (of which he served only 22 months). He was banned for life from the financial sector. Milken also had prostate cancer and gave the remaining of his fortune to medical research.

Giuliani's life also took a new direction after the verdict. He leveraged his reputation for incorruptibility and intolerance for illegality and successfully ran for mayor of New York City. His name became even more famous after the terrorist attacks of September 11, 2001. More recently, he has been President Trump's lawyer, notably in the Stormy Daniels affair (a pornographic actress). He was also involved in the impeachment proceedings against Trump in 2019, seeking incriminating evidence against Hunter Biden, the son of Trump's political rival, Joe Biden, in Ukraine. Giuliani intervened on behalf of Milken with Trump, with whom he has been friendly for a long time; Giuliani also suffered from prostate cancer, and the two exchanged, among other things, advice on a healthy diet.

In February 2020, Trump pardoned the fallen Wall Street star, thereby erasing his conviction. Justifying this decision, a Trump spokesperson praised Milken's "innovative financial mechanisms." Trump himself, as a real estate mogul, had benefited from the junk bond market by financing most of the $1.2 billion cost of his Trump Taj Mahal casino in Atlantic City through this means. In less than a year, the casino went bankrupt. Subcontractors were not paid, many went bankrupt. Trump, on the other hand, managed to reach an agreement with creditors that allowed him to keep half of the Taj Mahal.

A Formula for Making Gold

Private equity: finding another activity that allows you to earn as much money in such a short time without inventing or creating anything would be impossible. And, as Wilbur Ross's career shows, it even allows you to make money by destroying companies. It was through Ross that Donald Trump reached an agreement with his junk bond creditors in the case of the Taj Mahal. Once president, the real estate magnate made his former savior the Secretary of Commerce of the United States. Trump used to enjoy calling the octogenarian Ross his "Wall Street killer," until the "killer" drew the president's ire for his tendency to doze off at official events. At the height of his glory, Ross was recognized as the vulture king. He built his fortune during the steel crisis by acquiring classic American companies – laying off some of the employees and cutting pensions and health insurance for those who remained – before selling them for billions. He became an expert at cashing in on state aid, exploiting bankruptcy laws, and using an impressive array of financial tricks. For thousands of steelworkers, this strategy meant losing their jobs and their health insurance. In the end, it all boiled down to OPM: Other People's Money. It was this "other people's money" that made Ross and his partners in large private equity firms, such as Blackstone, KKR, Apollo, and Carlyle, multimillionaires or, for some, billionaires.

Here's how it works. The private equity firm creates a fund and raises money from investors interested in such deals. These investors are wealthy individuals, foundations, sovereign funds, insurers, and, above all, pension funds... which often count among their contributors employees of the acquired companies. Then, the dealmakers search for a target. Once the right company is found, they pay a portion of the raised capital as a down payment, similar to buying a house. At the time of RJR Nabisco, 10% was enough, and later – until the 2008 financial crisis –, 25% was generally sufficient. After the crisis, caution was advised (at least for a while): down payments could reach 40%. Regardless, private equity firms borrow most of the money from banks, which then issue bonds related to the loan – mostly junk bonds. The difference from buying a house: it's the acquired company that is responsible for repaying the debt and paying the interest, not the private equity firm. The high proportion of borrowed capital acts as a return accelerator. A simple example to illustrate how it works: an investor buys shares for $40 and sells them for $50. Thus, he generates a profit of $10, which is 25% return on his invested capital. But if the investor borrows an additional $40 to buy twice as many shares, his profit will be $20, which is a 50% return, minus the interest on the additional $40 he borrowed.

According to the dealmakers, the acquired companies can easily repay high debts as long as they are part of an organization with superior management skills. The dealmakers even charge the acquired companies additional fees for this privilege! It is not uncommon for a private equity firm to take on new debt on behalf of the acquired company in order to recover the money borrowed in the form of dividends. The euphemism used to describe this looting gives an almost opposite impression: this process is called "dividend recapitalization" on Wall Street. "This method has never been very popular outside the private equity sector," noted Pitchbook, an online specialized journal, in an article from August 2019. The authors cite the example of Sun Capital Partners, which bought Shopko, a Wisconsin-based department store chain, for $1.1 billion in 2005. Over the years, Sun Capital's dealmakers repeatedly "recapitalized dividends," most recently in 2015, to the tune of $50 million. In January 2019, Shopko finally went bankrupt. Three hundred fifty stores were closed, and thousands of jobs were lost. Senator Elizabeth Warren, a fierce opponent of the financial sector who was still a presidential candidate at the time, argued for a cooling-off period: private equity firms should wait two years after acquiring a company before being allowed to take on debt on behalf of the acquired company. But her efforts did not succeed.

Until recently, the classic method for private equity firms to profit from their companies was to first "optimize" them using their proven methods – austerity plan, departmental liquidation, job cuts – and then, generally about five years later, sell them for a price high enough to make a profit. But this "exit," as the sale of a company from a portfolio is called, has become less easily accessible as successful IPOs have become more difficult. Another option is to sell to a competitor or a group that has a strategic interest in expanding its business with the company. But it is increasingly common for private equity firms to sell their companies to each other. This relieves them of the burden of having to convince shareholders or a potential buyer's board of directors of the value of the acquisition. Additionally, such a sale generates remarkable premiums and allows them to show their investors an example of a successful "exit." For the companies, however, this usually means even more debt.

No Wonder for Many Companies, Being Bought by a Private Equity Firm Meant a Death Sentence.

One of the most notable victims of these dealmakers is undoubtedly the Toys "R" Us chain, whose aisles filled with toys were a dream for children and a nightmare for their parents. Charles Lazarus originally conceived the idea for Toys "R" Us after returning from World War II. "At that time, everyone wanted to come home, have children, and live the American dream," he later recalled. Lazarus sensed that the children's toy market was booming. In 1957, he opened his first toy superstore in a suburb of Washington. Hundreds of stores followed around the world. Geoffrey the plush giraffe became the chain's mascot, easily recognizable by children from afar. The baby boom and Americans' enthusiasm for shopping malls helped Toys "R" Us become one of the most successful stories in the retail sector. But from the 1990s onwards, Toys "R" Us faced increasing competitive pressure. Walmart, with its Chinese suppliers and competitive prices, surpassed the chain and became the largest toy seller in the United States. Unable to establish itself in online sales, Toys "R" Us had to agree to an exclusive deal with a burgeoning Amazon.

At this stage, Toys "R" Us would have needed a new strategy. With a 14% market share, the company still had advantages over the competition. According to Businessweek, "it would still have been possible to rely on children's whining and tantrums to force their parents to take them to the store, especially if the outing had been made entertaining. If the stores had always been well laid out and offered reasonable prices, parents would have found it easier to give in to their children's demands." This could have been the future of Toys "R" Us. With proper management.

However, the promise of better management was at the heart of the offer from the three private equity firms that took over Toys "R" Us for $7.5 billion in 2005. It was the cream of the crop: KKR, real estate specialists Vornado Realty Trust, and Bain Capital, where Mitt Romney, the 2012 Republican presidential candidate, made his fortune. But it was all in vain: over thirteen years and seven CEOs, austerity programs and ineffective reforms followed one after the other without results. Only the debt steadily increased under the new owners' reign. Among other things, they converted a park of five hundred American branches into separate companies, to which Toys "R" Us had to pay rent. When Toys "R" Us filed for bankruptcy in September 2017, it turned out that the chain had to raise $400 million a year for debt service. In an environment marked by strong competition and very thin margins, there was little left to invest in new ideas. After bankruptcy, employees, many of whom had been laid off without severance pay after decades with the company, began to protest. Some founded the Dead Giraffe Society on Facebook, a nod to Geoffrey. One can find the following post there: "One day, our children will ask, 'Who were these people?' And we will answer with a smile that hides tears, 'They were people with whom we spent some of the most beautiful moments of our lives.'"

Whether Toys "R" Us could have actually survived the Amazon era of Jeff Bezos is uncertain. But the heavy debt burden undoubtedly increased the risk of failure. In their book, Eileen Appelbaum and Rosemary Batt cite studies showing that companies acquired by private equity firms are more likely to go bankrupt than publicly traded companies. Private equity firms do not take into account this higher risk. Probably, conclude the two researchers, because they are not held accountable for the repayment of debts of insolvent companies.

The "Most Dangerous Company in the World"

The formula for making gold has never been so popular. Private equity funds have multiplied sevenfold since 2002: they now have $2.5 trillion in "dry powder": that's what the funds collected from investors for shopping for companies are called. This amount represents the GDP of Switzerland, Turkey, Taiwan, and Poland combined. It needs to be multiplied even more to get an idea of the debts it will generate. In other words, private equity triggers a flow of credit securities. However, to buy these securities, investors are needed. Without other people's money, the private equity formula doesn't work. And that's where BlackRock comes in. Because even though the asset manager's investment in equities attracts the most attention, its activities on the bond side are no less problematic. BlackRock has literally invested trillions of dollars in credit securities. Without BlackRock, the dealmakers would have a hard time using their formula to make gold.

And what does BlackRock do with these credit securities? The asset manager has also found a magic formula to maximize their return: ETFs, BlackRock's most important innovation that is fundamentally changing the bond market. ETFs (Wall Street has a penchant for three-letter acronyms) stands for Exchange Traded Funds, these seemingly simple products that allow small investors to invest like professionals. What is often overlooked about them: ETFs thrive and prosper in the realm of shadow finance.

CHAPTER 6

ETFs: The World Upside Down

Anyone who thinks that investing money is in the right place when it is done on Wall Street or elsewhere in New York is mistaken. Only traders and bankers - the executors, ultimately - have remained there. On the badges of floor traders at the New York Stock Exchange, names like Malony, Maguire, DeLucca can still be found. When the Exchange opened its new building at the southern tip of Manhattan, cheap laborers were hired for messenger services on the floor. Jobs that were gladly accepted by New York immigrants - Italians and Irish, who often arrived shortly before from one of the transatlantic ships docking at Ellis Island, the immigration port. They climbed the ladder, and some small brokerage houses still in business today are still family-owned. As for the decision-makers giving instructions to traders and bankers, there were only two options for a long time: they were either found in Philadelphia or, more importantly, in Boston. That's where the old American aristocracy lived, the "Brahmins of Boston," as the American media liked to call them in jest. The J.P. Morgan family, for example, the legendary American banker, came from there. The rich East Coast dynasties, who, unlike the new rich on Wall Street, placed discretion and the "stiff upper lip" above all else, quickly sought a way to invest their inheritance profitably. This is how the first investment funds came into being. Edward C. Johnson seized the opportunity to open elite asset pools to a wider range of investors and founded Fidelity Investments for this purpose in 1946. Bostonians were among the first to offer retirement pensions. Fidelity grew into a multinational: its funds managed nearly $3 trillion by the end of 2019. With this model, fund managers ensure a significant increase in the assets entrusted to them. This gave some star status - like Peter Lynch, for example, who steered the destiny of the Magellan Fund, Fidelity's flagship, for thirteen years. Investors scrambled to participate in the master's brilliant investment moves. Sometimes, Fidelity closed the fund to new investors - it simply became too large. Magellan was so popular that it was the largest mutual fund with over $100 billion at its peak. It's the curse of success: the larger a fund is, the more significant the fund manager's profits must be for the counter to move, as they say in the industry jargon. There is another downside for fund investors: fund providers and managers demand money for their intervention. And this lowers the return.

The Brand-New World of Derivatives

Then John Clifton Bogle - better known as Jack on Wall Street - arrived. He had a revolutionary idea. Why not create a fund that would essentially operate on autopilot? Instead of hiring an expensive manager to make investment decisions, the fund would only replicate well-known indices such as the Standard & Poor's. The first stock index was created by financial journalist Charles H. Dow in 1896. The principle of the Dow Jones Industrial Average was quite simple: Dow took the twelve most actively traded stocks listed on the New York Stock Exchange, added their current prices, and divided them again by twelve to determine the average price (today the Dow Jones includes 30 companies). Dow's goal was to obtain a benchmark to measure not the individual stock prices but the overall stock market movements. The indices were later refined. With the Standard & Poor's 500, the weight of the companies in the index is weighted by market value. The S&P 500, whose origin dates back to Henry Varnum Poor's American railway register in 1860, is still the leading US market index with its five hundred American companies. Bogle developed Dow's index idea. He wanted not only to measure the market movement but also to map the market in a fund, so that investors could invest in the basket of stocks. In essence: the fund would buy and hold the stocks contained in the S&P 500. The fund would then be forced to fluctuate with the market, and its profits would only correspond to those of the market. No fund manager could thus harm investors with bad decisions and - most importantly - cost them fees.

The concept was not new in itself. Its principles had been created by two Nobel Prize winners. Economist William Sharpe had analyzed the relationship between risk and return and concluded that investors would do better to invest in the entire market. His colleague Eugene Fama developed the theory that stock prices reflect all relevant information available - therefore, no fund manager, however intelligent, can do better than the market in the long term. Based on these academic reflections, Mac McQuown, a financial engineer, tinkered for Wells Fargo Bank in California in 1971 with the first investment portfolio that mimicked a stock index. Bogle, however, is the one who continued to develop Sharpe and Fama's concepts for the needs of small shareholders. Bogle had fled his last employer, a long-established Philadelphia investment fund, due to a merger he had himself accelerated and which had deeply failed. Since he had little to lose, he launched his first investment fund in 1975, modeled on the S&P 500, the American stock index. And he received the sarcasm of the entire industry - his investment vehicles were named "Bogle's Folly." The mockery came mainly from the "Brahmins of Boston": "I can't imagine that investors would be satisfied with average results," said Ned Johnson III, the son of the former founder of Fidelity. But he was wrong: Bogle's folly, now known as the Vanguard 500 Index Fund, eventually caught up with Magellan, the flagship of the Johnson family. By early 2020, barely $17 billion had been invested in the Magellan Fund, while the Vanguard 500 managed over $500 billion. After the financial crisis, Paul Volcker, the former Fed chairman and a friend of Bogle's, declared that the only useful innovation in finance in the past twenty years had been the ATM. Looking back at the past forty years, there is a second one: index funds. Meanwhile, these have grown so large that actively managed investment pools will soon be in the minority. In September 2019, for the first time, more passive investor funds were invested than actively. And Bogle's assumption - that investors who bet on a mix of stock and bond index funds, despite all the ups and downs, achieve better long-term results than with any other investment - has since been confirmed by comparisons. Standard & Poor's, which publishes financial analyses, calculated in a study that 66% of active fund managers achieved worse results than the S&P 500. Over a five- or ten-year period, even 80% of managers lose to the index.

Bogle almost never knew his success. He had six heart attacks, and in the early 1990s, Vanguard predicted that the founder would not live much longer. The company therefore erected a memorial to him: a two-meter-high bronze statue, realistic, according to Bogle's wishes. His arthritic fingers can be recognized. But in 1996, he received a donor's heart - a young man's heart, he said, which rejuvenated him in the process. Bogle's revived vital spirit quickly led him into a dispute with his successor, whom he had appointed himself.

For Bogle, who passed away in early 2019, index funds were more than just a product. He did not become rich with Vanguard - at least, not by Wall Street standards. His fortune was "in the tens of millions," as he once revealed to the New York Times - money he would have earned by investing in Vanguard funds. This is also because Vanguard is not a normal company but belongs to all the fund's shareholders. Insurance mutuals were the model for this. Bogle saw himself as an advocate for small shareholders, whom he wanted to offer fair access to the stock markets and was all the more shocked to see what Wall Street then did with his idea.

The Ingenious Minds Behind Exchange-Traded Funds (ETFs)

———

Clever minds continued to develop index funds and created a new investment instrument, the Exchange-Traded Fund, or ETF. ETFs combine the advantages of index funds - the ability to invest at lower costs in a whole basket of stocks - with the "advantage" that the fund's shares can be traded like individual stocks. It's almost an invitation to speculation! This is what Bogle criticized, and it was exactly the opposite of what he wanted to achieve with his funds: to turn average workers into long-term investors. He feared that ETFs would lead small shareholders to play with their money. It would be like "giving matches to an arsonist," he once complained. The warnings of the index pioneer fell on deaf ears. ETFs have become the most successful new investment vehicles in recent decades. Providers are racing to create the most popular ETFs. "There are more ETFs than ice cream flavors at an Italian ice cream parlor": this is the magic phrase of financial advisors. In no time, there were only ETFs, which replicated major indices such as the S&P 500 or the Nasdaq 100, or later the DAX. With ETFs, stock indices could also be copied and traded like stocks. Thanks to this, Wall Street speculators' old dream of trading credits like stocks on the stock exchange became a reality. And it didn't take long for there to be ETFs on gold, silver, investing in water, real estate, or biotechnology. Meanwhile, there have been more and more of them. A product has rarely so quickly and deeply disrupted the global securities markets. The first prototypes date back to the early 1990s; by 2000, there were just under a hundred; by the end of 2010, there were no less than 2,500; by 2019, investors had already poured nearly $6 trillion into the world's 7,000 ETFs.

When Vanguard also began issuing ETFs, under the direction of a new CEO, Bogle resigned from the company's board of directors, which he himself had founded, in protest. But it was too late for Vanguard. Someone else had already taken the reins of ETFs: BlackRock.

BlackRock entered the ETF business in 2009. While banks and other competitors were still busy repairing after the Lehman crisis, Fink attacked and took over Barclays Bank's iShares division in a $13.5 billion deal. With Merrill Lynch's fund division, BlackRock had already integrated into the investment market. But iShares suddenly catapulted New Yorkers to the top. iShares were launched with the first ETFs of the early 1990s with the clear goal of attracting a wide range of small shareholders. In 2006, Barclays acquired the ETF division of Hypovereinsbank, becoming the market leader in Europe.

Despite growing competition, BlackRock has kept around 40% market share with iShares in the US and even 45% in Europe. In 2019 alone, BlackRock collected nearly $185 billion net, more than a third of total ETF inflows. "The overwhelming physical domination of the market by iShares," Morningstar's fund rating agency headlined its annual report for Europe in 2013. That year, BlackRock also absorbed Credit Suisse's ETF trading. BlackRock's ETFs are listed in London, New York, Hong Kong, Toronto, Sydney, Frankfurt, and Zurich. In Germany, BlackRock manages around half of the 150 billion euros invested by German investors in ETFs. At least, that's what emerges from an interview with iShares Germany's head on the finance site Citywire in March 2019. The overall offering includes 800 iShares ETFs, in which more than $2 trillion was invested by the end of 2019.

"With ETFs, you can invest and save cost-effectively and flexibly, for yourself and your family": this is how the iShares website boasts their advantages. And, of course, the new products have also allowed small shareholders to access securities and other assets that were previously only accessible to large investors or multimillionaires. Before the era of ETFs, for example, an investment in commodities, oil, or alternative energy sources was largely reserved for VIP investors. It is just as easy to invest via an ETF in Kuwait, copper, or telecommunications.

The Complexities of Exchange-Traded Funds (ETFs)

"Being an investment expert is not necessary to invest. Even less so with ETFs," explains an iShares online brochure, featuring a photo of a little girl - to show how easy it is. ETFs are said to be "transparent and easy to understand." From the perspective of an individual shareholder, this may be the case. But exchange-traded funds are by no means simple. In the end, they are derivative products, whose value derives from the underlying securities - just like the value of mortgage-backed securities, infamous since the crisis, which is based on the underlying loans.

Critics see potential problems in the construction of ETFs. The idea is particularly appealing: a basket of securities in which various investors can participate. But turning this simple principle into a concrete investment product requires complex transactions and mechanisms in the background. Without the active participation of market players - banks and brokerage firms - who continuously maintain the link between the ETF and its underlying values, ETFs cannot function. Take an ETF that tracks an index like the DAX. Investors buy ETF shares, and, due to demand, the ETF price increases more than the market value of the thirty DAX values on which it is based. Market players specially mandated by the ETF manager to maintain the price, which we'll call price administrators, note the imbalance and buy DAX securities, which they give to the sponsor. The sponsor then creates new ETF shares that meet the demand, and the ETF price falls. Because the price administrators buy the underlying securities, their prices rise. The ETF price thus again approaches the development of the underlying securities. The price administrators mandated by the sponsor act in the opposite way if the ETF price falls below the market value of the securities on which it is based. They buy ETFs and exchange them with the sponsor for the basket of underlying securities. They resell the securities in the market. Since ETFs are redeemed, their price rises, while the sale of the exchanged securities puts pressure on them. This is how the ETF and underlying securities prices stabilize again on the same line.

The mission of creating new ETF shares if necessary or dissolving them back into individual securities is largely taken over by banks. According to a BlackRock analysis from the fall of 2019, this includes names such as Goldman Sachs, Bank of America, Deutsche Bank, the Dutch ABN Amro, and the French BNP Paribas. Their "compensation," in a word? Arbitrage. They profit from short-term price differences between ETFs and securities.

But there are other people who benefit from ETFs on Wall Street. These are market players who ensure that there is always enough liquidity and that investors can buy or sell their ETF shares at any time, without surcharges or discounts. They also have their acronym on Wall Street: LP, for liquidity provider. They also earn their keep with minimal price distortions, namely between the supply and demand for ETF shares. This arbitrage is only possible with the controversial methods of high-frequency traders, with the appropriate computer assistance and intelligent mathematical software. Price differences are minimal - fractions of a cent. But computer programs can exploit them millions of times. In the end, this amounts to billions. Because ETFs have acted as a turbocharger on the stock market. ETF fund shares change hands four times more often than ordinary company shares. According to the ETF Trends specialized website, the total trading volume of ETFs in 2019 amounted to $98 billion... per day, in the US alone. At first, banks were also very active as LPs. In the summer of 2017, a message from Goldman Sachs caught Wall Street's attention. The investment bank announced that it would significantly reduce its LP activities. The bank did not comment on the reasons for this withdrawal. The most likely reason, according to Reuters, was competition from small market operators. While Goldman Sachs, as a bank, for example, must deposit capital for commercial transactions, following tightened regulations after the financial crisis, market operators acting for their own account are not affected by such restrictions. Their profit is therefore higher. There would be enough providers to take over the ETF price administration that will be abandoned by Goldman, according to a competitor bank's statement to Reuters journalists. However, this means that risks are migrating from a bank supervised by regulators to the world of lightly regulated shadow banks.

Take, for example, Jane Street Capital, headquartered in one of the glass towers of New York's financial district. It's not a bank, and even on Wall Street, it's only known to insiders. Yet, it now trades billions in securities through over 1,000 employees. According to their website, the transaction volume was $8 trillion in 2018. To generate this amount, all Germans would have to work for two years. Before the financial crisis, the company, founded in 2000 by three traders and a geek, was one of hundreds of prop shops, as these small private firms speculating on securities at their own risk are called. Today, it is one of the hottest addresses for traders on Wall Street. "If you succeed, you can retire at 30," reads a comment from a trader claiming to have worked for Jane Street on an online Wall Street forum. On the employer review site Glassdoor, others complain about gaining weight because the free food served there is too good. It's no coincidence that Jane Street's meteoric rise has paralleled that of ETFs. As a privately held company, Jane Street does not have to publish figures and remains opaque, like the entire sector. The financial information service Bloomberg calculated that APs and LPs earn $10 billion a year. This exceeds the $6 billion in fees received by ETF providers - providers such as BlackRock, Vanguard, or State Street.

The aftermath of the mortgage-backed securities debacle, which proved toxic, is still present: the global economy has remained so fragile that central banks have kept interest rates artificially low, more than a decade later. But Wall Street has found a new cash cow. This time, as the parties involved assure, nothing can go wrong.

An event, however, challenges the fairy tale surrounding a product purportedly without risks. On Monday, August 24, 2015, investors and traders nervously awaited the opening of the New York stock market after violent turbulence in China. The New York Stock Exchange bell had barely rung at 9:30 am when prices collapsed. The Dow Jones Industrial Average, which includes American heavyweights such as Boeing, Coca-Cola, and Exxon, lost 1,100 points in the six minutes that followed, wiping out nearly $1 trillion in market value. To prevent a total crash, the stock market had to pull the emergency brake and halt stock trading. That morning, regulators had to press the emergency stop button 1,237 times. Most cases involved ETFs. Some fund shares were in free fall. Compared to Friday's close, the ETF "Direxion Nasdaq100 Equal Weighted" lost 47%. The "SPDR S&P MidCap 400 Value" 51%. What's curious about this is that the stocks that were supposed to represent these ETFs dropped much less. Even more strange: ETFs based on the same index listed different values. For example, the "iShares S&P 500" ETF, which tracks the S&P 500 index, dropped by over 20% in the first minutes of trading - and thus much more significantly than the "SPDR S&P 500" - even though both ETFs contain the same stocks. Prices rebounded during the day, and the iShare ETF once again closely followed the S&P index. The near-miss was briefly mentioned in the news. But Wall Street professionals were shocked. "What happened with these ETFs, damn it?" wondered Corey Hoffstein, an investment banker from Boston, in an online comment. There is still no consensus on this. One thing is certain: the arbitrage of price administrators, a prerequisite for ETFs, did not work, at least temporarily. Sector representatives, however, are looking for the cause elsewhere. "Our structure works, it's the Exchanges that need to modernize their technology," says Reggie Browne, a former American football player who has become one of the most prominent ETF designers. The August debacle inevitably recalls a similar event five years earlier: the May 6, 2010 flash crash. At that time, the Dow Jones plunged nearly 1,000 points (to recover by the close of trading). During the flash crash as well, ETFs were the most affected by extreme price fluctuations.

On that Thursday, market participants were concerned about the situation in Greece, and the atmosphere was tense. But nothing explains what happened at 2:32 pm New York time: suddenly, stock prices started to drop rapidly. The stock of Accenture, a management consulting firm with revenues of $30 billion and over 300,000 employees, is an example of what happened: just before the drama, at 2:20 pm, Accenture's shares were trading at $40, then they fell without apparent reason. At 2:47:47 pm, the price was $30 - 7 seconds later, it had dropped to 1 cent. One cent! The Dow Jones, which includes large American companies such as IBM, Disney, Boeing, and Coca-Cola, dropped nearly 1,000 points in minutes: a trillion dollars suddenly evaporated. But inexplicable movements also occurred in the other direction: the share price of the auction house Sotheby's climbed from $30 to $99,999.99 and suddenly reached a market valuation of $6.8 trillion - more than the combined French and German GDPs. Then, just as inexplicably, prices normalized again.

The flash crash has been forgotten, as prices quickly returned to their initial levels. But its memory still haunts market participants and regulators.

Why is the flash crash particularly significant for ETFs? Among the transactions later canceled by the Exchange, more than two-thirds were ETF trades.

In a report on the first 2010 flash crash, BlackRock admitted that ETFs were affected by the "volatile market" during the collapse. From BlackRock's point of view, however, ETFs were not co-responsible; they were victims of the turmoil. A survey of ETF investors showed that the majority were only minimally affected by the crash and continued to trust the instrument, as mentioned in a BlackRock study.

A potential threat from ETFs simply comes from their popularity. Standard large indices are weighted - as described in the case of the S&P 500. This means that the company with the highest market value also has the largest weight in the index. In tech stock indices, for example, these are Apple and Google. When ETFs replicate the index, most funds are poured into the index heavyweights. In doing so, their market value and weight in the index increase even further. Investors do not spread their risk more widely through index investments. Instead, more and more capital relies on just a few stocks. A good recipe for intense price fluctuations that harm small shareholders.

The constant arbitrage between the ETF and the underlying securities is not without consequence for companies. "This can distort company valuations," says Itzhak Ben-David, finance professor at Ohio State University. He gives an example: Apple unveils a new iPhone, and the company's stock rises. But an ETF, whose basket of stocks includes Apple, does not increase as significantly - after all, it also contains other stocks that are not experiencing a price increase. This prompts arbitrageurs. They buy the ETF and sell Apple to pocket the difference. This again brings the ETF price closer to Apple's stock price. "But without ETF arbitrage, Apple's stock price would have increased more after the new iPhone announcement," says Ben-David. With ETFs, companies share the same fate, involuntarily. If, for example, there is bad news from a car manufacturer and ETF investors want to reduce their exposure, this affects - as a kind of collateral damage - a refrigerator manufacturer also in the index, but whose business has not experienced a decline. These differences from the real price would mostly be minor and short-lived, admits Ben-David. But they hinder the central function of financial markets, which is to allocate capital as efficiently as possible.

BlackRock has every reason to fear problems with ETFs. Just a broader discussion about the risks posed by ETFs could in itself be detrimental to the market leader, sparking doubts among clients or regulatory curiosity.

The Prince of iShares

Unlike his boss Larry Fink, who towers over everyone simply with his stature, one could easily overlook Mark Wiedman. Even on Wall Street, just a few years ago, people were still asking, "Wiedman... who?" But that has changed significantly. In the end, he is considered a potential successor to Larry. The fact that he headed the iShares division until 2019 qualified him for that role. Wiedman is an attentive listener and an engaging conversationalist. His colleagues tease him because while he can readily quote the English romantic poet Percy Bysshe Shelley, he struggles to name two teams in the National Football League. Wiedman rarely discusses his background. He grew up in Long Island, one of those suburbs where the white middle class moved in the 1970s and 1980s to escape the crime-ridden, graffiti-covered streets of New York City. "Exit 39 off the highway, in a quiet suburb and a modest house," he once described it to Bloomberg. Wiedman comes from a family of physicians. His father was still practicing at the age of 80. His mother taught nursing at the local college. Not only did Wiedman manage to secure a place at Harvard College, but he graduated magna cum laude. Then he went to Yale, the rival, to study law. But he was perhaps too impatient - and maybe not humble enough - for his initial plan of becoming a judge. After a brief stint at McKinsey & Co., he joined the Treasury in Washington. There, his former boss, Undersecretary of State Peter Fisher, joined BlackRock and brought him along. Initially, he was part of the original team advising central banks and governments after the crisis about their toxic assets. Then he got his chance - Fink appointed him head of the iShares division. Wiedman's mission was to integrate ETF-related activities into BlackRock and instill a New York way of doing things in the department. And he had to keep Vanguard's competitors at bay. The latter had entered the race late due to Bogle's reluctance. But due to the unique ownership structure - no shareholder siphoning off profits - the investment company could offer extremely favorable conditions, making it particularly popular with small investors.

All this obviously only spurred Wiedman on. He quickly made headlines in the rather staid, if not boring, sector of fund providers. One of his early moves was to ally with Vanguard's old Boston rival, Fidelity, and enter into a distribution partnership. But that was just the beginning. "Ambitious," titled the Financial Times in a 2012 profile; one should see this description of the iShares boss as a British understatement. Wiedman wants to fundamentally transform financial markets. This is the area with "the most interesting and intellectually revolutionary developments," he said in the same article. He likened ETFs to the introduction of containers in shipping in the 1950s, which completely changed the global transportation system.

What Wiedman envisions could completely and enduringly change the financial market - not only for small investors, but for large ones as well, for hedge funds, and even for exchanges. Wiedman sees ETFs as much more than just a variant of index funds, much more than a dynamic alternative to a savings account. He believes that sooner or later ETFs will replace the actual securities on which they are based - at least for investors. "The idea that insurance companies, which until now have bought individual bonds or derivatives, can now use ETFs as an essential element for their portfolios, is completely new," he said in the same article. As an example, he cited an American pension fund that BlackRock had helped liquidate positions in 2,000 different securities and invest the capital obtained in just four ETFs. In a later interview with Bloomberg, Wiedman talked about a large investor who, instead of holding 2,200 different bonds, merged his capital into only two ETFs. And the iShares client would have saved the fees of a bond manager, who had previously managed these positions, Wiedman rejoiced. The goal is clear: instead of investing directly in stocks, bonds, or commodities as done previously, large investors must now also invest through ETFs. A development from which ETF providers like iShares should greatly benefit.

But Wiedman went even further. In the summer of 2013, ETFs were tested again. The then Fed chairman, Ben Bernanke, had stated that the era of cheap central bank money was soon coming to an end. The end of the Fed's program was better known as "tapering" in Wall Street jargon. Market participants reacted like a 2-year-old whose daddy wants to take away his candy: there was a drop in prices after Bernanke's announcement, a "taper tantrum." Nervous investors mostly bought and sold one thing: ETF shares. According to iShares, the trading volume of High Yield US Bond, a US toxic bond ETF, exceeded $1 billion for the first time, and that was on a daily basis. The largest of the iShares emerging market funds even saw a trading volume of $5.6 billion in a single day during this "taper tantrum." Business had gone smoothly despite the strong wave that hit its ETFs, Wiedman summarized afterward.

However, it did not go smoothly for all providers: with certain ETFs, based on securities from emerging markets and less frequently traded bonds, the price administrators had to urgently procure the necessary securities. This led to failures. "Turbulence reawakens concerns about structural problems in ETFs," noted the Financial Times. Just on June 26, transactions worth $4 billion in ENF reportedly were not completed on time. This means that the trading partner could not acquire the agreed-upon securities within the specified time frame. The failures were even more significant on August 15, 2011: $6.6 billion. At that time, the euro crisis was rocking the markets. However, market participants downplayed the situation - the failures were just an operational hiccup, not a systemic risk to the market. Most transactions were ultimately to be completed without any issues with an additional timeframe.

Betting on ETFs: A Horse Race with Only One Horse

<hr>

Wiedman reacted differently than the skeptics. He did not see the "taper tantrum" as a warning but took advantage of the episode to write an open letter to iShares investors. In this document, he claimed that ETFs had withstood market pressure well. He also emphasized that BlackRock was working with forty-five price administrators in the United States, all of which were "leading global financial institutions" ensuring that even large orders could be processed without any difficulty. Then he came to his central point: the turbulence had not revealed any problems or systemic risk in Wall Street's latest favorite innovation. No, for Wiedman, it was proof that ETFs were improving the market. Yes, ETFs are actually the market. According to him, ETF prices would now be decisive for investors, not the underlying securities or stocks as before. ETFs would not passively follow the prices of securities; it would be the other way around. To put it bluntly: the world was about to turn upside down. What Wiedman casually pointed out in his letter raised eyebrows among the most cautious players on Wall Street. "iShares' claims make me nervous," declared a headline on the specialized ETF.com website, aimed at professionals. "With its ETFs, the company wants to compete with futures contracts and other derivatives and, to a certain extent, assume the role of individual stocks," it was written, almost incredulously. And the author of the article is not alone in whom Wiedman's enthusiasm for the basket of securities revives a bad memory. That of mortgage-backed securities. This financial innovation, in which Wiedman's boss, Larry Fink, played a leading role, was initially hailed because it allowed a wide range of investors access to previously hard-to-reach forms of investment, namely mortgages on American real estate. In this initial context, these investors actually thought that skillful securitization and financial alchemy alone could improve the quality of the underlying credits. Then the crisis happened from 2007 to 2008, and even supposedly secured loans collapsed. The pseudo-alchemy turned out to be a recipe for disaster.

The criticism led other representatives of iShares to quickly backtrack and significantly qualify Wiedman's claim. But he reiterated. Nearly a year later, he condescendingly declared in an interview with a representative of the asset management company Morningstar that ignorance is one of the biggest obstacles in the industry. In the conversation, he stated that the idea that the spreads between ETF prices and underlying values would pose problems was a "great myth," mainly spread by the press. It would be wrong to apply outdated measures, which were used to determine the value of traditional funds, to ETFs. In stressful situations, in particular, the price of ETFs would be "the real market," and the valuation of underlying values the "yesterday's price." If one follows Wiedman's arguments, ETFs will sooner or later replace engagement in individual stocks or bonds for the majority of investors. But that's not all: a BlackRock employee proudly declared that they were about to compete with the Chicago futures exchanges. Instead of futures contracts and options, large investors would use more and more ETF instruments in the future. "It's cheaper than using futures contracts from the Exchange." This vision could soon become reality. According to Greenwich Associates, a market research firm specializing in financial companies, 60% of institutional investors used bond ETFs in 2019, compared to only 20% two years earlier. Thus, the financial engineers at iShares who compose the ETFs increasingly determine what is traded on financial markets; and, above all, how it is traded.

And what if ETFs were the only horse in the race? Regulators are concerned about the exponential increase in these new derivatives. "ETFs have expanded into new forms of investment (bonds, loans, emerging markets, commodities), areas where transparency and liquidity are generally lower," says a study by the Financial Stability Board, an international body created by the G20 countries after the 2008 crisis to anticipate new dangers to the financial system. Recently, the European Systemic Risk Board (ESRB), a body created to monitor financial risks in the EU, issued warnings. In their June 2019 report, the authors identified several crucial and worrying effects of ETFs. First, the risk that the arbitrage mechanism between price administrators would no longer function, as during flash crashes. This could in turn have a negative effect on the underlying values. ESRB observers also fear that the highly appreciated possibility for investors to withdraw their money at any time could become a risk not only for ETFs but for the entire system. Turbulences in the markets are always dangerous when actors do not have time to react; then comes the domino effect. Traditional investment funds typically hold cash to be able to meet, if necessary, investors demanding their deposits. Hedge funds' contracts typically contain a clause stating that the investor must adhere to a certain period before being able to withdraw their money. These two securities help prevent the fund manager from being forced to hastily dispose of assets to repay jittery investors, which could potentially worsen market panic.

ETFs have no safety cushion or grace period: what makes them interesting is the promise to owners that they can withdraw their shares at any time. This works smoothly as long as there is always someone in the market to take the opposite position. In essence, an asset - stocks, bonds, fund shares - is liquid when it can be sold whenever wanted, without having to accept a sharp price drop. This is possible when enough buyers wanting to acquire the asset in question are on the market. Insiders fear that liquidity problems with ETFs could have serious consequences. In March 2015, Howard Marks, the co-founder of Oaktree, a fund specializing in alternative investment strategies, sparked lively discussions with a letter to his investors. The Wall Street veteran wrote that ETFs would be a case study for financial innovations leading investors to think that a "universal remedy," a product superior to traditional forms of investment, had been found. Such financial innovations, he said, always reminded him of the story of the gambler obsessed with the absolutely safe bet. "It's like a horse race but with only one horse. The player has bet all his money on him but in the middle of the race, the animal balked, jumped over the fence, and galloped away."

The Big Bond Bubble

———

Massive bond sales are particularly feared on Wall Street. This is because, unlike stocks, credit securities are not yet traded on a large scale on the exchanges. This is due to how bonds are issued. While stocks are shares of widely standardized companies that grant their holders more or less the same rights and can therefore be traded on public exchanges, trading platforms, and electronically, bonds are tailored to meet the needs of the issuing company, each with different rights and conditions. In short: stocks are off-the-rack, while bonds are bespoke. This is why bonds are still mostly traded by brokers over the phone at banks. Brokers collect offers from investors and make some themselves, acting as intermediaries between investors (and pocketing hefty margins!). But since the new capital rules came into effect, banks have also had to reduce their activities in these trading rooms. By 76%, according to Bloomberg's estimates. And something else happened: in recent years, the bond universe has exploded, along with the volume of corporate bonds issued. Investors can now choose from forty-six thousand different corporate bonds. By comparison, there are only five thousand different stocks listed on US stock markets. This further complicates the trading of credit securities. The ETF boom adds another layer. It is now possible to trade bonds like stocks through exchange-traded funds, making them more attractive to investors like hedge funds, who can use them as tokens for new speculative creations. BlackRock, in any case, sees growth potential there. "It took seventeen years for bond ETFs to reach a trillion dollars," explained Armando Senra, head of iShares Americas in September 2019. "We believe this amount will double over the next five years."

For some bonds, a single fund holds half of the issued securities. When so much of a company's debt is concentrated in one hand, the difference with the house bank is only in the eye of the beholder, or rather in regulatory differences. Bond market activities would already be "a bit bank-like," said Jeremy Stein, then a Fed governor, in May 2014, in an interview with the

Financial Times. "It may be the essence of shadow banks to give people a liquid right to an illiquid asset," he said about bond funds. Funds promise their investors that they can sell their shares at any time (thus, these shares are liquid), while bonds are notoriously more difficult to sell and buy on the market (the fund's assets are therefore rather illiquid). And as the old Wall Street adage goes, "Liquidity is like air, you miss it when it's missing."

BlackRock is acutely aware of the danger. In the fall of 2014, BlackRock published a study on its website. The authors - including Richie Prager - wrote that bond trading was simply "broken." It would be high time for an overhaul of this market. The title of the work, "Corporate Bond Market Structure: Time for Reform," reads like a bland political party program title. But in the industry, BlackRock's demands caused almost as much excitement as Luther's theses in Wittenberg. "Prepare for the next bond crash," warned the Financial Times. If BlackRock gets nervous, then the rest of the world should expect the worst. And Bloomberg asked, "What's worse? When big banks shake the market or when big bond investors do?" According to BlackRock's conception, the role of intermediaries, i.e., bankers, should be significantly reduced, meaning that bonds should be standardized as much as possible so that they can be traded electronically, like stocks. Ultimately, this would make bonds, i.e., credits, tradable like stocks. And thus increase liquidity. But for now, we are about as far away from landing a man on Mars - it is not impossible, but extremely difficult.

BlackRock's attack should be seen as a defensive measure. For the giant fund manager, a functioning bond market is undoubtedly of the utmost importance. In May 2019, Moody's published a scenario that could be Larry Fink's version of the horror movie "Nightmare on Elm Street," in which the killer Freddy Krueger terrorizes teenagers in the fictional town of Springwood, Ohio, first in their sleep and then also when they are awake. "Unexpected liquidity shortfalls in the market could be exacerbated by ETFs tracking fundamentally illiquid markets, such as high yield bonds," the rating agency's report says, which certainly has an interest in redeeming itself after its role in the mortgage-backed securities crisis. These ETF-specific risks could in turn "intensify systemic risks in the event of an exogenous shock to the entire system," according to the report's authors. In plain language: an unexpected event that scares investors, bankers, and traders could plunge index funds into a crisis and then drag the entire financial system down with them.

Less than a year later, a killer did indeed invade the world. The Covid-19 virus spread for weeks after being identified by Chinese officials in December 2019. But the financial markets remained calm until March 2020 - no, euphoric even! In February, the Dow Jones celebrated a new record high of 29,568 points. Wall Street has rarely experienced such a sudden turnaround as the one caused by the pandemic: you have to go back to 1929 for a comparable crash. Investors fled bonds, especially junk bonds: in the space of a week, they withdrew $55 billion from bond funds, according to Lipper, a fund rating agency. This is the highest amount since 1992, when Lipper began measuring capital flows. The "iShares iBoxx High Yield Corporate Bond" ETF, abbreviated HYG, the largest US junk bond fund, reportedly experienced its largest single-day outflow of investor capital with $1.6 billion, according to Bloomberg. Then another detail added to investors' and traders' chills. Some days, ETFs were priced lower compared to the bond prices they are supposed to reflect. Competitors' funds from Vanguard and Pimco were also affected. It is the task of price administrators to smooth out these price differences through arbitrage, which they do in their own interest, also benefiting. However, this time, given the volatility and uncertainty of the circumstances, administrators apparently feared experiencing losses themselves. As with flash crashes, a weakness of ETFs has therefore appeared: price administrators are not required to arbitrage. "This shouldn't happen, something's going wrong," according to an analyst from a fund company quoted by the Financial Times. Another warned that investors could lose confidence in ETFs. If there had been a rush on bond funds, they might have had to sell their bonds on the market in order to be able to repay investors who wanted to sell their shares. This would have caused cascading sales and, probably, a new credit crisis. The claws of the night were already scratching at Wall Street's door.

Fortunately for Fink & Co., help arrived just in time. From Washington. The US Federal Reserve immediately responded, with the same weapons that had been used in 2008 to prevent a total collapse. Fed Chairman Jay Powell again lowered interest rates to zero, injecting not billions but directly trillions into the repo market, and announced the purchase of government bonds, municipal bonds, corporate bonds... "and old junkers," as a Wall Street veteran mocked. To top it off, Powell stated that the US Federal Reserve would buy corporate bonds for hundreds of millions of dollars. He didn't stop there: on the purchase list were even bond ETFs! Until now, such measures had been taboo for the US Federal Reserve: it feared being suspected of wanting to save certain industries, or even specific companies, with public money. It is possible that the Fed bankers realized that the ECB had no such qualms. The announcement by the powerful masters of the dollar was enough to calm credit markets despite the increase in Covid-19 infections. Even if the Fed only bought bonds from companies with good solvency or less so before the pandemic, the implicit guarantee it thus gave also helped junk bonds - and mechanically the ETFs that went with them. "Confidence is back in the market," praised commentators on specialized CNBC and Bloomberg TV channels. Confidence that the Fed would do everything in its power to prevent an explosion of the credit bubble that it had itself inflated by flooding the market with cheap money.

Fresh money from investors, that's what a return of confidence means on Wall Street. And BlackRock benefits more than any other asset manager. Its bond and credit funds total $560 billion, half of the money invested in bond ETFs worldwide. On Monday, March 23, 2020, the Fed announced its intention to buy corporate bonds. On the same day, $1 billion flowed into BlackRock's "iShares iBoxx $ Investment Grade Corporate Bond ETF," according to a Bloomberg calculation. The next day, another $1.5 billion was added, an amount that would have earned BlackRock about $2.3 million, according to the Financial Times. Shortly thereafter, the Fed announced that it would also buy junk bonds.

This is the kind of happy ending that director Wes Craven would have wished for A Nightmare on Elm Street. The teenagers survived: in the end, it was just a nightmare. But the producers insisted that Freddy not be eliminated permanently. The motivation on Elm Street was the same as on Wall Street: $$$. No less than six sequels to the film were released in theaters afterward.

Speaking of sequels: who was hired to assist the Fed in its buying program? Any idea? Of course! BlackRock.

2008: The Sequel, that could be the title of this film. Today, as at the time, the New York Fed, which oversees the Federal Reserve's activities on Wall Street, is turning to experienced ghostbusters.

However, the news did not please everyone. "It's really scandalous," complained the director of an asset management company, presumably a rival. "BlackRock will manage funds and decide whether taxpayers' money will be used to buy shares of their own ETFs or not. There are certainly between a hundred and two hundred asset managers who could do this job, but BlackRock was chosen." During this March 30, 2020 interview with Financial Times journalists, the man probably used a less polite word than "scandalous." Fearing "BlackRock's influence on Wall Street," he did not want to give his name, as the newspaper explains, wisely indicating that the money managed by BlackRock during the Lehman crisis for the Fed had earned at least $12 billion for US taxpayers. During a conference call, when an analyst asked him if the Fed's purchases of ETF and corporate bonds had constituted a bailout plan for BlackRock, Fink replied sharply: it would be disrespectful to present the matter in that way. And he added that it was two strictly separate divisions of BlackRock.

BlackRock in every corner of the market

"BlackRock is everywhere," bankers, stock traders, and regulators declare with either complaint or open admiration. In a short time, Larry Fink's team has managed to infiltrate almost every corner of the capital markets.

The giant black firm is also increasingly charting its own, private path in securities trading. Instead of trading stocks on public exchanges, asset managers like BlackRock prefer to move to VIP markets. These dark pools are surrounded by an infernal aura. Even for insiders and regulators, these trading platforms are difficult to discern. "There's a reason why they're called 'dark pools' and not 'crystal lakes,'" comments a participant in an online Financial Times forum playing the role of Cassandra. Dark pools, initially meant to serve as protection zones for investors, were created in response to speculators who scoured global stock markets with ultrarapid computers and complex mathematical software to catch wind of large investors' buy or sell orders. If, for example, an investment fund issues a large buy order, it implies a price increase. If these lightning-fast traders get wind of it—thanks to algorithms tirelessly combing through financial markets—they buy the shares before the increase. The advantage for the lightning traders: they pocket the difference and make almost risk-free profits. The disadvantage for the investment fund: as the price increases due to the lightning traders' purchases, the fund has to pay a higher price for the order. For this reason, large banks began offering off-exchange platforms a few years ago to protect large investors from such maneuvers. Unlike public exchanges, where orders must always be made public immediately, on these platforms, clients remain anonymous. The orders and the price at which they were executed are then transmitted to the exchanges with a mandatory notification. Due to this anonymity, the term "dark pool" has become established on Wall Street for these trading platforms.

However, these shadow trading platforms have increasingly made headlines in recent years. Operators have used their opacity to serve their interests.

Unlike public exchanges, dark pools are subject to less stringent regulation. Participants essentially rely on operators' self-regulation. Due to the lack of transparency, more and more critics have spoken out. "You can imagine the liquids at dark pool parties: Dom Pérignon, Cristal, Bollinger...," muses a participant in an online finance forum under the pseudonym "Karl Marx."

In 2014, then-New York Attorney General Eric Schneiderman made serious accusations against Barclays Bank: while Barclays assured its clients—including investment funds and pension funds—that they could safely process their stock orders in the dark pool, without being cheated by traders who were too fast, the bank would secretly and discreetly invite these lightning traders into the dark pool and give them additional advantages over large investors who knew nothing about it. Barclays admitted to this and paid $70 million to settle the matter. UBS settled similar complaints with a compromise.

In fact, dark pools and lightning traders are the result of well-intentioned reforms. After the bursting of the internet bubble, U.S. regulators feared that American exchanges would fall behind. While Frankfurt and London were busy tinkering with electronic trading systems, Wall Street seemed to have missed the already-moving train. Floor traders—especially those at the New York Stock Exchange—stuck to traditional trading, partly because it offered lucrative advantages as intermediaries. Existing rules ensured that the majority of transactions took place on the exchange floor. In 2007, these privileges were abolished as part of the overall market reform, the Regulation National Market Structure (Reg NMS). The goal of the reform, to create more competition and promote electronic trading, was largely achieved: the share of non-electronic trading in the United States is now negligible. In over 80% of cases, no broker enters their orders into the machine anymore; computers interact independently using algorithms. And exchanges have reaped fierce competition. Today, investors can trade U.S. stocks in fifty centers. Nearly 40% of exchanges already take place outside the exchange. Less strictly regulated trading platforms lured their customers with faster systems, aiming, above all, to be cheaper. Thus, dark pools are among the biggest beneficiaries of Reg NMS.

How precise are stock prices?

The boom of the dark pool has left regulators doubtful about the success of financial market reforms. They perceive a problem even greater than simple manipulations to the detriment of clients: in their view, it is the very functioning of the market that is in danger. For many skeptics, exchanges are nothing more than gambling dens full of speculators. But exchanges play a crucial role: they provide capital to companies. And - in theory at least - companies obtain this capital only if they manage to convince investors of their prospects. The stock market's function is to distribute resources in our economic system, publicly and for everyone. It is essentially like crowdfunding, so popular among millennials - except that investors have the opportunity to share in the company's profits. No banker decides anything here in secret, no regulatory official acts alone. The prices at which stocks are publicly traded on the stock exchange are the same for fund managers and small shareholders. But with VIP trading platforms, this price democracy will soon be a thing of the past.

Mary Jo White, chairman of the Securities and Exchange Commission (SEC) of the United States during the Obama administration, stated at an investor conference in June 2014 that the share of "dark trading" was detrimental to market quality - especially regarding price fixing. "Transparency has long been the hallmark of the American stock market, and I am concerned about the lack of transparency in dark pools," she said. In other words, if ever-increasing order flows bypass public exchanges, to what extent do prices reflect the actual market price?

The migration of trillions of dollars to the dark pool kingdom has only accelerated since the SEC chair's warning. In January 2015, nine major American investment firms announced that they wanted to operate their own dark pool. Fidelity initially developed the project under the code name "Sakura," the Japanese word for cherry blossom. And who was on board? BlackRock. While there have always been trading platforms launched by investors, this time, the big players in the investment sector got involved together. BlackRock explains on its website: "We believe that dark pools are a valuable tool for executing large blocks of orders and trading stocks that have low liquidity due to their low volume." There are even more advantages when it comes to placing orders outside public exchanges. Advantages that can be expressed in dollars. In the meantime, the cherry blossom dark pool, renamed Luminex, is managed by a former BlackRock executive. In 2018, Luminex was named the "best dark pool" by an industry organization.

Furthermore, a dark pool is external. But large asset managers can avoid this inconvenience. Instead of using external trading platforms, investment companies exchange securities between their different clients, a practice known as "crossing" in Wall Street jargon, which has now become commonplace among the big players. For example, if pension fund A, a BlackRock client, wants to buy Microsoft shares and sovereign fund B, also a BlackRock client, wants to sell Microsoft shares, then they exchange their shares with each other. This avoids clients the fees of external liquidators, according to BlackRock's argument. And their clients are unlikely to be saddened if this means that Wall Street banks and brokers lose hundreds of millions in orders. The positive side effect for BlackRock: all these transactions remain on BlackRock's servers. In an internal letter, leaked to the Financial Times, it is written: "This platform will allow cost savings and exchanges between all assets; thanks to it, we become one of the largest trading centers in the world." In other words: the "largest dark pool in the world," a kind of private stock exchange, as once boasted by a BlackRock representative to a visitor.

If BlackRock were a water management company, it would serve households and businesses worldwide. It would operate wastewater treatment plants, reservoirs, and pipelines, it would build dams and collect water at locks, it would be active from maritime transport to steam turbines. In many areas - as a direct lender to companies, purchaser of personal loans online, operator of its own in-house dark pool, or sponsor of ETFs - BlackRock is not only active, but is deeply reshaping its market dominance or, at least - as during the comprehensive review of bond markets - is trying as much as possible.

It's no wonder the finance world is worried. "We are closely monitoring BlackRock," says a Goldman Sachs executive. And even he cannot help but feel some admiration for the rival. But all these developments and evolutions have largely gone unnoticed by the general public.

We could now see all this - the new balls that ETFs are for finance jugglers, the growing activities of shadow banks, private stock exchanges, and dark pools - as what Americans like to call "inside baseball." A multitude of details that only interest fans of this collection of statistics camouflaged as a sport. Whether Goldman Sachs, Deutsche Bank, or BlackRock has its finger on the trigger, isn't it the same thing? No. Because it's more than just a story of rivalry in the financial elite. In the case of BlackRock's restructuring of the markets, it's about how the financial system will play its true role in the future, namely how it will support our real economy. It's not just about bonuses and egos, but about financing companies, municipalities, governments. It's about who determines the conditions. And what risks that entails. One thing is certain: BlackRock is not only playing a major role in all these changes. It plays a gigantic, XXL role.

And the transformation of the financial market is just one construction site for the black giant. Fink and his colossus are also the engine and spearhead of an even deeper change. This affects the companies themselves and, ultimately, our entire economic system.

CHAPTER 7

Financial Capitalism 2.0

The visit of the New York financial magnate was eagerly awaited in London. It was so important for the City, wrote a journalist, that some representatives of the financial sector even took out life insurance on him at Lloyd's. The man now controls or influences more money and interests than anyone else in the world. "No one can estimate, probably not even himself, the responsibility and importance of this power," the article states. Yet, the 64-year-old man was almost unknown on Wall Street twenty-five years earlier. "Today, he manages almost as much income and expenses as the German Empire." It is about John Pierpont Morgan. The article was published in 1901 in McClure's Magazine, one of the first investigative publications, on the occasion of a visit by the New York banker to Great Britain. Upon arrival, he bought the Leyland shipping company, which maintained thirty-eight steamers in the Atlantic, and incorporated it into his empire. The British were shocked to see that the newcomer had conducted such a massive transaction as if it were, one could say, a "holiday pleasure," because it confirmed their fears: Morgan had the British maritime hegemony in his sights.

A prince of finance for a new age

Without the New York banker, the world would be very different. America owes him its large industrial groups that dominate the world - like US Steel, General Electric, AT&T, Westinghouse, Portland Cement. He is the ancestor of the largest American banking giant JPMorgan Chase and the investment bank Morgan Stanley. But above all: J.P. Morgan founded financial capitalism, of which Larry Fink is the heir. Unlike his contemporaries, such as steel magnate Andrew Carnegie, Morgan was not a self-made man. He came from a wealthy banking family. The Morgans arrived in New England in 1636. They fought alongside the revolutionaries in the War of Independence. Morgan's grandfather was still a farmer; he left interesting land properties in Connecticut. Morgan's father, Junius Spencer Morgan, became an apprentice in a bank and then worked for Peabody, a member of the New England aristocracy. Because he suffered from rheumatic fever as a child and was temporarily unable to walk, young J.P. was sent for a cure to the Azores. Like many children of the American elite, he then came to Europe to study. He learned French in Bellerive, Switzerland, then studied art history at the University of Göttingen and spent some time in Wiesbaden. His level of German was passable, it seems.

But Morgan's true calling was in financial affairs. He realized this when he joined his father's bank in London in 1857. McClure's Magazine notes that he became very familiar with foreign trade and the currency exchange market. But above all, "he saw the credit system in its widest context." Morgan was not a conventional banker: he did not see himself in the role of a simple lender. Raising capital was only a means to an end. The young banker quickly rose to join his father - as an equal partner, not as a subordinate. Morgan, a massive man, made a strong impression. His contemporaries reported that he was like a gust of wind blowing through the buildings. Unlike his discreet successor Larry Fink, everything in his life was oversized. His love affairs had a bad reputation. Yachts were his passion; the bigger they were, the better. His private ship Corsair was bought by the US Navy and used in the war against Spain. He smoked the thickest cigars - real Hercules' thighs, as his detractors liked to say. Because of a skin disease, his nose became deformed in the ugliest way possible, turning purple - his many enemies liked to mock him for it. That's why there are virtually no photographs of Morgan: all the official portraits were retouched.

Morgan intervened several times to prevent Wall Street and America from collapsing. In February 1895, he took the train from New York to Washington. Without announcing himself, he showed up at the White House and asked to see President Grover Cleveland. The latter brushed him off. But Morgan explained that he would wait for the president to receive him, no matter how long it took. Cleveland received the banker the next morning. The United States was in the midst of a deep economic crisis. The American financial system, based on the gold standard, was on the brink of collapse. Morgan's offer: the Rothschilds and he would buy 3.5 million ounces of gold in Europe and in return receive a 30-year gold bond from the Treasury. Cleveland, backed into a corner, agreed. According to financial historian John Steele Gordon, "Morgan acted almost like a Central Bank - which did not exist at the time." And the intervention of the Wall Street magnate ultimately brought about a turning point for America. However, the rescue was not selfless, as Morgan also benefited from the transaction, which was sharply criticized by many of his contemporaries. In his satirical history of the United States, It all started with Columbus, Richard Armour summarizes the role of the banker with disdain: "This Morgan is known as J.P. to distinguish him from Henry Morgan, the pirate." Morgan, on the other hand, saw himself more in the tradition of the money lords, like the Medicis.

He passionately collected books - including a Gutenberg Bible - and works of art. He built a classical-style library on elegant Madison Avenue in Manhattan. His "study room," now open to ordinary curiosity-seekers, would have done honor to a Renaissance prince. The walls are covered in red damask, the sofas in red velvet. Morgan had the ceiling carved wood from a Florentine palace, and original stained glass windows from medieval churches adorn the windows. Next to them are originals by Memling,

Tintoretto, and Cranach, which all museums would like to own. One could easily roast a beef in the fireplace. For Morgan's office, where he liked to sit during the last years of his life to browse the treasures of his library, it would not be surprising if an entire oak forest had to be cleared. It was there, on November 2, 1907, on a windy Saturday night, that Morgan locked in the fifty most important bankers and financiers in New York. Because that year, Morgan once again played the role of Captain America.

At that time, there was a financial crisis similar to that of 2008. A Wall Street house, Moore & Schley, had miscalculated investments, and the creditor bank threatened to cut credit lines. If Moore & Schley had fallen, the multiple credit relationships with other Wall Street houses would have led to the collapse of many. The entire financial system would have been swept away - which would have also affected Morgan's empire. So Morgan bailed them out. But his fortune was not enough. He then gathered all the big names on Wall Street that night. It was only when they agreed to provide the necessary bailout capital that Morgan reopened the heavy double doors. Outside, dawn was breaking. Without Morgan's intervention, the United States would have plunged into another financial crisis.

However, this did not silence his detractors. Twenty-five years after his death, writer John Dos Passos wrote bitterly: "War and panic on the stock exchange, machine gun fire and arson, bankruptcies, war bonds, hunger, lice, cholera, and typhoid, that's the ideal time for growth, according to Morgan."

Dos Passos was alluding to the early days of Morgan's career, when he did business with both sides of the American Civil War. Then Morgan discovered the railroads. It was the equivalent of internet stocks when they first appeared; Morgan saw their potential. It was only with the railroads that American domestic trade could develop. Companies fiercely competed for new routes and goods, they had almost limitless capital needs and therefore often made bad speculations. An ideal opportunity for the entrepreneurially ambitious financier. He specialized in mergers and acquisitions, for which he organized capital. He controlled the newly formed conglomerates, in which he retained stakes. A term quickly emerged on Wall Street to describe what happened to acquired companies: they were "Morganized". John D.

Rockefeller can claim to have created the largest monopoly of his time with his Standard Oil. 90% of the oil produced in the United States passed through his refineries. Thanks to this, he amassed a fortune, a fortune still unmatched to this day. It amounted to 1.5% of America's economic output, or $340 billion in today's economic circumstances. According to reports, when Rockefeller learned, after Morgan's death, that the banker had left "only" $80 million to his heirs, Rockefeller exclaimed in disbelief, "And to think he wasn't even rich!" But with Morgan, it was about much more than wealth; his influence on the entire economy extended far beyond that of Rockefeller. Morgan succeeded in structuring capital on a scale never before achieved by anyone.

This visit to London in 1901, which caught the attention of McClure's journalist, followed Morgan's legendary feat: the creation of US Steel. There had never been a company like this before. It had a capital of over $1 billion and 250,000 employees - "a million souls live off the company, almost an entire nation," marvels McClure's. Morgan succeeded, like a Dr. Frankenstein, in assembling this colossus, but out of pieces of steel. Through a secret pact, he persuaded Carnegie to sell him his steelworks for $480 million. US Steel was supposed to weaken the leading powers of the steel industry - Britain and Germany. The goal was not only to dominate the steel sector, but also the entire infrastructure market. It was the founding years of America - the needs for bridges, ships, railways, and steel beams seemed endless. US Steel was Morgan's masterpiece. Despite all the bankruptcies and crises, the company still produces steel in its factories today.

Morgan used his position as a lender to actively influence companies. "Once a banker gets a seat on the board of directors, he will hold on to it tenaciously, and normally his influence will dominate, because he controls the supply of fresh money," his contemporary Louis Brandeis hammered in his book Other People's Money. Brandeis was a Supreme Court justice and a fierce fighter against cartels and monopolies, Morgan's archenemy. With a handful of New York bankers, he controlled the affairs of virtually all major American companies of his time. Representatives of J.P. Morgan's banking establishment temporarily held seventy-two directorships in forty-seven large companies. He had nothing against "a little competition," he condescended when questioned by an inquiry committee about his monopoly ambitions. The expression became legendary. A caricature shows Morgan with a bulbous nose, a big cigar, and an even bigger belly. Next to him is a glass full, as high as a barrel, as big as a reservoir, with the label: "Monopoly Whiskey," and a small bottle of soda labeled "competition" - of which a splash would not dilute the monopolistic drink. Morgan didn't think much of competition. His representatives, for example, sat on the boards of both General Electric and its rival Westinghouse. There were similar cross-connections in the railroads. From the banker's point of view, competition "between the left pocket and the right pocket" made little sense.

The managers' revolt

A side effect of Morgan's influence was that New York became the capital of capital. The great industrialists were drawn to the Hudson because they wanted to be close to the financiers. It was a golden age for them; they built palaces modeled after the aristocracy. If you stroll along Fifth Avenue, you can see them. Before building his villa, Biltmore, with two hundred and fifty rooms, central heating, a swimming pool, and a bowling alley, railroad heir George Vanderbilt II had visited the castles of the Loire. The society lady Mrs. Stuyvesant Fish even threw a lavish party for her dog, adorned for the occasion with a $15,000 diamond collar. This was more than ten times the average annual income of the vast majority of Americans at the time. Workers revolted, with over a thousand strikes just in the 1880s alone. Brutal confrontations erupted repeatedly, resulting in deaths and injuries. Four rebellious workers were hanged after an attack in Chicago, during which a policeman lost his life. The peak of these troubles was the strike of the Pullman Palace Car Company, best known for its luxurious sleeping cars furnished with padded furniture, a library, and all the comforts with which the oligarchs could travel across the country. The company was also one of the largest railroad companies. During the Recession of 1894, Pullman cut wages and raised rents in its worker colony. As a result, two hundred and forty thousand workers from twenty-six states went on strike. The company managers received support from government troops, who suppressed the protests. Many strikers were arrested and blacklisted. They could not find employment again.

The American labor movement only resumed fifty years later. Resistance grew, not only in the cities, where workers were packed into barracks. In North Dakota, an open revolt erupted against the "predatory speculators" from New York who, according to the locals, had ruined farmers there. To escape Wall Street's influence, North Dakota eventually founded a state bank in 1919, which still exists (cited repeatedly by activists). Although the labor movement was suppressed, under increasing political pressure, Washington began to act against cartels and trusts with regulations and then legal proceedings.

But, in the end, the upheaval came from entrepreneurs, not workers. Business leaders gradually rid themselves of banker control. This helped group leaders: in America, securities would soon no longer be reserved solely for the wealthy and those with the right connections. The first securities purchased by broader segments of the population were war bonds, that is, government bonds. Indeed, to finance World War I, the US Treasury sold war bonds - liberty bonds - not only to established investors such as banks or large private investors, but also to small investors. Advertising posters and appearances by Charlie Chaplin, as well as organizations like the Boy Scouts, helped draw attention to the new offer, appealing mainly to patriotism. This strategy worked. Of the 23 million Americans who invested in the famous liberty bonds, many were first-time investors. Americans then transferred this newly acquired confidence in such investments to large American companies like General Electric, AT&T, and the new automakers Ford, General Motors, and Chrysler.

Morgan and his financiers were replaced by the new caste of executives. Certainly, the same faces could be seen on the boards as before (they are still mostly white and male to this day), but they owed their influence to their belonging to the executive elite of the company and not to their access to capital. This is where the paths of America and Europe temporarily diverged: public shareholding never developed much on the Old Continent, so companies funded by stock remained a minority. For example, Germany has fewer than five hundred listed companies, fewer than Bangladesh. To this day, most companies in Europe are funded by banks.

How BlackRock Became the New J.P. Morgan

The financial capitalism of Morgan's golden age is experiencing a renaissance. But its dimensions have greatly increased. Instead of bankers, it is now asset managers who control the system. "Financial capitalism 2.0," as Gerald Davis of the University of Michigan named it in a thesis defended in 2012: "How BlackRock Became the New J.P. Morgan." Occupy Wall Street protesters and Tea Party members are certain: big business is responsible for today's social inequalities and economic uncertainty suffered by ordinary people. It's the opposite, says Davis. The power of big corporations is broken. Financial capitalists reign again. And that's exactly why job security is wavering, as is the social fabric.

If it had been designed for that purpose, there would have been no better way to complete the circle. The large publicly traded companies that J.P. Morgan had once pushed were at the heart of the economic boom of the 1950s and 1960s and the development of the middle class. In the 1970s, one in ten Americans worked for one of the twenty-five largest American companies. These companies created millions of jobs for "average Joe," the name given to the average American, who quickly owned General Electric refrigerators, an AT&T telephone line, a General Motors or Chrysler car, equipped with Goodyear tires and fueled by Standard Oil or Texas, ate General Foods (now Kraft) foods, and used Procter & Gamble cosmetics. It was the "American way of life": the small home you own, a car, two children, and the ability to pay for their decent college education. Those who were additionally employed by the heavyweights benefited from company health and retirement insurance. This still distinguishes America from Europe to this day - on the Old Continent, the public sector mainly covers social benefits. However, the generosity of American employers was a calculation: with these benefits, they wanted to ensure their power. But then globalization arrived, and especially the opening of China.

The success of large American companies after World War II fueled the belief that not only could they easily dominate the domestic market, but they could also dominate the world. Representatives of the American economy demanded the opening of the Chinese market for their own interests. The turning point came in 1972 with Nixon's visit, a notorious anticommunist, to China - a turning point that American composer John Adams even immortalized in an opera ("When I shook Zhou Enlai's hand, on that bare expanse in front of Beijing, the world was listening," Nixon sings in the first act of his aria). Beijing, then known in the West as Peking, showed interest. The result turned out very differently from what the leaders of large companies had imagined: the Chinese took advantage of the opening to flood the United States with cheap competing products. Suddenly, the social benefits of American workers became a costly disadvantage in the international struggle for market share. General Motors, for example, was the largest private provider of healthcare in the United States before its 2009 bankruptcy: nearly a million GM workers, retirees, and their families depended on the automaker. This cost GM an additional $1,400 per car.

Companies thus began to seek ways to rid themselves of this responsibility. It was the right time: Ronald Reagan, with his cowboy-worthy market economy credo, was president. The state helped companies by favoring individual capitalization retirement savings plans, called 401(k)s after the corresponding tax regulations enacted in the early 1980s. The big difference from company funds, which had been the dominant model for years, was that the pension was no longer guaranteed by the employer. In this new model, the employer only pays contributions or supplements for individual savings plans, and in times of crisis, they can even stop doing so. The risk thus shifts from the employer to the employee. 401(k) savings plans made average Joe and average Jane more or less involuntary participants in the stock market. These new shareholders were very different from Wall Street professionals or the wealthy heirs of Boston Brahmins. They mostly entrusted their savings to retirement investment funds - preferably to well-known large companies such as Fidelity, PIMCO, Vanguard, or later, BlackRock. This was the beginning of the rise of fund managers. In the 1950s, there were fewer than a hundred funds with about a million shareholders in the United States. Today, there are over ten thousand. In 1989 - just ten years after the introduction of 401(k) savings plans - private investment funds in the United States already managed over $1 trillion. In 2019, the amount was about $9 trillion, nearly twice Germany's gross domestic product. This is a massive concentration of capital in the hands of fund managers.

"The Twelve's Problem": this is how John Coates, a professor at Harvard University, named it in his eponymous book, which made headlines in 2018. With the victory of index funds, private equity, and globalization, control of most companies - we are talking about the largest multinational corporations, some of which are richer and more powerful than states - would be in the hands of a dozen men. In 2008, the big three - BlackRock, Vanguard, and a third, State Street, which is also an American index provider - held an average of nearly 13% of all major industrial companies, retail chains, banks, and insurance companies in the United States, as calculated by Bloomberg Businessweek. Ten years later, this share was 22%, or nearly a quarter of all large companies in the country were in the hands of three investors. Nearly 17% of the DAX belongs to the three North American funds. According to Coates, this is just the beginning. Even if the trend of index funds were to weaken, they would still hold, directly or indirectly, the majority of large publicly traded companies. In May 2020, for example, nearly 17% of Apple, the world's most valuable company, belonged to the big three. In 2009, it was only 9%. Such dominance even frightened Bogle, a stock market pioneer. The big three could alone dominate the stock market, he warned in an article for the Wall Street Journal in January 2019, just before his death. Such concentration is not in the national interest, he added.

The fixation of managers' objectives on profit maximization and endless cost reduction, on competitive advantages and market share, has become so widespread, so assimilated, that it would seem there has never been anything else – as if these were original components of capitalism. But this is the result of a revolution that began over forty years ago: that of shareholder value. A movement that changed companies, the economy, and society at least as fundamentally as 1968 and its aftermath. While in the early 1970s, students were protesting on the campuses of Harvard and the University of Chicago, their management school classmates, the supporters of the capital revolution, had case studies in their backpacks.

The prophet of financial capitalism, Milton Friedman, who taught at the University of Chicago, received the Nobel Prize in Economics. According to him, the only social responsibility of companies would be to use their resources to increase profits. Milton was responding to demands from the May 1968 movement, which called on companies like General Electric to be more committed to environmental protection and social responsibility. Such demands would have led to "pure socialism," as Milton declared in a 1970 New York Times article. Milton touched a nerve with investors. At that time, corporate America was in crisis. With the rise of Japan, American producers were facing powerful competitors in the domestic market for the first time. The oil shock and the ensuing inflation exploded prices, and unions, which were still strong at the time, demanded higher wages as compensation. Companies responded with a wave of mergers and acquisitions. This gave rise to bloated conglomerates, whose promised profits mostly did not materialize. Shareholders were unhappy. Spurred by Friedman's theories, an army of turnaround specialists and optimizers got to work.

This was the time for consultants. With their rigorous analyses, the minions of calculation were tasked with uncovering inefficiency and potential cost-cutting measures. The Boston Consulting Group, McKinsey & Company, and Bain & Company – which were later involved in the Toys 'R' Us debacle – were their breeding grounds: it was in these consulting firms that many young and ambitious business school graduates began their careers. They discovered the business market, where companies stood in relation to the competition, where they would find their biggest growth opportunities. It was primarily applied work: information had to be gathered from employees, suppliers, and customers, bills and orders had to be scrutinized, and endless data had to be entered into the rudimentary computer programs of the time (this was when the foundations for later digitization were laid). Consultants often ended up being hired by the companies they advised and thus helped the ideas of shareholder value to gain ground in the 1980s and 1990s. If Milken's junk bonds provided the capital for private equity acquisitions, it was Milton Friedman who provided the finance sector with the philosophy that continues to guide it to this day. Consultants became corporate hunters. Because even though they received substantial fees, in the event of success, the majority of the profits eluded them and went to the owners of the company, the shareholders.

The "Number Cruncher" from the Bain and Boston Consulting stables went through all departments with their pocket calculators, from purchasing to production to sales, to make processes simpler and more efficient. Private equity is the combination of Wall Street balance sheet extraction methods with those of cost hunters from consulting. It is the ruthless application of shareholder value thinking to all areas. The sole objective of private equity is to increase the profit of the owners – whether jobs are created or eliminated afterwards is just a side effect. The practices of the "locusts" have had a significant impact, far beyond the activities taken over by private equity firms. Competitors' chief executives copied their methods. Shareholders promised them high success bonuses in the form of shares. This was so that the interests of the owners and managers would coincide: managers were no longer to be employees simply collecting their salary, regardless of the company's results. And the argument of shareholder value – the value of the shareholder – also applied to management.

Encouraged by new technologies, factories and then management departments were "leaned out." The triumphant march of the shareholder value concept was not limited to America either: outsourcing to low-wage countries, for example, quickly became common in Germany. The underlying convictions are much deeper than cost-benefit analyses or laser-like focus on problem-solving. The essential idea of shareholder value is that the purpose of a company is first and foremost to provide increasing profits to the current owner or shareholder. This is the primacy of capital.

Where is the value?

If this capital has become increasingly volatile in this constant pursuit of maximum profit, so has the institution that is the company. US Steel and J.P. Morgan's railroads had enormous capital needs to invest in metal or tracks and build a sustainable organization. Today, companies are less institutions than a collection of patents, logistics, and contracts, which can dissolve more quickly.

In this regard, Gerald Davis has an impressive example. In 2007, when YouTube began to become popular, the "must-have gadget" was the Flip Video camera, a flip camera. It allowed individuals to quickly and easily create videos, edit them on their computers, and send them to their friends. The camera was relatively affordable, costing about $100. The "Flipcam" became – for a short period at least – a generic name like "Bic" or "Kleenex." The company selling the camera had not had to build a single factory, let alone hire workers, as it was Asian subcontractors that manufactured the camera. In 2009, the camera supplier held 20% of the market but had only a hundred employees, Davis reports in his case study.

The same year, the founders sold their company for $600 million to internet infrastructure giant Cisco. Two years later, Cisco stopped selling it: the Flipcam was dead. What happened? The camera function of new smartphones replaced the Flipcam: no one needed an additional device anymore. Less than four years elapsed between the beginning and the end of the story. "Unlike the disappearance of a company like Kodak, which had been a major employer and charitable donor for over a hundred and twenty years before going bankrupt, the disappearance of Flip left virtually no trace," Davis says in a sober conclusion.

To explain what is happening with companies in financial capitalism 2.0, Davis draws on concepts from physics in his study. The functions of the company would be subject to the centrifugal forces of outsourcing. On the other hand, on the shareholder side, the centrifugal forces would now – after the end of "morganization" – have changed direction, those that once ensured a distribution of capital owners to a broader base of shareholders. Stocks have become increasingly concentrated in the hands of fund managers over the past few decades. They are not the owners themselves – they are the investors in their funds or the members of pension funds who have mandated them – but only intermediaries. But they are the ones who direct the invested capital. And they do so with one goal: to maximize profits in a relatively short period, because they themselves are under enormous competitive pressure. Fund providers earn their money and can retain or attract new investors only if their funds and underlying values are higher than the market and competition. While John Pierpont Morgan generally pursued a strategy in his stock purchases – if only to hold a monopoly in the sector – fund holdings do not generate such unifying force. In actively managed funds by a manager, the goal is to select the most profitable companies or strategies. In passive funds such as BlackRock's iShares, clients cannot define at all which company shares the funds buy or sell. Because most investments are in index funds (over 80% of the shares BlackRock holds), investment in companies follows the set stock index. This means that if BlackRock clients buy more DAX ETFs, BlackRock must invest more in DAX companies. And if they sell their "iShare-Core-DAX" ETF shares, then BlackRock's ETFs withdraw their capital again.

This has made corporate capital more volatile. Significantly more volatile. Thirty years ago, institutional investors held their securities for about five years on average. Today, the normal holding period is five to nine months. One to two years are now considered "long term" by professional investors. This is generally too short for managers to successfully implement fundamental changes in their companies. Companies have had to adapt. They must take care of their lenders and deliver the desired performance within the desired timeframe.

Europeans, Germans in particular, like to believe that financial capitalism 2.0 – that is, the dictatorship of the financial market – is primarily an American phenomenon. After all, the stock market does not play a central role in

Germany's economic processes. Small and medium-sized enterprises still mainly finance themselves through bank loans and less with bonds. The new shadow banks, the rise of fund managers: all of this would be the problem of the "Anglo-Saxons," as German politicians like to explain. This is a mistake. From the financial market's point of view, Germany has long been a colony. Stakeholders are based in London and New York. From this perspective, the German economy is indeed the chessboard, but not the place where decisions are made.

CHAPTER 8

From Deutschland AG to Germany Inc.

If there is a place that represents the German version of industrial capitalism, it is the Villa Hügel in the Bredeney district of the city of Essen. The construction of Alfred Krupp's villa, which could rather be described as a castle, began in 1870. The son of the manufacturer Krupp had previously lived in the factory premises – as was customary at the time. The first Krupp had more or less succeeded with the manufacture, among other things, of tools and presses for minting coins, but Alfred succeeded in breaking through with the treads for the expanding railroads. With success came the desire for social ascent: Krupp wanted to escape with his family from the immediate vicinity of his steelworks, which with their soot and dirt constituted the basis of his prosperity. After more than three years of construction, the Krupps finally moved in. Bismarck had been chancellor for two years already. The villa, with its two hundred and sixty-nine rooms, surrounded by a 28-hectare green park and offering a panoramic view, became the family seat and emblem of the Ruhr barons. Alfred's successors added tennis courts, riding facilities, and a bowling alley to the splendid building. At certain times, more than five hundred employees took care of the residents' well-being. Imagine Downton Abbey, the fictitious castle from the popular British series, but much larger. Krupp steel became a reference worldwide, even if it was not always well regarded. Armaments became the main activity for the "king of cannons" Krupp. When the last family member to bear the name, Alfried Krupp von Bohlen und Halbach, died on July 30, 1967, he bequeathed everything to the Krupp Foundation "for charitable purposes." The foundation became a major shareholder in the steel group. Alfried Krupp's confidant, Berthold Beitz, took over the reins of the foundation and the group as general plenipotentiary. This did not change when Krupp merged with its former rival Thyssen in 1997, despite protests from employees. Beitz, nicknamed the "patriarch of Deutschland AG" or, more affectionately because of the Krupp logo, the "lord of the rings," was the last survivor of the era of "Rhenish capitalism," characterized by personal relationships and reciprocal shareholdings.

It was at the time when the villa Hügel was being erected that the foundations of Deutschland AG were also laid. It was the era when large joint-stock companies were emerging. The period before the First World War was a golden age for the German economy. Paul Windolf counted in a 2013 study that there were two thousand two hundred and eighty-six relationships between the two hundred and fifty large companies of the time. This is how these gentlemen – there are almost exclusively men in these commissions today – met several times a year. Because they represented, as directors, the interests of different companies at the same time, the clique of supervisory and management boards acted as a total supervisory body, according to Windolf.

Banks, Dresdner Bank and Deutsche Bank in particular, played a central role in the network. J.P. Morgan would easily have recognized his system during a visit to Frankfurt. Carl Klönne, for example, was a member of the Deutsche Bank's board of directors at the turn of the century. He also sat on the supervisory boards of Siemens, Allianz, Rütgers Chemicals, Gelsenkirchener BergwerksAG, and seventeen other companies at the same time.

In the early years of the FRG, the director of the Frankfurt-based Deutsche Bank, Josef Abs, assumed the role of primus inter pares: first among equals. During his tenure, Abs sat on thirty supervisory boards. In many of them, he even held a leading position. He liked to let it be known what he thought of these fine men's clubs. "The kennel is for the dog, the supervisory board for the cat," was one of his sayings. In addition to the Frankfurt bankers, the Munich insurers Allianz and Munich Re also controlled the post-war German economy. They set up a system of shareholdings in the largest industrial groups in the country. Until a few years ago, they decided who joined the supervisory board and the executive board. Deutsche Bank not only wielded its power directly through its own shareholdings. It also voted on behalf of its custodian clients, who had given it the right to vote for their shares. And often, the people in Frankfurt decided on loans while also being the house bank. The position of chairman of the supervisory board of

Germany's largest automaker, Daimler, was, so to speak, an inheritance for the director of Deutsche Bank. Chancellor Schröder, who felt at ease in the company of bosses, jokingly referred to himself as the "CEO of Deutschland AG." But nothing could really be done in the German economy or government without the agreement of the bankers from Frankfurt. It was an informal conduct: we know each other, we meet regularly. At the congresses of the Federation of German Industries (BDI) and the Stifterverband für die Deutsche Wissenschaft, the Union of Founders for German Science, for example. Or at the popular entrepreneurs' conferences in Baden-Baden: the top executives of German companies always meet in the spa town "to get to know each other," as Manager Magazin once put it. In the summer, Deutschland AG meets in Bayreuth at the Wagner festival or in Salzburg, where they retire to the luxury hotel Goldener Hirsch after the festival.

Until the 1990s, the men's club succeeded in dominating the German economy and isolating it from abroad.

The network protected managers from the influence of financial markets. Interdependencies and, above all, the strong integration of banks into the management of large companies meant that capital was "more patient" and "friendlier" than in the American variant of capitalism. Germany appeared as the "counter-model to American market capitalism," as political scientist Martin Höpner wrote in his 2007 habilitation thesis. There, no fund manager banged on the negotiation table as a shareholder, none demanded more profit, higher dividend payouts, or more severe austerity measures. Hostile takeovers were simply unthinkable. Economic historians argue that the integration of employee representatives on the supervisory board is only possible in such a context. In the United States, employee representation has always remained a problematic institution.

However, the principle of "one hand washes the other" often led both to remain dirty. There was the scandal surrounding the Philipp Holzmann AG company. Just a few days after its 150th anniversary, the largest construction group to date had to admit to losses of several billion, which had remained hidden until then. Despite a rescue plan from the Schröder government, Holzmann filed for bankruptcy in 2002. The accusations against the management and supervisory boards – of issuing false invoices and engaging in speculation, among other things – were settled by an amicable agreement. There was also the bankrupt real estate shark Jürgen Schneider, who cost the banks 5 billion marks with his fictitious empire and ruined many artisanal businesses.

Then, in 1999, the British mobile phone company Vodafone took on Mannesmann, a heavyweight in the DAX whose origins date back to the first seamless steel tubes by the brothers Max and Reinhard Mannesmann in 1886. After a month-long battle over the takeover, the German group lost. In February 2000, the supervisory board finally approved the acquisition. "The Düsseldorf agreement also marks the end of Rhenish capitalism. With this system based on consensus and employee representation, German companies had successfully resisted attacks from abroad," wrote Der Spiegel at the time. It was the first hostile takeover bid of a traditional leading company. The bulwark of Deutschland AG had been collapsing for some time. Globalization had played a role: to survive, German companies had to internationalize. They had not only started selling outside of Germany but also increasingly producing there. Almost half of Siemens' employees will soon be abroad. But, above all, the heart of Deutschland AG's power, Deutsche Bank, was changing. They threw in the towel. Under the chairmanship of Josef Ackermann, who, because of his role as chairman of the supervisory board of Mannesmann, had to appear twice in court during Vodafone's attack, the Frankfurters sold their stakes in the industry one after the other after the turn of the millennium. Shortly before the takeover, Ackermann – along with other members of Mannesmann's management and supervisory boards such as former CEO Klaus Esser and former IG Metall union president Klaus Zwickel – received bonuses, the legality of which was questioned. In the first trial, the defendants were convicted and the appeal trial was dropped in exchange for payments of several million. This was the most spectacular economic trial of the post-war period. It's no wonder that the motto in the towers of Deutsche Bank in Frankfurt was all the more vehement afterwards: to refocus on the core business, i.e., banking finances. At Daimler, for example, the bank held just under 12% until 2004. By the end of 2006, it was down to 4.4%, and by 2009, 2.5%.

The end of the German version of industrial capitalism

It was politics that ultimately accelerated the downfall of Deutschland AG. Within all parties, the model of cross-shareholdings between banks and industrial groups came under increasing criticism in the 1990s. Not only did the liberal FDP party see it as a growth-inhibiting problem, but the SPD and the Greens also viewed it as a cartel of executives. It was the red-green coalition government, precisely under the self-proclaimed honorary managing director Schröder, that abolished the capital gains tax in 2001 and thus made the sale of shareholdings fiscally attractive. The power network, which had survived two world wars, began to dissolve more and more quickly. Lothar Kempel from the Max Planck Institute for Societal Research in Cologne examined this using figures from the German Monopoly Commission. In the mid-1990s, there were still sixty-two capital interdependencies between the top two hundred and fifty companies. At the heart of the network were still the financial service providers, Deutsche Bank, Allianz, Munich Re, and Dresdner Bank. In 2006, there were only thirty-nine such cross-connections left. In 1996, Deutsche Bank executives still held thirty-two supervisory board mandates. Ten years later, there were only four left.

The Villa Hügel also went through this change of era. The patriarch of the ThyssenKrupp group, Berthold Beitz, who still went to his office when he was approaching 100 years old, died on July 30, 2013 – forty-six years exactly after his friend Alfred Krupp. Just a few months after Beitz's death, the Krupp Foundation lost its blocking minority in the supervisory board. ThyssenKrupp, which had been losing money for years, had swallowed up billions in assets in the United States and Brazil and was in the sights of hedge funds demanding a capital increase. The foundation, led by Beitz, could no longer keep up. With a 25% stake, it had so far called the shots in the steel group, preventing hostile takeovers and dismantling for decades.

Instead of three supervisory board positions at ThyssenKrupp as before, the public utility foundation could only fill two. As the foundation's share fell, the other major shareholders increased theirs: the Swedish hedge fund Cevian, the American fund company Franklin Mutual... and BlackRock, the nexus of the new "Germany Inc."

It's not only among the heavyweights of the DAX that well-established owners – families, foundations, or other companies holding a stake for strategic reasons – have slammed the door. The farewells of these reference shareholders have also accelerated significantly for medium-sized companies, the traditional backbone of the German economy. In a study, the consulting firms Cometis and Ipreo examined the ownership structure of companies represented in indices other than the DAX, representing smaller companies. The result: in the SDAX – an index that includes, among others, Puma, Heidelberger Druck, and the car rental company Sixt – the share of major shareholders was 42% at the end of 2014. Twelve months earlier, this share was still 47%. For the MDAX – whose fifty values include the optician chain Fielmann and Osram AG – this figure was only 34%, and had also decreased by 4% in a year. The new shareholders mainly come from North America, Great Britain, and Scandinavia (Norges Bank Investment Management, the Norwegian state pension fund, is one of the largest institutional investors in Germany). Among the top ten investors in SMEs are, besides DWS, the asset management branch of Deutsche Bank, and Allianz Global Investors, no more than two German financial companies. At the time of the study, BlackRock was involved in MDAX companies with nearly 1.2 billion euros – almost twice as much as a year earlier. And this amount only concerned the fund that BlackRock actively manages. Overall, the share must have been even higher at the time, as 14% of MDAX values were held by index funds, i.e., passive investors (or ETFs). And BlackRock manages around 80% of its funds as a passive investor on average. Little has changed since. This makes New Yorkers one of the main financiers of medium-sized German companies, at least those listed.

The new lords of the DAX family have brought their own customs and practices. This has caused some unpleasant surprises for members of the old

Deutschland AG. For example, when Deutsche Bank CEO Josef Ackermann wanted – as was customary at the time – to smoothly transition from the management board to the supervisory board chairmanship in 2012 – to crown his career – foreign shareholders refused to give their consent. Ackermann gave up, allegedly because he was still too busy with the consequences of the crisis in the time he had left as a board member, and therefore could not prepare for the new role. BlackRock remained silent on the matter because, as a major shareholder of Deutsche Bank, it does not comment on companies on a case-by-case basis as a matter of principle. But insiders report that BlackRock, as one of Deutsche Bank's largest shareholders, would have prevented Ackermann's transfer to the supervisory board chairmanship. The Frankfurters had lobbied hard for their boss on several occasions – in vain. The person responsible at BlackRock allegedly gave them a clear answer: "No!" Ackermann had apparently thwarted New York's personal plans.

Larry Fink openly praised "his" favorite candidate, Anshu Jain. Jain was considered a product of the London City (which cost him a lot of sympathy in Germany). But the man from Jaipur, India, had started his career on Wall Street. Familiar with this culture, he was welcome at events where Wall Street bigwigs congratulated themselves. Other foreign bankers, on the other hand, couldn't even watch. "Anshu has done a fantastic job," Fink also raved to the New York Times in June 2011. "He would make a very good CEO of Deutsche Bank." On the other hand, Ackermann's favorite candidate for his successor was former Bundesbank president Axel Weber. On June 1, 2012, Jain was appointed co-chairman of the management board of Deutsche Bank (with co-chairman Jürgen Fitschen, who mainly had to present a familiar face for "their" bank to those Germans who had a problem with Jain, an Indian, as chairman of Deutsche Bank).

A shareholder revolt also threatened Wolfgang Mayrhuber, long-time CEO of Lufthansa, who already saw himself at the helm of the company's supervisory board before the annual general meeting in 2013. But his brief switch from manager to controller did not sit well with American investors in particular, far from it. They threatened to vote against the Austrian at the shareholders' meeting. Mayrhuber was still elected, but at the very last minute and with such a narrow majority that it was embarrassing. Such a thing could not have happened within the old boys' club in the past. In the former Deutschland AG, conflicts were resolved with a nice dinner or a discreet phone call. "Deutschland AG protected many. Today, all companies are exposed to all winds," noted a former banker who had long worked in one of the major companies.

Serving on the supervisory board has become an uncomfortable position. "In the Anglo-Saxon world, investors send 'their' representative to the supervisory board to protect their interests. This is American-style corporate governance. And of course, this is what they also want to establish in Germany," explains Peter Dehnen, a lawyer specializing in consultations for supervisory boards. According to German law and German corporate governance, this is not allowed—the supervisory board is part of the "internal organs" of the company and, as such, it is independent; its sole responsibility is the well-being of the company, just like all the other parties associated with it—including the staff. Dehnen observed such great despair among business controllers that he founded their own advocacy association, the Association of Supervisory Boards in Germany, with more than a hundred members. Once a year, they meet to discuss topics such as "digital change and corporate governance," "strategic competence," or "personnel competence." At previous meetings, much work was done on the "future forum" on the "board model"—all presented by German television icon Sabine Christiansen. In any case, it's a more packed agenda than the luxurious menu at the "Goldener Hirsch" in Salzburg.

An entire industry has emerged with the aim of teaching German executives how to properly manage their new American owners. This is how a group of consultants regularly meets in Düsseldorf to work on the correct interpretation of the latest writings of Lucian Bebchuk. Bebchuk, a Harvard professor, is considered a guru of corporate governance. "Sooner or later, everything that is practiced in the USA will end up here," which motivates the participants, explains Burkhard Fassbach, one of the circle's initiators. No one wants to be caught off guard. Fassbach specializes in supervisory board liability issues, a field that did not exist in this form in Germany until recently. Meanwhile, disputes between shareholders and the supervisory board, or between the management board and the supervisory board, are now part of everyday life.

The investor relations function—often noted as IR—is also part of the conquests of financial capitalism 2.0. This function is most often attached to the management board. It emerged with the increase in funds for major shareholders. Firms hire IR managers to maintain their relationships with shareholders: their main task is to satisfy them. After the farewells of the main shareholders of the former Deutschland AG, over 80% of DAX values have become floating, and their shares are freely traded on the capital market. This means that it is enough for a fund to hold shares in the single-digit percentage range to have an influence on the company (see our example of the startup manufacturing plastic ducks in chapter 2!) "If we compile a list of our top 10, an investor holding 1% is already considered a major shareholder," says the IR manager of a DAX company. One of the difficulties for IR is that it is no longer as easy to know who is an important shareholder and who is no longer. Admittedly, there are mandatory notifications on voting rights as soon as the stake exceeds certain thresholds with the BaFin, as stipulated in the Securities Trading Act. But these reports only give an approximate idea. To know precisely, the IR regularly calls on specialists to know the real ownership situations. These shareholder detectives then run after investment banks and investors and call deposit banks that have been granted voting rights by their clients. In addition to a list of the largest shareholders, IR also wants to know who is buying the shares of their company—or who is selling them, and if possible, why. Is the entire sector unpopular with investors, and has the fund manager therefore liquidated the share? Or is he showing dissatisfaction with the company itself? Such questions must be filtered by number crunchers. Because IR must ensure that the share price does not experience violent fluctuations—ideally, it should regularly move upwards. But since German companies have been exposed to the turbulence of the global capital market, this has required interventions and some skill. Surprises are not desirable. Like a decline in sales, for example. This should not take investors by surprise. If bad figures appear on the screens, it is already too late. Then, Wall Street's proven maxim applies: "Sell first, ask questions later!" No investor wants to be upset afterwards because they did not liquidate the loser's stock in time. IR must therefore carefully prepare its major shareholders for unpleasant messages. But it must not give them concrete figures in front of other shareholders—this would be insider trading. So caution must be exercised. Good shareholder tamers must be able to manage stock price movements by simply making allusions.

Meetings where IR and its management board members personally meet with major shareholders are part of the daily life of the new Germany Inc. These meetings are generally organized by banks, mostly in a hotel in Frankfurt. If you expect, for example, to be able to chat with the gentlemen and ladies of BlackRock over appetizers, you will be very disappointed. Major investors prefer to rent a suite in the hotel. From there, they then invite the boards of directors of German companies for appointments. From time to time, business leaders—especially CFOs—go on a "roadshow" to visit their major foreign shareholders. They then head to London or New York. For this occasion, banks once again take on the role of tour operators. They also pay the bill. Banks hope that this will be offset in the long term through fees and commissions, and that they will in turn be considered in future orders from companies and investors. Bankers organize a complete and hassle-free trip: they ensure that board members get their appointments with important investors and arrange appropriate accommodations and transportation (it must be a Mercedes S-Class or a comparable model!) However, British supervisory authorities now care more about these arrangements, demanding greater transparency about who pays whom and why. The new service providers have taken the leap into the void—former bankers have almost rebranded themselves as independent travel agencies specializing in investor roadshows. An insider, however, fears that it will become more difficult for smaller companies to meet their investors or to get to know new ones. They will rarely be able to afford these expensive trips. So far, the investor indirectly pays for the smaller ones through bank fees. In larger companies, regular meetings are required. The IR manager of a DAX company, for example, reports that BlackRock would like to see the CEO, or at least the CFO, twice a year in London, twice in New York, and twice in Edinburgh (analysts and fund managers managing BlackRock's engagement in Europe are located in the Scottish capital). These interviews took place at the time of the research for the first edition. It remains to be seen how roadshows and IR meetings develop. For now, it seems that London, despite Brexit, will remain the point of contact in Europe, especially for Anglo-Saxon investors. Nevertheless, the new EU financial regulation (MiFID II) and, above all, the long-term consequences of the Covid-19 pandemic are likely to change many habits again.

However, the fundamental principles will not change. In modern corporations, democracy reigns—at least officially. Shareholders determine the supervisory board, which in turn determines the management board. At the annual general meeting of shareholders—which takes place at the beginning of the year for most companies—shareholders vote on management proposals and shareholder requests. The most important task of IR is to prepare the general meeting so that it runs smoothly—that is, it goes in the direction of the management board. Ideally, from the point of view of investor relations and managers, shareholders should let the management board's proposals pass without too much discussion. To prepare, IR services prepare hundreds of responses to potential questions. Large groups also hire external consultants to optimize the program. During preliminary discussions, IR employees gauge the mood of the shareholders. They try to cut off in advance small shareholders' associations, which could disturb with their annoying demands. However, the biggest dangers are not the old grumblers or complainers. "Imagine, it's the annual general meeting of shareholders, and nobody goes there": this is the nightmare scenario for companies. Like citizens in secondary elections, one of the problems is the indifference of many shareholders who simply abstain from voting. "The attendance at the AGM is a real issue for us, as a company, otherwise a 6 to 7% participation can quickly become a blocking minority. If 30% of our capital is present at the AGM, we are already satisfied," says the experienced investor relations manager of a German financial group.

Even in large DAX companies, it was not uncommon for attendance to be below 50% in recent years. And that's already a reason to rejoice! The problem with low attendance: if only a small part of the voting capital is present, it weakens management. Or, worse, the votes are enough to already cause small ripples to form a blocking minority and thwart the plans of the management board. Or a candidate for the supervisory board is snubbed and rejected, or—worst case—an attempt to increase capital fails. Such a shame makes headlines, causes turmoil, and in any case, a slide in the share price. Everything that IR seeks to prevent.

At the annual general meeting of Deutsche Bank in May 2019, only 34% of shareholders were present—even though it was about the uncertain future of what was once the world's largest bank. In the end, the leadership duo of CEO Christian Sewing and Chairman of the Supervisory Board Paul Achleitner were not questioned, even though the votes were— at 75 and 71%—far from the values to which German corporate leaders are accustomed. Without the grace of the lords from across the Atlantic, they would have been even lower. "Ultimately, it is obviously the major shareholders of the bank, BlackRock, Katar, and Cerberus, who—certainly due to the lack of alternative candidates—voted for the current management of the house," writes the German television channel ARD on this subject. During the Covid-19 crisis, shareholders once again closed ranks. At the virtual annual general meeting held in May 2020, Achleitner, chairman of the supervisory board, as well as Sewing, CEO, received the usual percentages of votes: 93% and almost 99%, respectively.

Under the influence of the Californian special unit

A special unit with forty-five members exercises the rights of shareholders for the BlackRock empire. Its members ensure that BlackRock's interests are taken into account by managers worldwide. They are spread across seven offices, in six countries and three regions of the world. Their headquarters is an office in San Francisco. All roads lead there, specifically to a red-haired New Zealander named Michelle Edkins. She holds the reins. The BlackRock super nanny took over the position in 2010 and is now trying to get BlackRock to adopt a clearer line on corporate governance. Corporate governance became a keyword after the scandals of Enron and Worldcom in the early 2000s, during which thousands of people lost their jobs and investors hundreds of billions. At the Texan energy company Enron, elected "America's most innovative company" by Fortune magazine for six consecutive years, it turned out that profits existed only on paper and were a kind of trick with derivatives. At Worldcom, CEO Bernie Ebbers simply falsified the accounts and bought himself a ranch the size of New York City three times over and a herd of twenty-two thousand cattle. Investors and regulators swore that such scams would never happen again and that better controls should be implemented in companies from now on.

Following the thousands of companies in the portfolio is now the main mission of Edkins' department. With her special shareholder commando, she has even developed their own jargon for their mission. If a supervisory board holds too many mandates for different companies, then it is guilty of "overboarding". According to BlackRock troops, the department is too busy to sufficiently deal with each company. Another term: "engagement," which has a military undertone in English. At BlackRock, this means that an analyst will be sent to verify that the company in question is doing the right thing. Company bosses can at least expect to receive insistent calls. Each year, nearly fifteen hundred companies in the BlackRock empire receive a visit from a colleague from Edkins' team or at least a few calls - 1458, according to the 2019 annual report. "Refreshment," is not a thalasso cure for tired supervisory board members but measures that may apply when "engagement" has not had the desired effect. In this case, BlackRock believes that personnel turnover may be necessary. At least, that's what the New York Times described in 2013 in a breathtaking account of Edkins' troop. "Our experience has shown that managers react strongly to direct approaches," Edkins said, pleased, to the specialized magazine Pensions & Investments. This is not surprising - which supervisory board does not listen attentively to one of its largest owners? And, very often, BlackRock not only plays this role, but also that of a major creditor, holding bonds and loans. You can hardly have more cards in hand.

However, all this happens in the background - like everything else at BlackRock. "When two parties wage war in the newspapers, it serves no one." This is how Larry Fink explains his preference for discretion in the foreword to the 2012 corporate governance annual report, which summarizes BlackRock's activities as a major shareholder. Two pages later, BlackRock's shareholder philosophy is bluntly discussed: "We do not publicly discuss how we approach a company because it does not need to make headlines to protect the interests of its shareholders." This means that BlackRock's wishes and demands to managers remain behind the scenes. Only those directly involved know exactly what is discussed with business leaders during "engagements" and what influence they have.

One of the few cases where BlackRock's wishes were made public took place in May 2014, as part of American pharmaceutical giant Pfizer's attempt to buy its Anglo-Swedish rival AstraZeneca. Pfizer was mainly interested in tax benefits with the merger. The American company planned to create a special holding company and move its headquarters to London. This could have saved them hundreds of millions of dollars. The takeover failed, AstraZeneca declined. Pfizer withdrew because, in the UK, the buyer must wait several months before being able to make a new offer. BlackRock, a significant shareholder in AstraZeneca, urged its board of directors to renegotiate with

Pfizer, once the legal waiting period was over. At least that's what an insider wrote on the New York Times Dealbook blog.

Anticipating the wishes of Fink & Co. is better than waiting for a call or a visit from a BlackRock representative: if you want to maintain good relations with the giant, it is preferable to keep them regularly informed. His company wants "a dialogue," Fink said in 2012 in a letter to six hundred board members of companies in which BlackRock was involved. If management refuses to meet BlackRock's expectations, things can get uncomfortable. "We will vote against the management if we conclude that our direct approach has not yielded results," says BlackRock's ten-point action plan for contact with companies. Supervisory boards that see one of their major shareholders turn against them are on thin ice.

One-way information

The London branch of Edkins' team handles German companies. But these companies must share this attention with other countries. Initially, there were five employees. Five more were hired in 2018; BlackRock proudly announced this in its annual report. Together, they handle BlackRock's stakes across Europe, the Middle East, and Africa – the so-called EMEA economic region. If we take the relevant stock indices for this region as a basis, more than six hundred companies are listed there. For comparison: other service providers, who make money by exercising shareholders' rights, such as the British Hermes Equity Ownership Services, manage a significantly higher number of companies: "One of our employees, for example, handles about ten to twenty companies. If you want to manage a company properly, a larger number is not possible," as Hans-Christoph Hirt, director of Hermes Equity Ownership Services, explained in an interview for the first edition of this book. Responsibility increases when you have a stake in a company. "If we hold a 3% stake in a large company, then the dialogue is intense." In any case, BlackRock's Corporate Governance teams receive support from the parent company, namely stock analysts and fund managers who introduced the shares into the portfolio. For some German companies, these are the contact persons. For example, the IR manager of a DAX chemical company has never dealt with Edkins' troop, but with the analyst responsible for the chemical sector. The companies concerned, however, remain in the dark about the criteria for this responsibility. Another Investor Relations manager complained of never knowing exactly who is responsible for him at BlackRock. Another wrote in a report that it is not easy for him to know which department exercises the right to vote for BlackRock at the general meeting.

Company representatives do not want to speak publicly about their relationships with BlackRock. It would probably be easier for them to talk about their personal lives. Who would want to upset one of their largest shareholders? (BlackRock is often the largest.) Only once assured of absolute anonymity did IR managers from DAX companies of various sizes and sectors agree to have confidential discussions. None of the respondents is a newcomer: they have all been doing this work for years, sometimes for decades. Everyone agreed on one point: BlackRock considers information to be a portable debt. BlackRock representatives expect companies to come to them if they have crucial questions. But the flow of information is one-way. It is not only at BlackRock that this is the case. Shareholders do not have to tell the company if they sell the share or why they are doing so. They also do not have to explain why they increase their stake. It often takes six to eight weeks before companies learn that something has changed with their major owners. "Absolute transparency is expected of us, but funds do not have to tell us anything," complains the IR manager of a healthcare company. Not even the number of voting rights attributed to a passive or active engagement. This makes a real difference, as passive votes are linked to index affiliation and are therefore only settled if something changes in the index. "To get this information, we have to pay additional providers!" complains a representative of a financial group.

In the end, all the representatives of German companies and investment professionals interviewed agree: unlike other large investors, BlackRock at least strives to fulfill the most important shareholder obligations, such as recording votes for the general meeting in a timely manner and then voting at the meeting. "Professional" or "informed" were terms frequently used to describe BlackRock's representatives. No one complained of a strained relationship; everything was "hyper-normal," as described by the IR manager of a DAX chemical company. As a result, Fink's corporate governance troop attaches importance to the formal requirements of good corporate governance. This includes, for example, respecting a "cooling-off period" before a former board member can switch to the supervisory board. Or the requirement to place more women on the board. But, if you look at the glass as half empty: at one of the largest shareholders of German companies, there is generally little more than this minimal commitment. In the 2013 corporate governance report from BlackRock's team, something entirely different is written. "We build relationships with the companies in our portfolio to develop mutual understanding about performance, strategy, and risk reduction," the brochure explains under a beautiful title: "Taking the long view."

In the 2019 report, the corporate governance troop describes some examples – always anonymized – of their operations. Once, they would have negotiated with a European pharmaceutical company repeatedly accused of corruption. In recent years, the group has been accused of alleged bribes in Turkey, the United States, and South Korea. BlackRock's snoops suspect "fundamental problems in the corporate culture." "We will monitor future investigations and, if necessary, we will come back," the report says.

BlackRock seems to often get crucial information for its interventions through the press. Siemens, for example, came under severe criticism from environmentalists in early 2020 because the company accepted an order to provide railway signaling technology to the Carmichael coal mine, one of the largest in Australia, operated by the Indian conglomerate Adani. The order volume was 18 million euros, a modest sum compared to the group's revenue of 87 billion euros in 2018. At the annual general meeting, Siemens CEO Joe Kaeser was accused of contributing to global warming with such projects. BlackRock, one of the company's major shareholders, sided with the critics and later stated that the company's management had not clarified the "broader risk" associated with the engagement. However, BlackRock itself held $144 million in investments in the Adani group at the time, as discovered by Market Forces, an Australian climate protection initiative. The only subsidiary of the group in which environmentalists have not been able to find any trace of BlackRock investment is Adani Green, specializing in renewable energies. Statistics clearly show that BlackRock focuses on the United States: according to BlackRock, 42% of Edkins' troop's "engagements" took place there in 2019, compared to 27% overall in Europe, the Middle East, and Africa and 31% in Asia. According to the report covering the year from July 2018 to July 2019, eight hundred fifty-five "engagements" took place in America during this period, two hundred sixty-one in Great Britain, three hundred in continental Europe, the Middle East, and Africa, three hundred ninety-seven in Japan, and two hundred thirty-seven in the rest of Asia and the Pacific. According to the 2013 corporate governance report, BlackRock voted in sixteen thousand one hundred twenty-four general meetings, of which two thousand five hundred seven were in European companies. The proportion was similar the previous year.

A problem that all expensive brochures and information-filled websites cannot hide: new big capitalists can only truly focus on the companies they own. Because fulfilling the role of a shareholder properly means investing. An investment that large fund companies must or should provide not only for a single company, but for the thousands of companies in their portfolios. In dozens of countries, following the current regulations. The bureaucracy alone associated with this – such as correctly registering voting rights – costs in terms of personnel and money. Costs that a fund provider can only pass on to its clients in the form of fees and under certain conditions. Because asset managers are in fierce competition. BlackRock is itself a listed company, and its shareholders want to see profits and stock prices rise. It is not surprising that large fund companies interact with the companies in their portfolios in a targeted manner and limit themselves to the essentials with all others.

Fink's call for constant dialogue with the leaders of his portfolio companies can also be interpreted as an admission that even BlackRock cannot get information from every manager.

At the time of research for the first edition of the book published in 2015, these scruples did not arouse much interest. Now, an increasing number of academics and (more annoyingly for BlackRock) regulators are looking into these issues. Lucian Bebchuk, the corporate governance guru mentioned earlier, for example, studied the corporate governance activities of the big three with a Harvard colleague, Scott Hirst. The result: index fund managers are encouraged to keep their level of control and oversight of their investments as low as possible. And they are equally encouraged to mostly adopt the preferences and positions of these companies' executives. The reason is simple: the more an index fund manager deals with the specific performance of each company and its managers, the more it costs. Moreover, if the company becomes more successful thanks to such interventions, the competition will also benefit. BlackRock likes to highlight "informal engagements," calls, and backstage meetings between fund managers and the executives of portfolio companies. However, Bebchuk and his colleague found that these informal contacts occur too rarely and with too few companies. "The 'informal engagement' of the big three cannot therefore be an appropriate substitute for other instruments of stewardship," they conclude.

Critics say that the big three are also responsible for the skyrocketing executive pay packages. In a 2018 study, Ryan Bubb and Emiliano Catan, professors at New York University, showed that mega-funds rarely oppose managers on controversial issues such as compensation, mergers, or acquisitions. In the case of mergers, BlackRock voted for in 79% of cases, and Vanguard in 85%.

BlackRock is certainly the largest fund management company facing the problem, but it is not the only one. Large funds should theoretically attend the general meetings of all companies in which they hold a stake. And that's not all: they should also know all the items on the agenda and have an opinion on them. Items such as executive compensation, dividend amounts, or a future capital increase. As shareholders, they should have formed an opinion in advance about the candidates for the board of directors or supervisory board. And, of course, have evaluated the company's performance. And all of this, not just for one company, but for hundreds or even thousands, in different countries. The most convenient thing is to delegate this work to someone else, namely "proxy advisors." The invention of this new activity is credited to Robert Augustus Gardner Monks, born in 1933 into a Boston "Brahmin" family (his wife was from the industrial Carnegie dynasty). Monks explained his commitment against the omnipotence of managers and abuses of all kinds by an experience he had in the early 1970s. While visiting Maine, he noticed a foam on the surface of the Penobscot River that was destroying vegetation on the banks. He discovered that the toxic wastewater responsible came from the Great Northern Paper mill, located next to the river. A few years later, Monks, now head of a Boston bank, remembered the incident. The bank held voting rights for its clients, and Monks was supposed to fill out the voting documents accordingly. As usual, he began to automatically approve the management's proposals. Until he came across the Great Northern Paper file: the company he remembered as polluting. "That's when I realized that I was part of the problem myself. Fifty or sixty people like me could actually change something. I began to think about shareholder ownership in a truly human way," Monks later told Fortune magazine. This die-hard Republican went to Washington after Ronald Reagan's election. There, Monks became the pension funds inspector. On the spot, Monks quickly realized that pension funds did not have the necessary staff to individually deal with each company in their portfolios.

For this reason, Monks founded Institutional Shareholder Services (ISS) in 1985. Better known by its acronym ISS, the company is still today the leading provider of services related to corporate governance. ISS has been acquired several times and now belongs, ironically, to the private equity firm Genstar Capital. According to its own figures, ISS handles 10 million votes for actual shareholders and represents voting rights for over 4 trillion shares. The number two in this market of shareholder whisperers is Glass Lewis, a subsidiary of a Canadian pension fund.

Today, ISS is an integral part of the industry corporate governance has become. Not exactly what Monks had in mind. On behalf of pension funds, hedge funds, or investment funds like those of BlackRock, proxy advisors analyze the agendas of the relevant general meetings and evaluate the candidates for the board of directors and supervisory board. They then advise their clients on how to vote on the various items. Measures are guidelines for corporate governance, such as limiting the accumulation of positions on the supervisory boards or a "cooling-off" period for transfers from the executive board to the supervisory board. But there are also specific client requirements - such as environmental protection or social criteria - which proxy advisors take into account in their analyses. However, even proxy advisors cannot do this work without help. For example, ISS has a highly regarded software system in the corporate governance sector, which sifts through the agendas of general meetings and automatically develops recommendations. According to ISS, these are always checked by human analysts. Funds are not obliged to follow the recommendations but do so most of the time. Why else would they pay millions in fees to ISS or Glass Lewis? At the same time, proxy advisors have gained influence through their activities. In Germany too. They are the "secret power" of the DAX, for example, claimed the Frankfurter Allgemeine Sonntagszeitung in April 2015. Shortly thereafter, in May, they provided proof. Before the annual general meeting of Deutsche Bank, ISS advised its clients to vote against a discharge of liability for co-chairmen of the executive board Anshu Jain and Jürgen Fitschen. Glass Lewis recommended abstaining. Among other reasons, the advisors cited the $2.5 billion payments for the bank's involvement in the Libor interest rate manipulation scandal as one of the reasons for their choice. Normally, the discharge of the management board is a routine matter. There, it became a historic vote of no confidence. Alternatively, acceptance rates are common, as was once the case in the Soviet Union - 90% and more. At this memorable general meeting, Jain and Fitschen each received only just 60%. A few weeks later, the two board members resigned. The tough game of the proxy advisors had evidently had consequences.

This new power of the proxy advisors, which has almost become autonomous, apparently does not suit Fink & Co. Fink formally warned the managers of "his" portfolio companies not to take for granted that BlackRock would blindly follow the recommendations of ISS & Co. "We draw our own conclusions, regardless of the proxy advisors," Larry Fink wrote in 2011 to managers of large American companies in which BlackRock holds shares. "We vote based on our own guidelines, which reflect our mission as fiduciary agents and guardians of our clients' economic interests." Which means: we, BlackRock, are the real lords, and the types at ISS and Glass Lewis are just our service providers. In the end, it's worth only what we decide. However, BlackRock evidently cannot do without the assistance of consultants: reports and information from insiders reveal that BlackRock is still one of the clients of proxy advisors.

The joke is that in the end, representatives elbow with representatives. The power of ISS, just like that of BlackRock, ultimately rests on the absence of the real owners: the investors. And that's a problem.

Financial Surrealism: Capitalism without Capitalists

Investors play a fundamental role in our market economy system: they decide which companies can grow and which ones must close shop. In their own interest, they want to give their money to companies with the best prospects. Shareholders choose from investment options, thus ensuring the best possible distribution of available capital. This also means that they constantly monitor companies and verify if they are actually using capital profitably. In exchange for their investment, shareholders receive securitized rights - they are entitled to a portion of the profits and are allowed to define management.

This is the ideal version. We are moving further away from it. In financial capitalism 2.0, the link between owners and companies has transformed into an increasingly long chain. The intermediate links are professional administrators who act on behalf of the real investors. The phenomenon has a name: it is the "separation of ownership from ownership." It sounds like a reference to Magritte, who wrote "This is not a pipe" under the image of a pipe. But financial surrealism has long been part of everyday life. The extension of the investment chain leads to additional intermediary costs, both for the system and for the investor, while control over decisions moves further away from those who bear the risks and reap their potential economic benefits, according to a 2013 report from the Conference Board of New York, an institute close to businesses. For example, a pension fund assigns a management order for a portion of its funds to an asset manager like BlackRock. Who then distributes them to various fund managers. This may include a hedge fund, which in turn buys passive ETFs to speculate on the market. Each of these intermediate actors wants to be paid and, in turn, protect their own interests, which do not always align with those of the real owners. This growing "separation of ownership from ownership" causes serious upheavals, argues Leo E. Strine, a former Delaware Supreme Court justice until 2019. Previously, Strine had been a judge on the Delaware

Chancery Court for a long time. His voice carries weight, as this court has a major impact on global corporate law. In a highly regarded speech in 2007, Strine warned that the separation had given new power to representatives, with "risks for the individual investor, but also for the prosperity of our nation." The problem with the increasing dominance of asset managers is not that they steer companies in a certain direction. At least, that's not the biggest problem. The growing problem is that they don't really care about the fate of most companies in their portfolios.

An anecdote illustrates this well: in March 2015, BlackRock almost bought the Australian company Monadelphous Group. By mistake. Because BlackRock held more than 20% of the civil engineering group through its funds. According to Australian stock exchange regulations, an investor whose stake exceeds 20% must submit a public takeover bid for the entire company. BlackRock apologized and cited incorrect evaluations by index publishers, who allegedly miscalculated the corresponding indices on which BlackRock's funds were based, so that BlackRock bought too many shares and exceeded the critical limit. "Our internal control recognized the problem, we reported it to the regulator and acted accordingly," justified BlackRock in the Financial Times.

Deutsche Bank is a much more problematic example of the consequences of owner-administrator. For years, the big bank has staggered from one scandal to another - toxic mortgages, Libor manipulation, money laundering, and other unappetizing allegations, so often formulated by the authorities that raids by investigators in the towers of Frankfurt have become routine. The bank had to pay out billions time and again. But this apparently left major investors unmoved, for years. BlackRock, still one of the largest owners with a stake of over 3% (as of January 2020), remained a spectator as the share price of the last German bank of global significance fell below 10 euros; a spectator to the attempts of several unlucky boards of directors to change the situation with successive economic plans. In 2019, the bank lost nearly 6 billion euros; it was the fifth consecutive year it was in the red. Christian Sewing, CEO since April 2018, plans to cut another eighteen thousand jobs, or nearly 20% of the workforce. And once again, Deutsche Bank is offloading its toxic securities and loans to a "bad bank."

In recent years, authorities and organizations have developed catalogs of corporate governance rules and voluntary agreements to cement the breaking point between investors and companies, so important for our system. There has already been the British Stewardship Code, then the United Nations developed the "Principles for Responsible Investment," which also take into account social and environmental issues. Japan has established seven principles of good corporate governance and Germany has designed the corporate governance code. Certainly, all these initiatives are well-intentioned and useful. However, an OECD study sought to understand why, despite all these efforts, the engagement of large owners still leaves much to be desired. The conclusion, which is thought-provoking: while, for some investors like hedge funds or private equity funds, active engagement would be a necessary element of the business model, for others, it would simply represent an additional cost. "In the first case, there are no rules, and in the second, the rules will hardly do more than tick off lists," the study states. In other words, the fundamental problem remains, there is simply more bureaucracy. Then, there are conflicts of interest. For example, when an asset manager hesitates to deal with the board of directors of a company in its portfolio because it also hopes to receive the mandate to manage the company's pension fund. "This makes many investment companies hesitate to formulate too aggressive demands," noted Simon Wong, a partner at the London-based investment company Governance for Owners, in a 2011 comment for the "Harvard Law School Forum on Corporate Governance." Because a tacit threat from the company's side to award the contract elsewhere is sometimes enough, as Wong has seen in his consulting experiences.

At BlackRock, the separation between the two business sectors is clearly regulated, the company asserts. Fink personally swore to this to Fortune magazine in July 2014. However, he admits to having received calls from business leaders, including friends and acquaintances, demanding that BlackRock vote in their favor. This puts him in an impossible situation, complains the boss of BlackRock in *Fortune*. It pisses me off, a comment that cannot simply be translated as "annoy."

Headlines like "The Shadow Man Who Rules the World" or "The Secret Lords of the DAX," which imply almost remote control of companies, miss the point. Contrary to these fears, the problem with the new Germany Inc. is not that BlackRock or major foreign shareholders are shopping in companies and then pulling the strings of the board of directors. Apart from aggressive hedge funds, whose strategy includes this approach, fund companies simply do not have the capacity for such micromanagement. Faced with German companies, BlackRock is like a New York real estate tycoon striving to exploit his properties abroad as profitably and smoothly as possible. The business leaders correspond in this comparison to the property managers, who regularly transfer the rent to the owner and maintain their building in good condition. As long as the manager proves to be reliable, there is no reason to intervene. This laissez-faire may be pleasant for the latter. But at some point, the building no longer yields enough in the portfolio or needs a long and complex renovation, so the owner sells it, simply. In the worst case, to a demolition company: a private equity firm.

ETFs, "Worse Than Marxism"

This doesn't mean that the concentration of owners has no impact. One of the consequences of these widely dispersed holdings by large fund managers like BlackRock is that different companies in the same sector often belong to the same group of owners. In the case of an ETF issuer's investment in a sector index, this is even by definition necessary. For example, in the case of rival American pharmacy chains CVS and Walgreens, the three largest owners are identical: BlackRock, Vanguard, and State Street (as of May 2020). "How does this common ownership structure influence competitive behavior?" wonders finance researcher Martin Schmalz, a professor at the University of Oxford. In other words: do CVS and Walgreens avoid a price war that would allow them to gain market share, because it would ultimately harm the common owner or, at best, be pointless? One could also wonder if the same monopoly effects prevail in the era of financial capitalism 2.0 as in the era of John Pierpont Morgan.

Harvard professor Einer Elhauge considers index funds, in any case, the greatest danger to competition. "Their influence is much greater than their shares suggest. Because they participate in shareholder votes much more often than individual shareholders." Larry Fink, Mortimer Buckley, the CEO of Vanguard, and Ronald O'Hanley, the CEO of State Street, do not meet in a back room somewhere, enjoying a Macallan Highland Single Malt and a Cuban Cohiba cigar to negotiate a deal. No, all of this is arranged much more subtly.

Schmalz examined this new type of oligopoly in a study conducted with his colleagues José Azar and Isabel Tecu, published in September 2014. He looked at American airlines, their prices, and passenger traffic on certain air routes. He took the acquisition of iShares by BlackRock in 2009 as a starting point. This acquisition resulted in a greater concentration of the owners of companies serving certain air routes, supposed to be in competition. The result: tickets were about 5% more expensive and the number of passengers about 6% lower than in a case where the airlines would have belonged to different owners on this route. The decrease in the number of passengers means that prices do not seem to have increased due to higher demand. Especially in sectors with a limited number of competitors, the following applies, according to Schmalz: "Shared ownership, combined with the axiom of shareholder value maximization, implies an incentive for companies to reduce the quantity in portfolios, increase prices, and thus, the associated loss of well-being for the national economy." Said in a less academic way: while shareholders benefit from ownership concentration, it is consumers who pay. Schmalz believes that fund representatives, when they talk to company executives, are very likely not aware that they are distorting competition. It is enough, for example, for the fund representative - who also knows the competitive situation well - to give the board of directors the indication to aim for higher margins instead of fighting for more market share.

Another study, conducted by José Azar, showed that in the banking sector as well, competition was tamer when credit institutions had large index funds as co-owners. This leads to higher fees for customers and lower savings rates.

The study on airlines in particular caused a sensation in the industry. BlackRock commissioned its own study, which concluded that the three academics had overestimated the impact on prices by ignoring the fact that the airlines were temporarily insolvent after 9/11. This is important: the shares of a bankrupt company are removed from the corresponding index and the funds sell the shares. In other words, the potential influence of large index owners on the behavior of airlines could not have been observed. They would very well have taken this downtime into account, Azar, one of the authors of the study, retorted when confronted by Businessweek journalists with BlackRock's criticism. The economist stuck to his findings.

Keeping in mind that BlackRock holds stakes in different competitors in many industries, the potential problem begins to emerge. It is not surprising that BlackRock reacted nervously. What worries its executives: the theories of academics have attracted the attention of competition regulators.

In November 2019, pharmaceutical giants Bristol-Myers Squibb and Celgene wanted to merge. Rohit Chopra, one of the members of the Federal Trade Commission (FTC), the US antitrust watchdog, voted against the $74 billion merger. One of the reasons for his opposition was that many investors held stakes in both the buyer and the target being sold. While it is true that Chopra, a Democrat in this predominantly Republican authority, did not succeed, his colleagues seem to have taken his concerns more seriously. In January 2020, Bloomberg reported that when evaluating mergers, the FTC also questioned companies about their communication and interaction with large fund owners. In this regard, Europeans are already further ahead. When chemical giants Dow Cheminal and DuPont wanted their merger to be approved by the EU in 2017, the question of cross-shareholdings arose during the authorities' decision-making process. The EU ultimately imposed conditions: DuPont had to divest part of its pesticide business, without which the authorities would not have allowed the marriage between the two behemoths.

In a response provided for the new edition of this book, BlackRock emphasized that it was a "small number of scientific studies" dealing with the issue of a monopoly or oligopoly of owners. "The results of these studies do not provide conclusive evidence of a link between common ownership structures and prices, let alone a plausible causal mechanism." As a precaution, they add: "Voices have been raised calling for measures against us based on the claims of these early studies. However, since the theory, questioned by many, is still being debated, it would be premature to adopt the proposed measures."

On the one hand, BlackRock & Co. do not have the means to control each individual company (except occasionally, when there is a particular interest in doing so). On the other hand, corporate governance requirements ensure that all companies adhere to the same guidelines and standards. "The silent road to servitude: why passive investment is worse than Marxism": that was the title of a defense manifesto by active fund managers, published in 2016 by analysts at Sanford C. Bernstein, a New York investment firm. ETF supporters dismissed this critique: Sanford's analysts, as advisors to active investors, could not be impartial. The manifesto nevertheless caused concern on Wall Street. Here is the thesis: instead of directing capital to investments where it can be most productive, able to create the most jobs and raise the overall standard of living, passive managers distribute funds according to a predefined key, which is the index. And why would passive investment be worse than Marxism according to Sanford's analysts? Because at least Marxists had a vision they wanted to achieve.

And if BlackRock had a vision to achieve? Which would be a good cause, a noble goal recognized by all?

A Green Fink

A gala dinner in the City of London, well-dressed people seated in front of silver plates. But this is not just any meeting between traders and financiers out to enjoy their expense accounts. On the contrary, these are members of Extinction Rebellion, radical environmental activists, who have set up in front of BlackRock's offices. The dishes served: banknotes. A poster hangs above the table: "When the last tree has been cut down, the last fish caught, and the last river polluted, then you will realize that you cannot eat money."

The activists have targeted the asset manager with their protest because, according to their calculations, BlackRock is the largest investor in coal, natural gas, and oil, with over $300 billion. Other environmentalists have followed suit, accusing the asset manager of investing billions of dollars in companies that pollute, deforest, and contribute to greenhouse gas emissions. With its billions invested, BlackRock would be the "biggest driver of climate chaos," as explained by an initiative called BlackRock's Big Problem, supported by a network of environmental activists like Friends of the Earth and the Sierra Club, the largest nature conservation association in the United States. Former US Vice President turned environmental activist Al Gore took aim at BlackRock at the United Nations Environment Conference in Madrid in December 2019: according to him, major investors like BlackRock must decide whether or not to continue funding the destruction of human civilization.

Fink took up the pen. In his January 2020 letter to corporate leaders, he wrote: "Climate risk is also an investment risk." Then he announced something concrete: "We will exit investments that present a high sustainability risk, such as holdings in thermal coal producers." Jonathan Donges, a climate researcher based in Potsdam, Germany, presumes that Fink's letter could change the investment culture worldwide. "With BlackRock's announcement, the financial system has definitively moved closer to a possible tipping point in the climate context, if it has not already been reached," he says. Fink, our climate savior! What largely falls by the wayside, however, is that Fink only refers to funds whose securities are actually chosen by BlackRock's managers. Such disengagement is not possible with index funds. And BlackRock only wants to withdraw from companies that generate more than 25% of their revenue from coal. The economic news agency Bloomberg cited Glencore as an example. This commodity giant - of which BlackRock's Fund, with around 6%, is one of the largest shareholders (as of January 2020) - is indeed one of the largest coal suppliers; however, revenue from the most harmful fossil fuel to the climate amounts to only 10% of Glencore's total transaction volume.

In his letter to corporate leaders, Fink justifies his group's reorientation less with a green conscience than with business interests: it would mainly be its clients - major pension funds, insurers, and foundations - who would have demanded more attention to sustainability issues from BlackRock. The Japanese pension fund, for example, withdrew some of its investments from BlackRock in 2019 because it wants to base its investment strategy on environmental and social criteria. At the same time, green investments have become increasingly popular, especially among young investors. In 2019, inflows into so-called ESG index funds quintupled to $20 billion. BlackRock also wants to double the number of sustainable funds in its range to reach one hundred.

But what will be the effects of this consideration for clients' environmental and climate interests in the future? Fiona Scott Morton, a professor of economics at Yale University, is skeptical about its practical implementation, and even smells a risk to democracy. Her viewpoint is reported in an article in the major German national daily Die Zeit: "Of course, we are delighted that such a powerful investor now wants to push companies towards more climate protection, but what if it were a controversial goal, such as increased use of facial recognition and artificial intelligence, or a restriction of press freedom?" Fink has no democratic legitimacy, he does not represent society as a whole, but only the layer of those who own financial assets. From Scott Morton's point of view, large investors like BlackRock should not use their influence for political purposes but, on the contrary, it is politics that should regulate companies and investors. Especially since, in the current legal context, no one can hold Fink or BlackRock accountable if the fund provider fails to achieve its climate protection goals.

Chapter 9

Aladdin, a Djinn in the Orchard

4,425 kilometers separate Wall Street from Wenatchee, almost an entire continent. A whole world, in any case. Wenatchee is located in the extreme northwest of the United States on the Columbia River, which winds its way south through the forests of Canada. The jagged ridges of the Cascade Range rise above Wenatchee, and the Pacific Ocean stretches three hours' drive away. In spring, the peaks are still covered with snow, while the blossoming of fruit trees begins on the lower slopes. Wenatchee, with its 30,000 inhabitants, proudly claims to be the "world capital of the apple." There is a tourist center about apples, a hiking trail through the orchards, and in April, the apple blossom festival for eleven days. If you go up a narrow street leading east, you will pass small houses with neat gardens. A sign hanging on a fence says "Honey for Sale." The road runs along equestrian parks, orchards, and a small airfield until it reaches two beige, flat, and new buildings. They are surrounded by a two-meter-high fence, and the black steel gate is closed. Half a dozen cars are parked in the parking lot. Cameras monitor the area. Foreign vehicles parked too long attract the attention of a guard in uniform, who emerges from the building after a few minutes. No logo, no company name indicates what is happening inside the compound.

Here, on a former wheat field, Aladdin stores, selects, calculates, and arbitrates an endless series of numbers and formulas in its thousands of processors. Seven days a week, twenty-four hours a day. Aladdin is BlackRock's electronic djinn. Like the genie in the lamp in the tales, Aladdin has made its legendary success possible. It is what keeps BlackRock going from the inside. It is the basis of its growing power.

BlackRock does not keep the existence or significance of Aladdin a secret. On the contrary: the public relations department even produced an advertising film about the electronic superbrain. It shows dynamic young people of different origins and skin colors evidently BlackRock employees. They sit in shirt sleeves in New York taxis, stand in front of London's Big

Ben and typical double-decker red buses, pose with their hair blowing in the wind in front of the Golden Gate in San Francisco or the skyline of Hong Kong. They tell us in a serious voice what Aladdin's daily work looks like: creating over 1.8 million reports, monitoring interest rate movements in Europe - just like droughts in the American Midwest - and then querying silver prices in Asia. Recording at the same time how 4 billion shares on the New York Stock Exchange change hands, even settling twenty-five thousand commercial transactions and, on top of that - watch out! - avoiding three thousand investment disasters.

Because that is Aladdin's real task: determining the effects of all this information and events on fifty-five thousand investment portfolios and thus on their security; portfolios that Aladdin constantly and tirelessly watches over. Aladdin is supposed to protect them from unpleasant surprises and, above all, unexpected losses. It thus monitors $20 trillion. This is also information that BlackRock proudly presents. Funds equivalent to the GDPs of China, Brazil, and France combined pass through its computers. A sum that no government or institution in the world can dispose of otherwise.

If the creators of the advertising spot intended to impress the viewer, they succeeded - even if not necessarily in a positive way. The advertisement becomes downright scary when Aladdin speaks to us through BlackRock employees - almost making them its human avatars. They utter phrases such as "I am Aladdin, and I find the numbers behind the numbers" or "I am Aladdin, and I know what I know. Everywhere, and right now." Aladdin is smarter than any algorithm, more powerful than any processor, assure us Aladdin's human spokespersons. In short: Aladdin is a new type of intelligence, explains Larry Fink, who also appears in the film. Aladdin is celebrated by BlackRock as a collective genius, a gifted hybrid being, part human, part technology.

Hundreds of people have worked on the programs that make up Aladdin for more than two decades. Aladdin now consists of an army of hundreds of analysts, technicians, and programmers and thousands of computers that perform billions of calculations per day. An installation that would make NASA jealous. Aladdin needs all its capacity to calculate the value of stocks, bonds, currencies, or credit securities contained in multi-billion-dollar investment portfolios, all this every day, every hour, every minute, and sometimes every second. At the same time, Aladdin precisely examines how this value should change if the environment changes - with the economy, for example, or sales figures, when currency rates plummet, or when oil prices rise. This sounds much simpler than it is because the securities that investment institutions and investors juggle are complex constructions. Most are pools with thousands of different investment products, securities, real estate, fund shares. It is therefore extremely complex to detect the true value of the investment... and where the dangers lie.

The advantage for Aladdin's clients: whoever can withdraw their positions and risks scattered around the world by pressing a button gains a decisive advantage in the billions at stake on Wall Street, which are always faster. They can buy or sell in time, pocket profits, or avoid losses. "It's a kind of MRI for institutional investors' investment portfolios," explains Rob Goldstein, the guardian of the "genie of the lamp," to visitors.

Becoming One with the Machine

Internally, Rob Goldstein is often described as a "child prodigy." Tall and gangly, he exudes the enthusiasm of someone who only recently stopped playing video games and still has his first Commodore 64 from the 1980s in his garage. Only the gold watch and gold-rimmed glasses stand out. Goldstein is a pioneer at BlackRock. He has spent almost his entire adult life at Fink's side since joining BlackRock in 1994, two weeks after graduating from college. It was a time when BlackRock was still the Wall Street equivalent of a small garage startup. Today, he is the Chief Operating Officer and head of BlackRock Solutions. Those are his official titles. But Goldstein is primarily the guardian of Aladdin.

Behind the name from the Arabian Nights lies a legend that pales in comparison. Aladdin stands for Asset, Liability, Debt and Derivative Investment Network. It was Freddie Mac, one of the first clients, who proposed this fairy-tale acronym to name the platform.

Aladdin's beginnings are just as prosaic. The global superbrain has its origins in the computer that used to be located in BlackRock's first office kitchenette. The first programs that ran on the device were tinkered with at the time by BlackRock's co-founders and MIT whiz kids Bennett Golub and Charlie Hallac, early BlackRock employees. Legend has it that once, they wanted to print data but there was no printer paper in the office. Just a stack of green paper. What began as a makeshift solution became a tradition, and Aladdin's printouts are still called the "green package" internally.

If one wishes, Aladdin is Larry Fink's paranoia about risk, rewritten in 25 million lines of computer code. That's roughly the same number of lines of code that Facebook needs to manage its billions of user profiles. Microsoft Windows, considered by geeks to be one of the most complex, if not the most complex, programs, has about 45 million lines of code.

Early BlackRockers noticed that credit securities, compared to those Larry Fink issued in the pioneering days, had become increasingly complex. There were more and more risk tranches that investors could acquire. In addition to mortgages, other credits were now bundled together, such as car loans or student loans. Wall Street bankers were increasingly resorting to "financial engineering," making it increasingly difficult for buyers of securities to determine profit and loss potential. Initially, BlackRock used these analyses for its own transactions. However, clients, who wanted the system to analyze their loan portfolios, gradually came forward. As described above, the breakthrough came with the conglomerate General Electric. Aladdin's guardian, Goldstein, was part of the team that unwound the infamous Kidder Peabody portfolio for GE. The corresponding data was stored on a floppy disk, a disk that still sits framed in Goldstein's office today. Like a rock star framing his gold record. Or a nobleman a photo of his ancestors.

There has never been anything like Aladdin. To better understand what is happening in the superbrain, imagine what it would be like if, instead of sifting through hundreds of billions of transactions and financial market data, Aladdin monitored our daily chaos. It could be used like this: Aladdin takes care of waking us up in the morning. Since it has analyzed past data to determine how long it takes to shower, get dressed, prepare breakfast, spread bread, and pack school bags, it has compared this duration with subway schedules. It then compares the schedules with the actual arrival and departure times of the stations, which it has collected over the past months or even years. It checks current weather data and recommends not forgetting the umbrella and rubber boots if there is a high probability of rain. Finally, it calculates whether it is enough to walk normally to the subway station and what happens if the son's favorite sweater is not found at the last moment or if the father has to turn back to fetch his cell phone. Aladdin can thus prevent the risk of being late to school or work. Aladdin would not only do these calculations for one family but for all families in the school, and even for the entire academy. Other risks are more complex: for example, if a taxi driver loses control of his vehicle during an illegal maneuver and ends up on the sidewalk, it is a rare but not impossible risk. A deadly risk. In the world of finance, this would be, for example, the fact that mortgages in the United

States are massively defaulting. A risk that many thought unlikely before 2007 - much less likely, in any case, than being hit by a taxi. But Aladdin must also detect these rare but devastating risks, and in a timely manner - so that BlackRock and its clients can avoid them.

But Aladdin is more than a computer program and much more than a database. Aladdin, the superbrain hidden in the apple orchard, is the harbinger of a future that belongs to machines.

The room is dark, only the small squares of smartphone screens sparkle here and there. It could be the set of Alien, the classic Hollywood science fiction film. The billboards arranged on the stage, on which one can vaguely distinguish the limbs and head of a mannequin, also contribute to the eerie atmosphere. "Art," explains the moderator after greeting the four to five hundred people sitting on folding plastic chairs, at the event entitled "Rise of the Machines." It could also have been called "Waiting for Ray Kurzweil." One of the visitors is named Alan S. Like most, he has come only for him. He even took a red-eye flight from San Francisco to arrive in time for Ray Kurzweil's conference in New York. "Ray is the philosopher of technophiles," explains Alan, whose t-shirt bears the URL "singularity.net." The term technological singularity describes the moment when artificial intelligence will surpass human beings. Physicist and mathematician John von Neumann, one of the participants in the Manhattan Project and co-inventor of the atomic bomb, was the first to use the term in the 1950s. Science fiction author Vernor Vinge made it known. Ray Kurzweil is now one of the great prophets of the singularity. The septuagenarian is considered a genius by his fans, the self-taught man holds nineteen honorary doctorates and has successfully founded more than half a dozen companies. Time featured him on a cover, an honor he shares with, among others, Pope Francis and Mikhail Gorbachev. According to Kurzweil, whose profession is best described by the term futurist, by 2045, artificial superintelligence will be able to surpass its human creators. His book: The Singularity is Near: When Humans Transcend Biology. He does not question the likelihood that this prediction will occur but rather when it will happen. Because Kurzweil is certain that man and machine are merging.

A gray winter day, Kurzweil's fans gather in a trendy club on the unglamorous outskirts of Manhattan. But their idol will only make his appearance at the climax of the event. Before him, other futurists will share their forecasts with a receptive audience. Among them is Jincey Lumpkin, sex columnist for the Huffington Post and Chief Sexy Officer of the startup Jucy Pink Box, offering online lesbian porn. Lumpkin is also a lawyer and a devoted fan of Kurzweil. By 2047, she claims, robots will have intelligence similar to humans and will become our sexual partners. It is important, says the lawyer, to quickly raise ethical and legal questions, to know, among other things, to what extent a robot would have its own will or if it would be permissible to rape it. Her presentation is followed by a short film about a future astronaut stuck with a robot as his only companion. The latter has a secret fondness for robot porn. Things go wrong - in the end, the robot destroys the fuel ducts. Finally, the big moment arrives: the moderator announces the star of the day, one almost expects a fanfare. Then a balding, thinner, older man takes the stage. He wears a dark suit and comfortable shoes, reading glasses hanging around his neck. Kurzweil, who takes a hundred pills a day, supposedly to prolong his life, looks older than in his press photos.

Kurzweil is an experienced speaker. As the excited chatter continues in the now crowded room, he displays the first graphs on the screen using his remote control. He describes his theory, according to which the brain could be understood as a hierarchical pattern recognition system. It would thus be possible to artificially simulate brain function. This would be the next step in human evolution. The technological progress made to date confirms his thesis. Kurzweil talks about cloud computing, Google's driverless car, stem cells, IBM's Watson supercomputer, the fight for internet freedom, smartphones. He can rarely resist pointing out that he had already more or less predicted today's achievements years or even decades ago. But at the time, he was dismissed as a crackpot.

That's not really the case anymore. Larry Page, co-founder of Google, hired him as Chief Developer for Artificial Intelligence. With the latter, Kurzweil is to develop a new type of search engine. At a tech company conference in Silicon Valley in the summer of 2014, Kurzweil expressed optimism, as usual, about creating an artificial assistant in the not-too-distant future that would not display links, as Google does so far, but would be able to provide a fully formulated answer. "You'll be able to talk to it like a human being," Kurzweil explained to journalists. Kurzweil not only wants to teach computers to find words in a text, but he wants them to understand the text like a human being. Watson, IBM's young superbrain, is the one that has come closest to this goal. It successfully competed against human opponents on the American quiz show Jeopardy in 2011. But, like before, Watson's AI remained based on the ability to analyze more data than anyone else and to discover patterns. Kurzweil wants machines to grasp the deep meaning of words. When Watson reads the sentence, "John sells his red Volvo to Mary," it does not understand that it is a property transfer. Kurzweil's machines must be able to understand such logic.

Kurzweil considers the rise of the machines, which he had predicted, to be absolutely positive. He hopes to live long enough to be able to download his biological brain onto a computer and thus become immortal. In Silicon Valley in particular, where thousands of engineers, software developers, mathematicians, physicists, and cyberneticians work daily on increasingly intelligent and faster machines, the majority are in Kurzweil's camp.

But not all futurists are as convinced that this cyber-era will be all rosy. The guru of physics Stephen Hawking, precisely, warned against self-sufficient superbrains before his death. His contributions to the theory of relativity and to the physics of black holes have sparked controversy. He held the Lucasian Professorship of Mathematics at the University of Cambridge for over thirty years. In his book A Brief History of Time, he presented his vision of an endless universe without a creator god. Hawking's message is the triumph of science over religion. He was a staunch advocate of space colonization - in his view, humanity should even use genetic engineering for this purpose. The physicist suffered from amyotrophic lateral sclerosis (ALS), a rare degenerative motor neuron disease, and therefore moved around in a wheelchair. After losing the ability to speak, he communicated via a computer program he controlled with eye movements. His skepticism towards artificial intelligence is all the more remarkable. The completion of a fully developed artificial intelligence could spell the end of humanity, he astonishingly warned in an interview with the BBC in 2014. "As soon as humans develop an artificial intelligence that continues to develop itself, it could reinvent itself faster and faster."

One could always say that Hawking is a scientist judging the tech industry from his ivory tower of academia. But with Jaron Lanier, one of the pioneers of the internet, it's different. He developed the first applications for virtual reality - a term he coined himself - without which none of today's video games would exist. And it is precisely Lanier, with his long dreadlocks and hippie look, who has become the Cassandra of the tech industry. In his books, he calls for resistance against the glorification of computers. But his doomsday scenario for the future is very different from Hawking's. He does not fear the tyranny of self-sufficient machines, but the tyranny of people through machines. And all around us, in our daily lives, he detects the harbingers of this domination. The owners of the machines - that is, the owners and pilots of tech giants like Google, Facebook, Apple, and Microsoft - have enriched themselves at the expense of workers and the middle class. The saga of artificial intelligence serves only to disguise people's real contributions to these technological empires, to extract their value. Lanier argues that the data and information used by Silicon Valley giants for their purposes are not provided by a machine but by the users themselves, by people. The masses create big data without being remunerated for it. Artificial intelligence does not exist, Lanier told American tech journalist Kurt Andersen. "It's just a modern word for plutocracy." But critics like Lanier and Hawking and optimists like Larry Page and Ray Kurzweil have something in common: they all believe that, sooner or later, it will be possible to build machines capable of thinking like humans. The question is no longer whether this will happen. The question is rather: who will control them?

Cyborgs Dominate the Markets

It was 1:07 p.m., New York time, on April 23, 2013, when the Washington office of the Associated Press news agency posted the following tweet: "Breaking: Two explosions in the White House, Barack Obama injured." In a matter of milliseconds, the stock market crashed. No human could have reacted to the news as quickly: these were machines specialized in searching for information streams on the internet, using keywords that could move financial markets. The combination of Obama and the White House with the word "explosion" triggered an alert on search engines. Other computers, responsible for trading securities such as stocks, received the message and quickly began issuing sell orders. This time, however, the artificial market guardians' search went wrong: the presumed AP tweet actually came from the Syrian Electronic Army, terrorist hackers supporting the Bashar al-Assad regime. The digital terrorists hacked the AP's Twitter account and sent the false news. A few minutes later, the AP stated that the message was false. But for the stock markets, the AP's denial came too late: over $200 billion in assets had already been wiped out by the stock price plunge. Human traders, such as those on the New York Stock Exchange trading floor, for example, had been skeptical of the message - but their reaction time was much slower than that of their computer colleagues. The incident shows who now dominates the stock market: machines. Or bots, as Wall Street affectionately calls them. Computers now account for nearly 80% of stock trading and currency operations, and almost 50% of operations involving government bonds. (As described above, BlackRock is one of the largest instigators of electronic bond trading.) The famous - or rather infamous - high-frequency traders, the HFTs, are traders who, thanks to their huge computing power and intelligent software, are almost as fast as light on financial markets and make profits. Big banks have also undergone electronic upgrades in recent years. Human traders are no match for bots. "The traditional trading floors, those gyms filled with traders who own villas and BMWs - that will soon be a thing of the past," explains a longtime Wall Street expert who prefers to remain anonymous, considering his clients. Bots don't demand bonuses. HFTs are simply what's done today, says the IT head of a large international bank, who also prefers not to be named. It's not just about trading. Computers have long been composing messages for other computers, which are then "read" by yet other computers - which then make investment decisions. As was the case in response to the hacked AP Twitter account. Computer programs analyze quantities of data that were unimaginable until recently - not to mention the subsequent analysis of data streams. These processes are increasingly taking place without human intervention. Just a few years ago, Wall Street was an industry where experience and relationships were important; today, it's about having the right algorithm, and connections are electronic. "The machines have taken over Wall Street. Artificial intelligence, mathematical models, and supercomputers have replaced human intelligence, human thought, and human practice": that's the conclusion drawn by Tom C.W. Lin, a professor at Temple University Beasley, who addressed "cyborg finance," as it is called, in a thesis dating back to March 2014. Cyborgs are half living beings, half machines. That's how BlackRock describes Aladdin in its promotional video - part human intelligence, part technology. Automation is accelerating and taking more and more ground from human actors. Since the financial crisis, banks and other financial institutions have cut hundreds of thousands of jobs. If this had been an industry like the automotive industry, the radical dismantling would have led to protests over job loss due to automation. Instead, there was only a sadistic pleasure, and even that only when there was a reaction. Because public opinion did not forgive the banks for the crisis, the digital revolution in the financial system received little attention, outside of those directly affected. This is a mistake, as the digitization of our financial system has huge consequences for all of us. Cyborg finance was born over forty years ago. At that time, young scientists - physicists, mathematicians, computer scientists, and chemists - found that research positions were becoming scarce. The technological competition between the Soviet Union and America culminated with Sputnik and, ultimately, Apollo 11. But then the Vietnam War devoured American funds, and government research was reduced. For many recent MIT or University of California graduates, Wall Street became an alternative. Instead of tinkering with plans for future colonies on Mars or searching for new sources of energy, they quickly began tinkering with yield models and hedging strategies. And earned much more. Later, when the Soviet Union finally fell apart, a fresh batch of well-trained new scientists followed. Initially, traders mocked the newcomers by calling them "rocket scientists" - they didn't think the "missile inventors" would outsmart their intuition and experience. But that fundamentally changed over the past decade. In trading rooms, the Russian programmer became the typical Wall Streeter instead of the original Irish or Italian broker. The days when the Dow Jones, the stock index of American heavyweights such as IBM and Exxon, set a new record, when traders crowded the counter at Harry's Bar at the southern tip of Manhattan, when the day's winners bought a round for the others, are over. Today, Harry's Bar is a chic restaurant serving martinis in the afternoon and Kobe beef hamburgers. None of the former regulars go there anymore. Instead of meeting at a bar, their successors prefer to meet other programmers - at a hackathon, for example, a kind of software developer brainstorming party where they spend a day or even a week working on projects, fueled by a stack of take-out pizzas.

The rise of quants is unstoppable

The term refers to the methods used to understand the market: quantitative analysis. It is difficult to know who first used this term. One thing is certain: since quants entered Wall Street, they have been responsible for almost all innovations in the financial sector. With their formulas, data collections, and powerful computers, they have increased the volume of transactions, the speed, and the impact of financial markets. Financial instruments such as credit derivatives would hardly be conceivable without "rocket scientists." All in all, the Quant family is also responsible for the fact that disasters in these financial markets have such rapid consequences on the economy and society. Quants are well aware of their influence. But they would not feel responsible for the financial system, at least that's what Aaron Brown, risk management manager at the $180 billion AQR hedge fund, one of the largest quant funds until 2017, claims. "My job is to find the best technical solution that serves my investors or my employer - or myself, when it comes to my money," Brown wrote in an article in the specialized magazine Risk Professional. But he acknowledges that if many quants followed this motto, it would revolutionize the entire financial system and create winners and losers. "I don't know if this leads to a global catastrophe," writes Brown with somewhat refreshing honesty. He only has a "slightly mystical belief" that knowledge is better than ignorance, progress is better than immobility, and that good technological developments lead to good outcomes. His conclusion: innovation in the financial sector is irreversible, and its inventions should not be judged by standards different from those of other economic sectors. It's not fair to love your iPod, Brown complains in his essay, and to hate collateralized debt obligations (CDOs, which became known to finance laymen during the crisis). It is also unfair to rejoice in the availability of Viagra but not be satisfied with exchange-traded funds (ETFs). To praise the anti-lock braking system but demonize high-frequency trading in return. If there is one man who can be credited with the rise of quants, it is Edward Oakley Thorp. As a child, Thorp, known as Ed, attracted attention with his pranks. Once, he threw paint in the public pool, which had to be completely drained. Later, his antics became more useful - his gift for mathematics emerged. He became a doctor of physics and began teaching early on as a professor at the tech stronghold in Boston, MIT. But it turned out that Thorp had remained true to his penchant for pranks, even as a scholar. He was particularly interested in gambling. In the early 1960s, he developed the first portable computer with a colleague. This would have been a huge success in itself, at a time when computers still occupied entire floors. But Thorp had a very specific goal in mind. He wanted to use the portable computer to calculate in advance the path of the ball on the roulette table. Thorp had conducted corresponding experiments with balls and roulette wheels to deduce a formula. In the casino, it was planned that Thorp would provide the computer with data on the progress of the game - on which numbers the ball stopped, how often it landed on black, on red, etc. The computer would then derive a forecast for future wins. His calculations were then to be transmitted by radio to a wireless receiver at the ear of a partner at the roulette table, who would then place the appropriate bets. Not surprisingly, the two researchers armed with their computers were kicked out of the casinos. Thorp had more success at blackjack. Thanks to complex computer calculations on the mainframe IBM 704 of his university, Thorp developed a model for card counting. He believed that with this, especially towards the end of the game, he could predict the dealer's cards with a high degree of certainty. To test his method, he wanted to go to the gambling havens, Las Vegas and Reno. He received a stake of $100,000 from a professional gambler with dubious connections, who had read about the crazy gambling professor in the newspaper. In the book Thorp wrote about this trip, he simply calls him Mr. X. Later, Thorp explained that if he had been aware of Mr. X's dubious connections, he would never have approached him. This time too, Thorp & Co. were thrown out of a few casinos because they were winning too often, and managers suspected a system. Thorp grew a beard, but found that the casinos had already warned each other about "a bearded player." Thorp's experimentation was nevertheless successful. One weekend, he won $11,000 with his method. At the time, it was an impressive sum! And, even more decisive: he had proven that what was previously considered unpredictable - but as the result of chance - was absolutely calculable. In

1966, the mathematician, who was then in his thirties, summarized his ideas in a book: Beat the Dealer6. The book immediately became a bestseller and sold over 700,000 copies. Casinos were forced to change their blackjack rules. But then Thorp had the idea that his discovery could change not only Las Vegas but also the whole world. He thought that profits could be made using a computer program in the world's largest casino as well: Wall Street. Just as the rule for players in Vegas has always been that the casino wins in the long run, on Wall Street, it was generally believed that no investor could beat the market in the long run. But here too, Thorp found that it was possible to make a forecast for future prices through information about price fluctuations and other factors. Shortly thereafter, the mathematician got on the bandwagon and published a book in which he presented his "scientific system for the stock market." And he didn't stop at theory. He made a fortune with his hedge funds. According to his own statements, his investments earned him 20% for nearly thirty years, thanks to his method. Thorp is the man who showed what scientists could achieve in the very real world of high finance, who were sometimes considered nerds outside their lecture halls. Many followed his example.

The quants contributed to the 2008 disaster. Without their formulas, it would not have been possible to create a flow of new securities from auto loans, credit card debts, and mortgages. It would not have been possible to place bets on their default and to create new securities from them - namely, credit derivatives. The quants not only helped build a new generation of financial instruments. They also developed computer programs with which the risks associated with these new inventions were tested. But the underlying thought models of both the new financial instruments and the tests were based on assumptions that later proved to be incorrect and inadequate. Unlike in mathematics or physics, the ancestral terrain of quants, actors in the financial market do not always behave rationally and certainly not consistently. The fact that models and simulations learn from the past to anticipate the future was therefore fatal to them: they ignored the possibility of extreme events that had never happened before. Situations that rarely occurred, but were all the more devastating. "During the crisis, two kinds of people were ruined," according to veteran speculator Henry Kauffman, who first worked for the Central Bank in the 1950s and then at Salomon Brothers for twenty-six years, "those who generally have no idea what is happening, and the others who knew everything." When you hear Monte Carlo, you think of the gambling mecca on the Côte d'Azur. But for finance insiders, Monte Carlo means something else. Namely, a computer simulation that can be used to explore future scenarios. A bit like rolling a die a thousand times and organizing the results by their probability. The first ideas behind Monte Carlo were developed by nuclear physicist Enrico Fermi. In the 1940s, Stanislaw Ulam and John von Neumann (the same Neumann who introduced the term singularity) took up his ideas when they were working on the atomic bomb at the secret Los Alamos laboratory. The name Monte Carlo comes from Neumann, because his uncle had frequented the casinos there. Quants transferred this method from physics to Wall Street. It quickly became very popular there. Indeed, thanks to it, new artificially assembled securities, such as CDOs, and new credit derivatives, such as CDSs (credit default swaps), for which there was no experience yet, could be evaluated, at least in theory. Without Monte Carlo, it was almost impossible to find a price for the products, and without evaluation, no market participant would have bought them. Rating agencies were and still are enthusiastic users of the mathematical dice game. During the mortgage boom, they used their Monte Carlo simulations, among other things, to assign their credit ratings such as AAA to mortgage-backed securities. Without these quality labels, pension funds and sovereign wealth funds would have refused to buy the new securities. But the weaknesses of the Monte Carlo models were precisely revealed with the mortgage securities. A rapid collapse of the real estate market across America seemed too improbable to be taken into account in the models. Critic of the latest financial innovations, Warren Buffett summed up his problem with such products and the underlying thought models as follows: "Give me a gun with a magazine containing thousands or even millions of chambers, but in which there is only one bullet. Then ask me how much I want to press the trigger once. I refuse, no matter what your offer. I don't see any real advantage for me if things go well, but a fairly clear disadvantage if things go wrong." In the finance sector, however, many are willing to accept such games. The failure of Monte Carlo did not lead to the disappearance of the method. Quants argue that the error did not come from the models themselves, but from the data that fed them. "Garbage in, garbage out" - garbage in, garbage out. And that's how Monte Carlo continues to be used. Among others, by Aladdin. And although their models have failed repeatedly and spectacularly, the quants have not been banned. "When a bridge collapses, we don't remove the entire civil engineering profession," grumbled Steven Shreve about critics of the "rocket scientists." Shreve is a mathematics professor at Carnegie Mellon University and mentors quants who want to do a PhD there. Shreve even admitted that during the mortgage boom, graduates of his program who were working on Wall Street contacted him, worried because they realized that complex financial products had long since exceeded the limits of their models. Shreve defends his quant colleagues. Ultimately, it is the bank managers and bosses who are responsible for the decisions, not the quants. They would have ignored the warnings of the quants to make as much profit as possible. Shreve sees the 2008 debacle as a dark but brief interlude in an irreversible ascent. Like many of his quant colleagues, he is convinced: quants will increasingly dominate the financial sector. "Even if many wish for it, we will not go back to a simpler time," he wrote in a blog post in response to criticism. In any case, banks and investment houses agree. They want to lure more quants into their ranks. And elite American universities provide them with them: in addition to Shreve's program, New York and Stanford universities in California offer the right courses. In Britain, China, and Germany, there are also opportunities to pursue a career as a cyborg.

What a kitchen mixer and interest rate forecasts have in common

Amazon is mostly known as a giant online store where you can buy everything from books and coffee machines to ski suits and printer cartridges. But the merchant has another business that promises even faster growth than its main activity. The subsidiary with the meaningless name Amazon Web Services - better known as AWS - was launched in 2006. Nearly ten years later, it reached $8 billion in revenue. In 2019, it was $35 billion. AWS's offering is to provide and manage the computing capabilities of external customers. A kind of external IT service. In the tech industry, the nebulous term for this is "cloud computing." For the tech community, the cloud is much more than a service: it embodies a potentiality. Before its arrival, companies were forced to create and maintain their own IT systems and software. With the costs that this incurred in hardware and personnel. There was certainly the possibility of outsourcing this to another company, but this generally involved complex contracts, long-term commitments, and high fees. The difficulty of accessing computing capabilities was a major obstacle for startups. The cloud changed the game. They were able to access significant computing power quickly and flexibly. And cheap. Cloud advocates expect an increase in innovation. Because the cloud reduces the risk of making costly mistakes. If a project fails, at least there are no unnecessary servers or long-term service contracts to be honored.

The use of the cloud has become so common that small businesses pay for services such as office supplies with a credit card. In Silicon Valley, venture capitalists sometimes distribute gift checks for Amazon Web Services as a friendly gesture to tech founders. The cloud is an integral part of the business model of internet companies like the streaming video provider Netflix. But old-school groups like Kraft Foods are also cloud users. Thanks to it, municipalities like the city of Miami operate their municipal services without having to expand public infrastructure. And even the CIA has become a customer of Amazon's cloud computing.

Amazon, with its kitchen mixers, and BlackRock, with its interest rate forecasts, have something in common: both companies have discovered that it can be profitable to make internal capabilities and resources available to external customers. Just as Amazon offers its servers to Silicon Valley startups, BlackRock offers large investors help with portfolio evaluation, stress testing, and, most importantly, access to a wealth of data that no one else in the world has. When BlackRock's tech guru Bennett Golub left MIT in 1984 with a doctorate in "applied economics and finance" and sought a job on Wall Street, he didn't immediately have luck. He was rejected by investment banks for months. No one knew what to do with his education. Until he was finally hired by a small bank, where a trader had started programming a model for mortgage valuation but had left without finishing it. Golub took over and, as he later told MIT students, produced one of the first models for new mortgage securities in three months at a rate of eighty hours per week. These CMOs that his future colleague and co-founder Larry Fink had launched. "When people asked me what I was doing, I could now say: I'm building CMO models and I have a PhD from MIT." It was a time when securitizations were becoming more popular and more complex. Suddenly, Golub became a sought-after man. Fink's employer, First Boston, hired him. Golub opened a division in his new company called "financial engineering." His reasoning: there were indeed engineers at work, and they were using software that was no different from the CAD-CAM systems, increasingly used in industry for automated production. With these programs, Golub's team designed mortgage securities tailored to investors' expectations. In just three years, the finance tinkerers securitized $25 billion in loans. At First Boston, Golub met mainly people who shared the same ideas: Fink, Kapito, and Novick. The idea of founding a company together was born. Shortly after the launch of BlackRock, Golub and the other BlackRockers realized that the analyses and models they were building for their own needs could be used to develop a new business branch. Aladdin was officially launched as an offering in 2000. Since then, more and more customers have come on board. Like in the corporate consulting sector,

BlackRock came to the rescue of the financial crisis. Until the 2008 debacle, maximizing returns was an absolute priority for large institutional investors. The crisis suddenly made risk management a hot topic. No executive wanted to be caught off guard again. Moreover, regulatory authorities began asking questions and demanding data on an unprecedented scale. However, very few large asset managers had enough staff and expertise to respond to these requests with the resources at hand. BlackRock's offer to use Aladdin's analysis tools and databases must have been a divine answer to a prayer. Since then, more than two hundred fifty institutional investors have become clients, including the world's largest investors, namely pension funds, foundations, insurers, sovereign wealth funds, and fifty central banks - knowing that there are one hundred seventy-seven central banks in the world according to the Bank for International Settlements. Even Deutsche Bank's asset management arm, a BlackRock competitor, now manages its capital through Aladdin's platforms. And according to a February 2020 Financial Times report, rivals Vanguard and State Street also use it. Few companies have such market penetration - only the search engine Google and the social network Facebook exercise comparable dominance. Let's stick with the GAFAM: according to a Financial Times report, Apple, Microsoft, and Alphabet, Google's parent company, also make calculations with Aladdin. BlackRock helps the richest companies in the world with their internal financial management. This results in more connections than among the protagonists of the Brazilian telenovela Escrava Isaura, whose plots and secrets of the beautiful slave Isaura held half the world in suspense during the 1970s. Thus, BlackRock co-founder Sue Wagner also sits on Apple's board of directors. This is exceptional: BlackRock, like all major fund managers, avoids sending its own representatives directly to the boards of directors of companies because otherwise insider trading regulations would apply and BlackRock's funds could no longer buy or sell shares of the company in question as freely. Wagner, it must be said, retired from BlackRock's operational business in 2012. "Sue is a pioneer in the financial sector, and we are thrilled to welcome her to Apple's board of directors," said Apple CEO Tim Cook when Wagner was appointed in the summer of 2014. Wagner is not the only link between the Wall Street colossus and the Silicon Valley giant: BlackRock's funds are among the largest shareholders of Apple.

Wagner also serves on the board of Swiss Re, one of the world's largest reinsurers. Swiss Re is also an Aladdin client, and former vice president Mathis Cabiallavetta now sits on BlackRock's board of directors. BlackRock is itself one of the largest shareholders of the insurance group. According to the Financial Times, Aladdin is the "central nervous system" for many major players in the financial sector.

Data centers like BlackRock's in Wenatchee consist of thousands of high-performance servers - computers stacked like drawers in cabinets taller than men. Just a few years ago, companies would buy one server at a time when they wanted to increase their capacity. Today, Microsoft, for example, orders its equipment by the truckload. Server cabinets are lined up, cables of different colors and carefully labeled emerge from them, bundled as thick as a bodybuilder's arms. Most of the time, the rooms are dark - light bringing unwanted additional heat - and deserted. The only noise comes from the machines. "If one of our technicians is tinkering in one of these units, it is difficult to find him," explains the manager of a data center owned by a large internet company. Diesel generators, the size of locomotives, come into play in case of power failure. BlackRock has three of these emergency diesel generators, each with a capacity of 2.5 megawatts. Together, they could power a small town.

What led BlackRock to install its electronic superbrain in the remote northwest also attracted the Wanapum Indians: the Columbia. For centuries, the "river people" tribe lived along the banks in reed huts. They lived off salmon fishing. But European farmers were taking more and more land. Eventually, engineers arrived and built dams. These dams blocked the passage of salmon that had been swimming upstream from the Pacific every year to spawn. Today, the descendants of the Wanapum live in modest houses built for them by the power company. Electricity providers now operate the dams, of which there are four hundred. They have been impounding the waters of the Columbia and its tributaries since the 1950s. These dams, which deprived the Indians of their livelihoods, are now the basis for a new industry in the Columbia Basin: data centers.

Yahoo, Microsoft, and Dell each operate their own football field-sized data centers in Quincy, a small farming town 20 minutes from Wenatchee. Telecommunications subsidiary T-Mobile has its server banks in the building next to BlackRock's. Electricity from the dam's turbines is unbeatably priced. It costs between 2 and 3 cents per kilowatt-hour in Wenatchee and neighboring communities - for comparison, businesses in the US pay an average of over 7 cents. The cool outdoor temperatures further reduce costs. This is fortunate: Aladdin's calculations involving billions literally overheat computers and cables.

Data centers like the facilities in Wenatchee and Quincy are the real, concrete, albeit often overlooked, side of our digital world. Data processing is now the most energy-intensive and fastest-growing part of our energy consumption. According to calculations by data center provider vXchnge, data processors consume 90 billion kilowatt-hours annually. This could power New York and its eight million inhabitants more than twice. By 2025, big data will already be responsible for over 3% of all greenhouse gas emissions - as much as airlines - and this share is expected to reach 14% by 2040 according to the American specialized magazine Computer World. However, according to environmentalists, systems like BlackRock's are exemplary, "ultra-efficient" and green, unlike the installations of small and medium-sized enterprises, which are mostly inefficient and involve huge consumption.

We, the users of the Aladdin network

Aladdin is expanding daily, every hour, every minute, every second. Because it is constantly fed with new data. And, most importantly, like at Google and other tech companies, because this data is voluntarily provided by users. In this case, these are major investors. Aladdin knows where capital is flowing on our globe, but also where it comes from. Even information about ordinary consumers can end up in the distant superbrain of Wenatchee. Unlike Google & Co., however, it's in anonymous form. But that doesn't really matter. "BlackRock's analytical model is capable of sorting very precise information, for example, the fact that people living near IBM offices often pay off their mortgages early," writes Fortune economics magazine admiringly about Aladdin's genius. The reason for this: IBM managers are often transferred elsewhere, so they sell their homes and pay off their loans before they are due. For Aladdin's clients, such information is worth gold: it means that mortgages granted to homeowners living near IBM pose a greater risk. A loan paid off too early is not good for mortgage-backed securities investors. Because it implies that the finely calculated returns on these mortgage bundles are no longer accurate. What can investors do with IBM's information? For example, they might speculate that they don't want mortgage securities from those regions in their portfolios. Banks would still like to resell them to get rid of them, since they are risky. This can result in it being more difficult and more expensive for buyers looking to buy a house in the vicinity of IBM to get a loan.

It is precisely the success of Aladdin that makes this system so dangerous. If traditional Amazon sector servers, online orders, were to malfunction, it would mean a loss in revenue for the company. And, probably, a delay in delivery for customers. If the lights were to go out at Amazon Web Services, it would potentially be a major nuclear accident for thousands of businesses. It's the same with BlackRock. Errors in the system not only affect the company itself: they spread throughout the client network and, in the case of Aladdin, hypothetically, to the financial system. BlackRock is certainly not the only provider of such a system, but none other has the global reach of Aladdin.

Analytical systems lead users to rely too much on machines. In the same way that we often accept the result given by a calculator without much thought. Or similar to how investors trusted the AAA ratings of rating agencies for toxic mortgage products - creditworthiness ratings they determined using their quant models. Who wanted to doubt the "rocket scientists"? We know how the story ends.

It should be noted that BlackRock still warned its clients to exercise caution. "It depends on how risk assessment models are used," explained Rob Goldstein in an interview with the Financial Times in July 2014. "The models don't tell the user: buy, sell, or hold this or that asset, they simply provide tools to enlighten them about that asset." In other words: BlackRock is not responsible for the conclusions clients draw from Aladdin's results. His boss Larry Fink's opinion is even more draconian: "If you think the models are right, then you'll be wrong," he warned readers of The Economist in December 2013.

This does not prevent BlackRock from offering models and programs. BlackRock Solutions, the division to which Aladdin belongs, generated $170 million in revenue in 2014; five years later, in 2019, nearly $1 billion. Fink wants to achieve one-third of the revenue with Aladdin by 2022. But the smarter and smoother the analysis systems work, the greater the risk that their users will blindly trust them. BlackRock may not be responsible for user behavior, but that does not diminish the risk of excessive trust in systems like Aladdin. The remarks of Goldstein and Fink, in which they call for skepticism towards models, are reminiscent of drug warnings that no one bothers to read. The only difference is that there are no safety standards in the risk assessment model industry, unlike the pharmaceutical industry.

And that's not the only threat posed by our cyberfinance system.

The conqueror's victory message arrived via instant messaging. "The Nasdaq is ours," wrote to his accomplices Aleksandr Kalinin, better known in his circles as Tempo. Kalinin was one of the hackers who discovered a vulnerability on the Nasdaq website in May 2007. The Nasdaq is the tech Bourse per se. 3,200 companies are listed there - including many major US tech stocks. Using the password reminder function for clients, Kalinin was able to access - through what's called a "back door" - the Nasdaq's internal electronic systems and managed to obtain the same rights as the system administrators themselves. "We have access to the servers and can do whatever we want with them," he wrote to his accomplices via instant messaging. He was visibly impressed: "The databases are of infernal size, I think they are transaction records."

The hacker gang got caught. US law enforcement agents accused Kalinin of illegally accessing Nasdaq computers via the "back door" until October 2010. In any case, authorities assumed that computers directly regulating trading had not been affected by the manipulation and that the Nasdaq had only suffered limited damage. One of Kalinin's accomplices was a certain Albert Gonzalez, aka Soupnazi, considered one of the strongest hackers. Gonzalez, who was sometimes an informant for the FBI, was already liquidating credit card accounts on a large scale at the age of 20, reportedly squandering the proceeds at a $75,000 birthday party. According to authorities, Gonzalez, who is currently serving a 20-year prison sentence for past offenses, was just one of the accomplices in the largest financial data theft to date. The other brains behind the operation, four Russians and one Ukrainian, hacked servers at over a dozen major companies in addition to Nasdaq systems, including Citibank and French retail giant Carrefour. This allowed them to steal the numbers of 160 million credit cards. Experts were impressed by the gang's organization and the length of time they managed to stay in the shadows. They set up, among other things, from their bases of operation in Russia, fencing platforms in Germany, Panama, and the Bahamas, to temporarily store the stolen data.

Cyberattacks are now part of daily life on Wall Street. And they are becoming increasingly dangerous.

It's no longer just about stolen credit card data or hacked private accounts. The threat now resides at the heart of global financial markets. In a survey published in the summer of 2013 by the World Federation of Exchanges and IOSCO, an international association of financial regulators, more than half of the exchanges surveyed reported being attacked by hackers. According to the study, cybercrime is at the top of the list of dangers for financial markets because they are increasingly reliant on information technology. In a study published in October of the same year, Aite, a consulting group for financial institutions, reported that on average, up to 150,000 pieces of malicious software code were being distributed every day. "Risks are multiplying too quickly for banks and businesses to implement a defense system," write the authors of the study. The American clearing services company DTCC also sounded the alarm. The company is a key component of the financial infrastructure. It is, so to speak, the distribution center of Wall Street – where the actual exchange of "securities for cash" takes place – once the stock exchange transaction is closed. Banks, exchanges, brokers, and major investment funds are connected to DTCC's financial transaction flow. If one wants to move the global financial markets, this is where it can start. In a DTCC report from August 2014, it is also stated that cyber risks are "the primary systemic threat to global markets and their infrastructure." Greater, for example, than the risk of a new credit crisis.

What frightens exchanges, banks, and authorities is that the nature of the attacks has changed: for example, the increasingly common ones where the websites and internet access of affected companies end up crashing due to targeted overload attacks – known as distributed denial of service (DDoS) attacks. According to DTCC experts, such attacks previously emanated from desktop computers and personal computers. Today, professional servers attack on behalf of cybercriminals – in some cases, involving thousands of highly capable computers. Before 2012, hackers' computers sent at most one to two gigabits per second to the website of the targeted organization. Today, companies are bombarded at a rate of 150 gigabits per second – roughly equivalent to fifteen times the capacity of a normal financial institution's website.

Even more insidious are cases where attackers infiltrate the system unnoticed to manipulate it from within. Such attacks, called advanced persistent threats

(APTs) in cyber jargon, primarily spy on their targets through social networks and use their findings to send their manipulation software, camouflaged for example as an email attachment sent to key employees.

The JPMorgan Chase attack in the summer of 2014 shows how professionally hackers operate. Strangers gained access to the deepest electronic infrastructure of the largest American bank and stole gigabytes of information, including about clients, before JPMorgan's IT staff discovered it. The means of the criminals were so advanced that experts suspected they could be linked to the Russian government and Vladimir Putin. The Russians denied it.

Just as they deny to this day deliberately manipulating the 2016 US presidential election. Not only did they conduct targeted campaigns designed to help Trump and harm Clinton, but the hackers they hired also gained access to internal information of the Democratic Party, whose publication disadvantaged Clinton during the election campaign. US intelligence services have officially confirmed this.

One thing is certain: for hackers, it's not always about financial gain. For example, the electronic attack on the Syrian army described earlier. And North Korea is suspected of hacking Sony Studios' servers and making public internal elements such as the remuneration of Hollywood managers and stars. The action would have been an act of revenge after Sony produced The Interview, a comedy in which two Americans – played by Seth Rogen and James Franco – plan the assassination of North Korean dictator Kim Jong-un. Although there are obviously many indications that North Korea may be involved, there will never be definitive proof. "Setting up a potential cyberattack is much easier to hide than setting up a physical attack," says the World Federation of Exchanges study. Moreover, such an internet attack is much harder to trace.

It is clear that hackers have discovered the world of cyber finance themselves and will ruthlessly exploit its weaknesses. "There are two types of American companies: those that have been hacked and those that don't know they have been hacked," said FBI Director James Comey in an interview with ABC

News in May 2014 after discovering that Chinese cyber spies had infiltrated dozens of companies. Comey then investigated Russian hacking attacks on Hillary Clinton and her party. President Trump fired him after taking office.

It would undoubtedly be tempting for hackers to crack a system like Aladdin: the collected data could provide them with decisive informational advantages in the markets. Even more terrifying is the possibility that nations hostile to the West could gain access to this data. Asked for the first edition of the book, BlackRock declined to comment on Aladdin's protection in the event of a cyberattack or specify if such attacks had ever occurred. For the new edition, the asset manager provided a statement indicating that "significant resources are invested to ensure the stability and reliability of Aladdin. As the primary user of Aladdin, we have the highest operational standards, which also apply to our clients."

The world through the lens of BlackRock

There is another risk posed by Aladdin, more difficult to grasp but no less worrying. It is related to how prices and movements are formed in financial markets. Ultimately, this only works if parties have different opinions about the future. Take, for example, a stock transaction: the seller believes that the price will no longer rise, or even that it will fall. The buyer, on the other hand, sees potential for growth. In the case of bonds, trading partners have divergent views on the future evolution of interest rates – or, more fundamentally, on the future evolution of the economy. The same goes for commodities, currencies. Different views are expressed in terms of transactions and prices – and their sum ultimately controls the market. A crash is nothing more than a herd instinct, which leads too many participants in the same direction.

It is therefore worrying that so many leaders of global capital see the world through the lens of BlackRock.

If a large number of market players interpret data using Aladdin, they also adopt the assumptions on which the analyses and models are based. "Buyers, sellers, and regulators can all make the same assumptions, simply because they consult Aladdin," worried The Economist. Moreover, the British magazine, the designated voice of the economic elite (and those who think they belong to it), is extremely positive about technologies and innovations in the financial market. However, in December 2013, the magazine again devoted a cover story to the subject. "The monolith and the markets," announced the alarming headline. Since 2008, even non-experts no longer need much imagination to envision what will happen when too many market players share assumptions that prove to be wrong at a catastrophic level. And what does BlackRock say about the fear that Aladdin may lead market players to see the market only through its "lens," and that this could trigger a herd movement? On this question, too, BlackRock had not wanted to comment in the first edition. For the new edition, the asset manager stated that Aladdin does not replace risk management functions in companies using the system, but only provides tools that managers can use to analyze the risks of their portfolios, taking into account their internal guidelines on these issues. It would be up to clients to integrate their own data and adjust possible models and analysis parameters according to their own economic outlooks and investment plans. The statement also notes that BlackRock and Aladdin are just one technology provider among many.

CHAPTER 10

Power Shift on Wall Street

Tourists, straying from Fifth Avenue during their shopping tour, end up at San Pietro feeling disoriented. At first glance, they think they're in one of those kitschy, slightly dusty Italian neighborhood bars. There are vases, figurines, and porcelain knick-knacks everywhere. Crystal balls hang from the ceiling, not really matching the rustic ceramic tiles with maritime motifs. The New York Magazine once wrote that it looks like the set of Martin Scorsese's mafia epic, Goodfellas. But as soon as one of the skilled waiters in white leads them to a perfectly set table, they realize their mistake. Not just because of the breathtaking prices or the tailor-made suits worn by their fellow diners. San Pietro is not your average ravioli and tiramisu joint (though both specialties are excellent here). The restaurant owned by the Bruno brothers from Salerno is the unofficial club of Wall Street magnates. Near the window, John Mack chats with foreign clients. The former Morgan Stanley boss, now a consultant and a banking gray eminence, is better known as "Mack the Knife" for the radical measures he used to keep his employees in an atmosphere of fear and terror. At the next table sits a regular, Joe Perella, the legendary banker, one of those corporate raiders who, in the 1980s, instilled fear in American corporate bosses and their employees with their aggressive takeover campaigns. Today, the gray-bearded man only eats vegetables, having converted to vegetarianism. In a subdued atmosphere, over a branzino crusted in salt and herbs – San Pietro's $43 fish specialty, next to the $48 veal loin with radicchio – deals are sealed, friendships forged, and enmities buried. It's a who's who of Wall Street. When bank bosses meet here, it's like a press conference. That's why journalists like Charlie Gasparino, who gathers the latest financial and political news for Fox Business Network, like to linger at the precious wood counter, waiting for the next big gathering. A few years ago, Fink could sit at a table here without being noticed. He wasn't yet part of the small elite group that occupies the "chairman row" – the coveted tables near the window. Now, not only does

Fink have his table at San Pietro, but Gerardo Bruno, one of the managers, also knows his fondness for fresh peas.

Yet, he is different from the other San Pietro patrons. He wasn't appointed to the position of chairman of a traditional house: he had to build his own empire first. Until he became so powerful that he is now a leading player among bank directors.

Our Retirement Savings: The Holy Grail on Wall Street

Fink owes his rise to the top and his regular table at San Pietro to his talent, ambition, and also, a bit of luck. However, his ascent would hardly have been conceivable without the irresistible rise of fund managers. The power shift began before the financial crisis, but since then, the movement has accelerated. "For a long time, asset managers were in the shadow of their cousins, the banks and insurers, but by 2020, they will definitely be in the spotlight," poetically describe the authors of a future scenario published for the sector by consulting firm PricewaterhouseCoopers (PwC) in 2014. Until the financial crisis, banks were the innovators, the drivers of development in the financial market. They brought ideas and a direction to follow. They had the ear of the political class. The crisis, loss of confidence, and the global wave of regulations that followed cost the banks their supremacy.

But new laws also apply to asset managers. The competition for the world's money is fierce. The questions of scale and scope become decisive in deals with investors; this is the only way that rising costs can be widely distributed. Global expansion increases expenses for marketing and sales in the sector. This increases the pressure. Those who cannot attract enough capital to survive in the global competition for clients and margins will either have to settle for the crumbs left by the giants or give up altogether. In 2018, the ten largest asset managers controlled 34% of global managed capital, and the top five nearly 23%. The Americans clearly dominate: eight of the largest companies come from the United States, only Allianz and Amundi are European.

BlackRock currently enjoys a huge advantage. Those who want to compete for distribution in the future must first and foremost succeed in emerging markets. By the end of 2016, 3.2 billion people belonged to the middle class, according to the Brookings Institution, a Washington think tank. Therefore, 140 million people are joining it every year – more than ever before in human history (all of this before the Covid-19 pandemic). The majority of this middle class will no longer be in Europe but in Asia. For now, the sector manages in Asia (excluding Japan) only a modest $7 trillion in assets and in Latin America less than $2 trillion – for comparison, in the United States, it is about $35 trillion and in Europe, $20 trillion. But most importantly for Fink and his competitors, growth rates in emerging countries have been much higher than in industrialized countries since the 2008 financial crisis. Between 2007 and 2017, capital inflows into Asian countries (excluding Japan and Australia) grew by an average of 12% per year. In Latin America, it also grew by 12%. In Europe and North America, growth was 4% over the same period. However, asset managers recorded net capital outflows in 2018. While they lost 5% in the United States and 3% in Europe, they only gained 2% in Asia, and Latin America continued to grow by 8%. Automakers and fashion houses have also targeted China. The country's spectacular economic growth over the past decade has created a new layer of urbanites, who are increasingly saving for private retirement or children's education. In the Middle Kingdom, financial managers are still grappling with bureaucracy and regulation. Access for foreign providers is limited.

BlackRock definitely wants to be at the forefront. As early as 2011, Fink insisted during a conference call with analysts and BlackRock shareholders that his company was progressing more slowly in China "than we would like." It was only after a waiting period that the black giant was able to receive a license in 2012 for direct investments in the Chinese stock market, reported the Financial Times. The 2018 annual report indicates that China is one of the largest future growth opportunities. Asia – mainly China – will account for 50% of global growth in invested capital in the financial management sector over the next five years. "Our goal is to become one of the country's leading asset managers." In China as well, Fink is counting on recruiting the right key figures, such as Wang Hsueh-Ming in 2013. A graduate of Columbia University in New York, she was previously at Goldman Sachs, where she achieved the coveted status of partner. Thanks to her good relations with the financial circles of her home country, she helped Goldman conclude two huge deals: the listings of China Telecom and the oil company PetroChina. In doing so, she worked closely with Goldman's CEO, Hank

Paulson, as noted by the Financial Times. Tony Tang has been running BlackRock's business in the Middle Kingdom since 2019. He has been able to pull the right strings toward Beijing. "With his extensive and in-depth experience in regulation and industry in China, Mr. Tang has been involved in cooperation with international regulators and initiatives to open up the Chinese financial market," the company's press release announced. But Fink's wish has not yet been fully satisfied; business remains challenging. In early 2020, BlackRock filed with Chinese authorities for approval for investment funds that Americans would like to offer to the Chinese market.

BlackRock and its funds have long been involved in the country. In recent years, American investment banks – as evidenced by the example of Goldman Sachs mentioned earlier – have helped the Beijing regime value state-owned enterprises and introduce them to the Western stock markets. For hundreds of millions of dollars in fees, of course. The guys on Wall Street dolled up these drab companies with "lipstick, mascara, pedicures, and blowouts" to make them look as much like Western companies as possible, according to Carl Walter and Fraser Howie in their book Red Capitalism. There always needed to be buyers for these securities. The black giant was ready, just as it had been for corporate bonds. For example, nearly 40% of the "iShares Emerging Markets" ETF was invested in Chinese stocks in May 2020. American regulators, including Jay Clayton, chairman of the Securities and Exchange Commission, warned that they could hardly verify the information provided by Chinese companies. In April 2020, Luckin Coffee, a Chinese rival to Starbucks aiming to offer cheaper lattes, admitted to accounting fraud committed by the CEO and other employees. The revenue of over $300 million was nothing but smoke and mirrors. Less than five days later, Tal Education, a tutoring company, reported that employees had falsified diplomas to inflate the numbers. A company press release stated that the matter had been turned over to local police. Luckin kept its place in the "iShares Emerging Markets" ETF until April 30, 2020, and Tal until May 29, 2020. "Once the lipstick is gone, it's not beautiful anymore," RealClearPolitics sarcastically commented on BlackRock's investment in China and these accounting frauds. This does not prevent BlackRock from advertising its expertise in the former Middle Kingdom. A website dedicated to "opportunities in China" explains what an investor needs to do business there: a "trusted partner who is not only an expert on China, but also has the knowledge, expertise, and judgment necessary to build portfolios that offer the best of the Chinese markets."

China is ahead of the West in one area: the merger of finance and technology. When e-commerce giant Alibaba offered a money market fund to investors, such a large amount of capital flowed into the fund in the first eight months that it quickly swelled to become one of the largest money market funds in the world. Another fund, named Yu'e Bao, which can be translated as "the remaining treasure," did even better later on. In 2018, this treasure fund had reached over $260 billion. However, seeing this growing competition for banks in a bad light, the authorities began to restrict the activities of the new finance giant. Yu'e Bao was called a "blood-sucking vampire" on public television.

In Silicon Valley too, interest in the financial sector is growing. Google, for example, is investing in online credit platforms. Apple made its debut in the fall of 2014 with Apple Pay, a digital payment method that allows users to pay their bill using their mobile phone, and then in 2019 with a credit card, Apple Card, in partnership with Goldman Sachs, following the motto: If you can't beat them, join them.

The new financial giants will be global, digital, and, above all, gigantic. And practically everywhere. BlackRock is at the forefront: the asset manager has partnered with Microsoft. Aladdin must be connected to Azure, the software giant's cloud, to enable new economies of scale, as stated in the April 2020 press release.

Even though Germans remain skeptical and reluctant about private investments, the rise of fund managers will not pass Germany by. The industry must invest its trillions worldwide. German companies and real estate are becoming investment objects for the new global middle class. This is already the case for the large companies in the DAX. ETFs are already heavily invested, and hedge fund interest is increasing. Among them, Cevian, the hedge fund that, after joining the construction group Bilfinger, quickly ensured that the CEO and the chairman of the supervisory board left. The Swedes are also on board with ThyssenKrupp. When Elliott Management arrived, the icon of the German industry eventually became the toy of foreign funds aiming to destroy the company. The hedge fund founded by Paul Singer, part of the "activist investors," enjoys a dubious reputation. In the battle for Argentine government bonds, Singer's team even tried to get their hands on the ARA Libertad, the Argentine navy's training ship. In early 2020, after years of pressure from hedge funds, ThyssenKrupp gave in and sold its elevator business. Meanwhile, Elliott also went shopping at Bayer and software giant SAP. Staff can expect budget cuts. "These are situations where there is potential for improvement and where the question arises of what the company can do to create more value for shareholders," said Franck Tuil, portfolio manager at Elliott, in the most straightforward way possible.

However, this movement will not be limited to publicly traded companies. Private equity firms have discovered the German middle class. In 2019 alone, there were eight hundred sixty-six acquisitions of German companies, with 46% by private equity firms. When a company changed hands during this period, it was usually to American hands, as a study by management consultants PwC showed. BlackRock now wants to expand into private equity as well. In August 2019, a BlackRock fund bought the Authentic Brands Group for $875 million – a company that holds brands such as Nine West or Juicy Couture, and licensing rights for Mohamed Ali and Marilyn Monroe, for example. Fink's entry into the market startled everyone, even the most seasoned business hunters. "BlackRock has let equity fund management fees go up in smoke. Will they do the same in private equity now?" worried a representative of the industry in the Financial Times.

The authors of the "Brave New World" study saw only one real problem for mega-managers: the growing distrust of individuals. The sector will need to gain society's trust as a whole, it is written. To avoid a backlash from regulators and citizens as there was after the financial crisis. In plain terms: otherwise, the financial titans could collapse in the same way as the big banks after 2008. As instruments, the authors suggest massive lobbying and public relations campaigns. They recommend establishing "close contacts with decision-makers and the media." "Relationships with policymakers" should be nurtured, not only at the industry level but also at the company level. It should be ensured that society recognizes fund managers as a solution and not as part of the problem.

For mega-fund managers, particularly BlackRock, the goal is to continue to grow, to bring even more investor money into their funds. Proximity to decision-makers opens up other opportunities.

Monica Lewinsky, Savior of the Retirement System

———

Wall Street is once again trying to divert the capital flowing into public and state pension schemes to land in its coffers. This attempt is considered the Holy Grail of the financial industry. If anyone can achieve this, it's Larry Fink. BlackRock is already the third-largest pension manager in the UK and has hired former Chancellor of the Exchequer George Osborne. During the early decades of BlackRock's ascent, Fink remained in the background. He rarely appeared in public. Even when success came, his company and he himself stayed away from the limelight. Interviews with the press were rare. That suddenly changed in 2013. Since then, Larry has appeared on all channels: on morning shows, in Washington, Madrid, London, and Berlin. He writes opinion pieces for the Wall Street Journal, gives interviews to the Spanish newspaper El País at the Ritz, talks to editors of Der Spiegel, explaining to them that Germans are too afraid to invest. He speaks to students, bankers, investors, and politicians. Sometimes, he even speaks at two events in a single day. Because Fink has a message to convey: our retirement systems urgently need reform. In the United States, Fink has even declared a retirement emergency. A national crisis! And the head of BlackRock has a ready-made solution: private provision - and more voluntary, but as a state constraint.

His favorite example is Australia. There, the government has made it mandatory to pay into a savings fund for retirement reforms since January 2014. Fink would like to go further. In the United States, in 2013, he publicly advocated that half of the contributions for public old-age insurance (12.5% of wages or salaries) be paid into private funds. Because social security would be just designed as an insurance and would be a "terrible investment". According to Fink, the fact that so many citizens still wish to cling to public systems is due only to their biased psychological perspective. Studies have shown that people consider the fear of loss more than the potential benefits of gain. According to him, this fear must be overcome. The multimillionaire likes to say that he himself is made up of 100% stocks. However, there is one subject that Fink only touches on in his reports, and even then, when he does: what the 2008 financial crisis did to the savings of many average Americans. Following the latter, many 401(k) savings accounts suffered losses of up to 30%. It remains to be seen what the Covid-19 crisis will do to the savings of ordinary people. The fact that Fink invites us to consider this risk in a slightly more relaxed manner is cynical.

Fink is also a proponent of extending professional life: "Why should we be unproductive for a third of our lives?" he asked in an interview in August 2013. "In my view, it is a blessing to work until 67 or 68." As for the fact that this simply means a reduction in retirement for many average workers, because they cannot find employment at that age and therefore must accept the pension cuts that go with it, Fink barely mentions it in the interviews and conferences he gives. He explains that retirement provision is a concern for him because he himself is approaching retirement age - he was born in 1952 - and because BlackRock plays a major role in global retirement provision. But it can be seen differently: inflows of savers play a decisive role in the future growth of BlackRock and the more they are diverted from public pots, the greater the chances that the industry leader will gain a disproportionate share.

Larry Fink is one of the most powerful voices in favor of privatization. But the attack on public pension systems has a long history - and BlackRock plays a kind of henchman role in it. Behind it lies an ideological struggle, the struggle of advocates of a libertarian economic order against advocates of the social state. Market radical economists want to reduce the role of the state. And this includes public protection systems. In America, in particular, the ideology has found more and more supporters among the barons of private equity, hedge fund titans, and major industrialists. With their huge financial means and thanks to sympathetic judges who have lifted restrictions on campaign financing, they enjoy ever greater influence over politics. In the United States, this struggle has been going on for decades.

In 1980, shortly before Reagan's entry, shareholder value guru Milton Friedman published a book in which he argued for "freedom of choice." He advocated gradually ending social security. Reagan was open to the idea, but the attempt failed: state pension schemes were too popular. Reagan simply reduced social security. But Milton's idea was not forgotten. In 1984, Stuart Butler and Peter Germanis of the libertarian Cato Institute - whose main patrons include the Koch brothers, later known as patrons of the Tea Party and organizations - developed a strategy document. The two Cato masterminds recommended using a "Leninist strategy" and a kind of guerrilla tactic against social security. Just as Lenin wanted to mobilize workers to finally collapse capitalism, they wanted to make bankers, insurers, and asset managers the advocates of privatization. They should gradually convince politicians of the disadvantages of public systems, while presenting private provision as superior. The finance industry volunteered as a logical partner.

The next opportunity came under the presidency of Bill Clinton. He recruited Erskine Bowles, a former Morgan Stanley banker, to be White House chief of staff. Bowles' mission: to finance social security, at least in part, through the stock market, and to reduce state benefits. With this reform, Clinton wanted to go down in history. The opportunity seemed favorable: the stock market was rebounding at the time, the American economy was booming. Health and Human Services Secretary Donna Shalala appointed a commission to prepare the proposals. Also present: Pete Peterson, co-founder of Blackstone and once a financier of Fink. Wall Street has never been as close to the Holy Grail as it was under Clinton. According to historian Steven Gillon, who later interviewed all those involved, there was already an agreement between Clinton and Newt Gingrich, who was then the Republican majority leader in the House of Representatives. "The President was ready to act against the will of his own party and campaign for Republicans to introduce private social security accounts," Gillon writes in his book The Pact.

But the Clinton affair with intern Monica Lewinsky triggered a scandal and impeachment proceedings. Although the president survived both, he dared not push controversial projects anymore. "Monica Lewinsky changed everything," Bowles himself said. This is how Lewinsky, who was only 22 at the time, saved the retirement system of American retirees.

The next serious attempt came under George W. Bush. With the slogan "ownership society," a society of owners, he campaigned for at least partial conversion of state old-age insurance into private savings accounts. But Bush ran into a wall: his attempt to abolish the popular protection among the elderly failed. Indeed, the voter turnout of older generations is higher. Abolishing social security has since been seen as political poison in Washington - like the "third rail," the name given to the third rail of the metro, which is responsible for electrical power. Anyone who touches the "third rail" receives an electric shock, usually fatal.

George W. Bush's failure led privatization proponents to change their approach. Frontal attacks were found to be damaging. Since then, they have been trying to achieve their goal indirectly. They warn of system overload due to aging and warn that the younger generation will miss out. That is why a combination with private benefits is necessary. But the average household budget is limited. The more it goes into private funds, the less lands in public systems. This leads to reductions in benefits. And this is how the dark prophecies of critics finally come true: public systems are shaken and are no longer sufficient to protect.

I've translated and proofread the text. Let me know if you need any changes or if there's anything else I can help with!

Under the presidency of Barack Obama, the discussion about reforming social security resumed. This time, reformers argued by pointing out the increase in US debt. They argued that, in the long term, social security could not be maintained without drastic cuts. "Fix the debt" was the motto of the initiative, which aimed to save the United States from over-indebtedness. "Fix the debt" was promoted by an old acquaintance: the late billionaire Pete Peterson, co-founder of Blackstone. Peterson's avowed wish was for reform, meaning a reduction in state old-age provision. As a lever, he tried to use budget crises in Washington. The initiative of the rich and powerful (alongside Fink, we find Jamie Dimon, CEO of mega-bank JPMorgan

Chase, as well as Jeffrey Immelt, then CEO of General Electric) met with some success. President Obama publicly considered a new formula to adjust retirement to the cost of living - which would have led to a insidious reduction. The proposal came from a committee very close to "fix the debt". During his second term, Obama introduced new savings contracts called myRA for employees who did not have a 401(k) plan through their employer. While myRA savings contracts were far from the mandatory savings plans Fink envisioned - they only allowed investment in government bonds - it was a first step in the right direction.

Donald Trump, on the other hand, abolished myRA savings contracts. This was not so much due to aversion to the privatization of retirement provision, but rather to Trump's obsession with abolishing everything his predecessor had introduced.

The privatization advocates' offensive was by no means limited to the United States. In 1994 - the year Clinton concluded the secret pact against social security with the opposition - the World Bank published a study entitled Averting the Old Age Crisis. The study sought to ensure that the idea of privatization gained ground internationally. The historical context was also favorable: the fall of the Wall, coupled with that of the Soviet Union, had made advocates of free markets the winners. The World Bank made it known, among other things, that it preferred to continue dismantling "dilapidated" public security systems in Eastern Europe rather than saving them. These same arguments had once been used to implement one of the most radical experiments with private pensions. It took place in Chile.

In the early 1980s, the South American country abolished public old-age insurance, financed by the pay-as-you-go system, and replaced it with private savings plans. From then on, employees had to contribute 10% of their monthly income to their individual account. The reorganization was costly and was paid for with public funds. It had been imposed because Chile was then ruled by dictator Augusto Pinochet. Behind the initiative was José Piñera, a minister Jef Pinochet, inspired by Milton Friedman's ideas. In the 1990s, other countries in the region followed Chile's example - Argentina, Costa Rica, and Mexico. Piñera was dubbed "the Pied Piper of Pensions" by the Wall Street Journal, and no one knows if the journalists were thinking of the dark German legend of Hamelin. Piñera is now a social expert at the Cato Institute in Washington, the libertarian think tank founded by the Koch brothers, heirs to a pipeline and refinery empire that became (infamously) famous for their political influence.

Chile was also a model for George W. Bush. The country was praised worldwide as an example of successful privatization - at least by proponents of neoliberal and libertarian theories. Pension funds accumulated over $200 billion, which is not insignificant for a country with a GDP of $280 billion. Many middle-class Chileans were satisfied with the system. But critics complained about the high management fees of private accounts, compared to the rest of the world. And when the first post-reform generation retired, deficits appeared. Many retirees complained that their incomes were much lower than those of their former colleagues who had retired under the old system. Many Chileans had earned so little that they remained below the minimum payout. The state had to intervene. Discontent with extreme social inequality in Chile brought Michelle Bachelet to power. At the beginning of her first term in 2006, the socialist tried to initiate a return to a public pension system, but failed. However, in 2008, the pension system was nevertheless supplemented by a solidarity pension, intended to provide basic security for retirees.

The private pension system in Chile faces similar problems to the pay-as-you-go system it replaced: young people take longer to train and Chileans are aging. This shortens the period during which they can contribute as active workers. And in Chile, too, uninterrupted and long-term employment is becoming increasingly rare. However, for the calculation to work, contributors must make their contributions consistently and with sufficient amounts. In the fall of 2019, the country was ablaze, notably because of the miserable pension situation. The new government promised further reforms. In this affair, there will nevertheless have been a winner: the fund sector, with which a whole population of savers was led, coerced, and forced. BlackRock, of course, is also part of the game. With over $8 billion in invested capital in 2019, the New Yorkers are the largest foreign fund provider in Chile.

Chile's successes and failures in restructuring a capitalized pension system are significant far beyond this South American country. Reformers worldwide should study Piñera's experience.

The issue of retirement in Germany and France

Germany also embarked on an experiment with private benefits. This is the "Riester" retirement, introduced in 2001: an attempt to escape the demographic trap. The numbers speak for themselves: the working population in Germany will decrease significantly from 2020 onwards, and according to projections by the Federal Statistical Office, will be between 34 and 38 million from April 2015 until 2060 (depending on the net immigration figure). For comparison, in 2013, there were still 49 million people aged 20 to 64. The population under 20 will decrease from 15 million to 11 to 12 million. On the other hand, the number of people aged 65 and over will continue to increase. In 2060, the group of over 65s will reach 23 million. One in three Germans will then be retired. According to a study by the German Institute for Economic Research (DIW), one in five German retirees could live in poverty by 2039. And the Deutsche Paritätische Wohlfahrtsverband, the German charity association, estimates that by 2025, 10% of retirees in Germany will be affected by poverty.

Retirement reformers in 2001 believed that a larger share of internal and private pensions could be a solution. Instead of aiming for a high pension level involving increasing contributions for those affiliated with the general scheme, adjustments were avoided. According to the plan, Riester pensions and company pensions were supposed to fill the resulting gap. But the Riester retirement, named after former German Minister of Social Affairs Walter Riester, did not meet all expectations.

While it now applies to 16 million Germans, many more would be needed to achieve the desired effect. And it is often people who hold other assets, such as real estate. It is precisely among those who would most need private retirement that gaps are felt. In addition, the different Riester products - capitalization retirement savings plans - are strongly criticized. The financial sector does not have a good image among the public. "Beware, risk of poverty in the elderly! Almost all Riester pensions fail," writes, for example, Stiftung Warentest, the German consumer association, in its Finanztest magazine at the end of 2013. Only five out of forty-two offers tested were valid in the eyes of the testers. A third of the contracts are no longer active.

"Riester retirement was a big mistake," says Rudolf Zwiener, retirement pension expert at the Böckler Foundation, close to the unions. Its balance sheet should not please Larry Fink & Co. : private old-age provision does not compensate for the decline in pensions. "Returns will not be high for long, they will continue to fall, and precisely with the recently concluded Riester contracts," explains Zwiener in an interview with Cicero magazine. This shows the development after the euro crisis. The cheap money that central banks used to flood the markets ultimately led to negative returns for bonds. In other words, savers also had to pay to lend money to the government or companies. Restructuring into equities is only possible to a limited extent for retirement provision products, as state-funded products must be deemed "safe".

The issue of private pensions is still relevant. In March 2020, in the midst of the Covid-19 crisis, a commission of the federal government, called "Reliable Generational Contract," presented the results of a two-year consultation. The committee members - mainly politicians from the government coalition parties, as well as a few experts - were supposed to develop projections anticipating what the retirement system in Germany could look like after 2045. Their proposals focused on key parameters: What will be the pension ceiling? How long will employees have to work? What percentage of their income will young workers have to invest? However, the committee members did not propose specific answers. The contribution rate, currently 18.6%, will have to be between 20 and 24%. The standard retiree will receive between 44 and 49% of their previous income as a pension. Maybe. Because the commission recommended convening "an advisory council for the pension system" which will be responsible for developing the main data. In other words, the retirement issue has been postponed, and it will be up to future governments to address it. Retirement is seen as a politically toxic issue, much like social security in the United States.

The idea of private supplementary retirement is gaining more traction. For example, an initiative from the government of the state of Hesse called Deutschlandrente ("Retirement for Germany"), resulting from an agreement between the CDU and the Greens, stipulates that employers should transfer a portion of salaries into a specific fund. The CSU, on the other hand, proposes a "starter kit" that grants each child up to the age of 18 a state allowance deposited into a pension fund. If the allowance amounts to 1,200 euros per year, the young adult will have already contributed 21,600 euros by the time they reach adulthood. However, BlackRock encountered resistance in France. Initially, everything seemed to be going well in that country too, with savvy decisions regarding the team. The French subsidiary is led by Jean-François Cirelli, former economic advisor to Jacques Chirac. Like Merz, he has worked as a lobbyist, among other roles for GDF-Suez and Engie. On January 1, 2020, French Prime Minister Emmanuel Macron, himself a former investment banker familiar with Wall Street, awarded him the rank of Knight of the National Order of the Legion of Honor. However, this event caught the attention of the opposition as it coincided with Macron's government planning to reform the pension system. Among other things, under this reform, high-income earners, with an annual income of over 120,000 euros, will be able to invest in private funds instead of contributing to public funds. Photos of a previous meeting between Fink and Macron at the Élysée Palace circulated. In a note to clients about the reform plans, a BlackRock analyst wrote about how disappointing the share of investments in stocks in the country was. (French households hold only 5% of their savings in company stocks.) This made headlines. Asked about it, BlackRock stated that Fink had met Macron on four occasions. The first time was in January 2016, in Davos... of course! At that time, Macron was still the Minister of Finance. Also present at the meeting were Mark Carney, former Goldman Sachs banker and then Governor of the Bank of England, and Tidjane Thiam, then CEO of Credit Suisse. The reunions took place at a meeting of international asset managers in October 2017, by which time Macron had become head of state. According to BlackRock, it was the President of the Republic who organized the meeting, where possible ways to attract investors to France were discussed. The next meeting was in July 2019, this time focusing on climate change. And finally, in January 2020, Macron invited Fink to the "Choose France" summit, attended by two hundred business leaders from different countries and sectors. BlackRock did not reveal whether Fink and Macron had met before, when the latter was still active as a banker.

Fink has never been closer to the Holy Grail. But to overcome the traditional aversion of the German political world towards speculators, they needed an ally on the ground. Just as they had hired former central banker and finance diplomat Hildebrand, BlackRock recruited an insider in Germany. Friedrich Merz, once a great hope of the CDU, lost the race for power to Angela Merkel. The lawyer's political career began in 1989 when he became a member of the European Parliament, before becoming a member of the Bundestag. In 2000, he became president of the parliamentary group of the CDU/CSU. His claim regarding a "dominant German culture" sparked strong reactions. But he is best known for his interest in economic issues. Merz advocates for restricting social benefits and "simplifying" the tax system: he made a name for himself by arguing that the surface of a coaster should suffice for a tax return. He seemed on track for the pole position when Angela Merkel outpaced him. Merz, willingly or not, had to settle for the vice-presidency of the CDU. But in 2004, he resigned. A year later, he joined the international law firm Mayer Brown. He remained a member of parliament in parallel, without clearly defining which of the two was his main activity: apparently, the possibility of a conflict of interest was not his primary concern. He announced in 2009 that he would withdraw from politics for a while. But he quickly found other occupations. The insurance company Axa and the Deutsche Börse knocked on his door, as did Stadler Rail, a Swiss manufacturer of railway equipment, and Wepa, a toilet paper producer: all wanted this familiar figure in political power to join their board of directors. At the same time, he chaired the supervisory board of Cologne-Bonn Airport. The list of his commitments is still long. Thanks to them, he became a millionaire, as he himself pointed out in an interview with the newspaper Bild am Sonntag: "Today, I earn about one million euros gross per year." Nevertheless, he considered himself part of the middle class. "When I hear about the 'upper class' or 'people at the top,' I think of those who have inherited a lot of money or a business and who only enjoy their lives. That's not my case." But it was Larry Fink who offered him his most controversial position: in 2016, Merz became chairman of the supervisory board of BlackRock's German branch. The New Yorkers left no doubt about their expectations: the CDU politician would have to assume a "broadly consultative role" for BlackRock in Germany, in which he would "encourage relationships with key clients, regulators and government agencies in Germany," the press release said at the time. In other words: Merz became BlackRock's first lobbyist in Germany. Now, Merkel's mandate is coming to an end. And Merz has quit his job at BlackRock to fight again for the chancellorship. But he seems to have internalized his New York boss's message long ago. Thus, one of his proposals was to force Germans to buy shares. In a publication for Zeit Online in the summer of 2019, he wrote that it would be important to involve employees more in the economic success of companies. In Germany, a "culture of saving in the form of shares" should emerge, "from which a share of the success of the market economy develops." And further: "I am now of the opinion that the legislator should seriously consider an obligation to subscribe to private, market-oriented capital benefits for old-age provision, in whatever form." In Manhattan, the prospect of seeing Merz as chancellor must have elicited a lot of anticipatory joy - he will steer Germany's savings book for them. However, New Yorkers have encountered resistance in France. Initially, everything seemed to be going well in that country too, with savvy decisions regarding the team. The French subsidiary is led by Jean-François Cirelli, former economic advisor to Jacques Chirac. Like Merz, he has worked as a lobbyist, among others for GDF-Suez and Engie. On January 1, 2020, French Prime Minister Emmanuel Macron, himself a former investment banker familiar with Wall Street, awarded him the rank of Knight of the National Order of the Legion of Honor. However, this event caught the attention of the opposition as it coincided with Macron's government planning to reform the pension system. Among other things, under this reform, high-income earners, with an annual income of over 120,000 euros, will be able to invest in private funds instead of contributing to public funds. Photos of a previous meeting between Fink and Macron at the Élysée Palace circulated. In a note to clients about the reform plans, a BlackRock analyst wrote about how disappointing the share of investments in stocks in the country was. (French households hold only

5% of their savings in company stocks.) This made headlines. Asked about it, BlackRock stated that Fink had met Macron on four occasions. The first time was in January 2016, in Davos... of course! At that time, Macron was still the Minister of Finance. Also present at the meeting were Mark Carney, former Goldman Sachs banker and then Governor of the Bank of England, and Tidjane Thiam, then CEO of Credit Suisse. The reunions took place at a meeting of international asset managers in October 2017, by which time Macron had become head of state. According to BlackRock, it was the President of the Republic who organized the meeting, where possible ways to attract investors to France were discussed. The next meeting was in July 2019, this time focusing on climate change. And finally, in January 2020, Macron invited Fink to the "Choose France" summit, attended by two hundred business leaders from different countries and sectors. BlackRock did not reveal whether Fink and Macron had met before, when the latter was still active as a banker.

A risk? What risk?

If you walk down 14th Street towards the East River in Manhattan, you will see huge brick towers looming ahead of you. Like a red fortress, the austere blocks stand out from the typical New York architecture all around. This is Stuyvesant Town, a 32-hectare residential complex comprising one hundred and ten buildings, named after Peter Stuyvesant, who established the former New Amsterdam in the 17th century as a center for trade (including slaves) at the southern tip of Manhattan and built a protective wall - now Wall Street. Together with its neighbor Peter Cooper Village, it forms the largest housing complex in the city.

And it became the stage for BlackRock's worst defeat in history. Nowhere else has the company made such a gross mistake. Exactly where Fink & Co. were considered particularly savvy: real estate financing.

Stuyvesant Town, or Stuy Town as New Yorkers call it, was built by the insurance company MetLife after World War II. At that time, as today, there was an urgent need for affordable housing in New York. Stuy Town - originally reserved for white tenants only - was intended to offer the middle class and civil servants, such as teachers, firefighters, and police officers, an alternative to urban exodus. The first residents were often war veterans. Peter Cooper Village, with its more luxurious units at the time, was intended for doctors, lawyers, and other professionals. MetLife was a good landlord, explains Susan Steinberg. When she moved into her apartment in Stuyvesant in 1980, she was thrilled. "I thought I was dead and now I was living in paradise." The concierges, permanent employees, quickly took care of repairs, and gardeners took care of the parks. Steinberg, longtime president of the Stuyvesant Cooper Tenants Association, had waited for her apartment for two years. The waiting time later increased to over twenty years, as the complex was very popular. From the living room window of Steinberg's apartment on the 11th floor, there is a view of the rooftops of New York and the Empire State Building. Although the skyscraper is only a few blocks away, it looks more like a distant backdrop. Twenty-five thousand people live in the city. "Life here was like in a small town, we had a community," explains Steinberg. She speaks in the past tense. Because the Stuyvesant she knew for thirty years no longer exists. According to her, the culprits are the investor BlackRock and its real estate partner.

During the real estate boom of the early 2000s, Stuy Town became coveted. MetLife decided to cash in on the real estate complex. The insurance giant sold Stuyvesant Town and Peter Cooper Village to the consortium formed by BlackRock and Tishman Speyer for $5.4 billion. It was an absolute record. In many ways, the deal marked the peak of the concrete gold rush of the early 2000s.

Many of BlackRock's good clients got on board, like CalPERS, the pension fund for California state government employees, which invested $500 million in the project. Sister fund CalSTRS, which manages the California teachers' pension fund, was also on board with $100 million. Singapore's sovereign fund invested $575 million. BlackRock's partner was Tishman Speyer, one of New York's big real estate dynasties. Rob Speyer and his father Jerry run the company, whose major commitments include the Rockefeller Center, the Chrysler Building, and the Messeturm in Frankfurt. Speyer Senior has good relations with Wall Street. After all, he served on the board of the New York Federal Reserve from 2001 to 2007.

Many tenants in the Stuyvesant complex had protection - their rent could not be raised. This allowed them to pay only a few hundred dollars for housing that would have cost them several thousand if it had been on the open market. According to tenant activist Steinberg, the plan was to increase the number of apartments that could be on the market as quickly as possible. But legal protection stood in their way. Tishman Speyer allegedly tried all sorts of legal maneuvers to get rid of tenants with rent protection, explains Steinberg. She shakes her head when it comes to the pension funds' involvement in the Stuy Town takeover. "Didn't they think that the consequences of such a deal would affect exactly the same kind of people as their members?" she asks. Ordinary workers, retirees, who depend on affordable housing. Did CalPERS and CalSTRS only consider the promised profit? In the new world of asset managers, such considerations have no place.

In the end, the investors' calculation did not work out. The tenants resisted, went to court. And won. In many cases, Tishman had to cancel rent increases. Added to this was the recession that followed the 2008 financial crisis. Rents in Manhattan fell. By 2010, it was clear that the largest real estate deal was at risk of becoming the largest real estate bankruptcy. Creditors pressured. Tishman and BlackRock decided to hand over Stuyvesant Town and Peter Cooper Village to them. The investors lost their stake. For CalPERS, it was $500 million. A bitter loss for the pension fund. Embarrassing for BlackRock: Californians, whose strategies are closely watched in the market, withdrew the mandate for the real estate portfolio from BlackRock.

Apart from the collapse of a well-established reputation, BlackRock came out with a relatively manageable loss of $112 million, the New York Times reported in January 2010. Tishman Speyer also lost $112 million. In the fall of 2015, Stuy Town was resold. To an old acquaintance: Blackstone. With its partner Ivanhoé Cambridge, the queen of private equity firms won the bid for $5.3 billion. And they struck a deal with the city: starting in July 2020, they will be able to start raising rents for 6,200 apartments. This should spell the end of the affordable oasis in Manhattan's real estate market. Stuy Town is now marketed as "luxury housing."

For Fink, Stuy Town is a sore spot. Everyone makes mistakes, Fink barked at journalists from Vanity Fair who dared to ask about the costly - at least, for clients - catastrophe. It gave him sleepless nights, the multimillionaire claimed. In the end, he concluded, his mother receives her pension from CalPERS.

Stuy Town is not the only embarrassing misjudgment for BlackRock. In June 2008, Bloomberg reported that BlackRock had bought shares in Lehman Brothers. "We have confidence in the bank and the management team," BlackRock President Robert Kapito commented at the time. Lehman's management reportedly had a reputation for being a real team, focused, with crisis management experience, and market confidence. Words that Kapito probably regretted, even more than the financial commitment itself, after just a few weeks. Because barely three months later, Richard Fuld's management team, whom he had praised, appeared before the bankruptcy judge. In June, when Kapito gave an interview to Bloomberg, Lehman was already going through strong turbulence. Lehman's shares had fallen by about 60% in the first six months - market players clearly lacked confidence in Lehman. In order to save himself, Fuld had already thrown his right-hand man, Joseph Gregory, and his CFO, Erin Callan, "under the bus," as they say on Wall Street. He blamed them for the crisis and then fired them.

As Fink rightly says, everyone makes mistakes. Nevertheless, the Stuy Town debacle and the Lehman error are important moments in BlackRock's trajectory, as they show that even BlackRock cannot escape the prevailing mentality and culture, despite the emphasis on "paranoid risk awareness" and the deliberate distancing from Wall Street, communicated.

The biggest bank robbery of all time

In November 2018, the newspaper Bild revealed a spectacular piece of news: BlackRock's offices in Munich had been raided by the police! According to the newspaper, this was linked to the CumEx scandal.

CumEx is probably the most lucrative bank robbery of all time. Except in this case, the thieves are bankers and the victims are taxpayers, notably in Germany, but also in France, Italy, and at least eight other European countries. According to estimates, the damage caused by this largest tax fraud in history amounts to 60 billion euros. Hundreds of bankers, traders, lawyers, and investors have been involved.

Bankers and traders set up a system of "dividend arbitrage": they moved packages of shares with (cum) and without (ex) dividends in an opaque and ingenious manner to create the impression that they had paid too much tax on dividends. Then, the same bankers and traders claimed reimbursement from the tax authorities for these supposedly paid taxes. In some cases, they didn't limit themselves to doing this only once but repeated the trick. At the same time, lawyers drafted sophisticated reports to prove that the procedure against the Treasury was entirely legal. A kind of carte blanche to protect themselves from any eventuality. Despite the efforts of the German legislator to counter these maneuvers, the CumEx machinery systematically invented new loopholes, consistently slipping through the net.

It is not known who carried out the first operations of this kind. However, it is certain that two bankers from the London branch of Merrill Lynch were among the first to strip dividends. Martin S., a mathematician who studied at Oxford, and Paul M. joined HypoVereinsbank before launching their own business thanks to their tax trick. S. was sentenced to 22 months in prison for tax evasion in March 2020, but the sentence was suspended due to his cooperation with the investigators. His colleague Paul M., of New Zealand origin, who, according to the media, liked to wear Hawaiian shirts, fled to his native country. Responding from there to journalists' questions, he denied any illegal enrichment and any preference for brightly colored clothing. Nevertheless, this unlikely couple had worked with Hanno Berger, a respected German tax lawyer, who is considered the mastermind of the affair. That is, until one of his former employees spilled the beans. In an interview with Zeit, the witness recounted that the people involved in this scandal shared a hatred of the state. He himself, coming from the provinces, admired the cosmopolitan spirit of his boss. Hanno Berger, the son of a pastor, shone with his humanistic education, his knowledge of Latin and Greek. They worked together on the 32nd floor of the Skyper, a skyscraper in the banking district of Frankfurt. "When we looked down at the street, we saw only very small people," said the man, who also testified in court. "That was the world, the normal world, from which we no longer belonged. We were at the top. Looking out the window, we thought, 'We are the smartest, true geniuses, and you are all stupid.'" Berger, one could say, went from being a saint to a sinner: at the beginning of his career, he worked for the state as a tax auditor at the regional Finance Directorate of Hesse, where he ensured that financial institutions paid what they owed to the Treasury. Following a raid on his law firm in 2012, Berger left the country for Switzerland. He considers himself a victim of a judicial scandal. In December 2019, the Wiesbaden court accepted the indictment against Berger. "Mr. Berger will face trial in Germany," his lawyer Gerson Trüg told the economic daily Handelsblatt. He also rejected the allegations of the Attorney General's Office as inaccurate. In May 2020, this case, like many other CumEx cases, is still in the hands of the German justice system. Among the stakeholders are German financial groups such as Deutsche Bank and Commerzbank, branches of American investment banks, but also the very traditional private bank M.M. Warburg & Co. In March 2020, the Regional Court of Bonn sentenced the Hanseatic institution to pay 179 million euros. Warburg has since appealed.

BlackRock's Role in the CumEx Scandal

Immediately after the November 2018 raid, a BlackRock spokesperson told the Deutsche Presse-Agentur news agency: "BlackRock is unconditionally cooperating with the authorities investigating the 'CumEx' transactions that took place between 2007 and 2011." It was only in 2016 that Friedrich Merz joined the asset manager as the senior supervisor for activities in Germany, meaning after the period of interest to investigators. Nevertheless, at the time of the raid, Merz was the chairman of the supervisory board and promised a "thorough investigation." However, this investigation has not taken place, at least not yet.

Therefore, at the moment, one can only speculate. Securities lending plays a key role in the scandal: it is the only way to actually make money with dividend arbitrage. The stocks used to justify the tax refund claims of the CumEx fraudsters were typically not part of their portfolios; they were borrowed. Otherwise, capital would have been needed to purchase them. However, making CumEx profitable required a lot of capital.

Securities lending is another obscure area of Wall Street. Large investors such as insurance companies, pension funds, and asset managers typically hold onto their stocks for the long term. However, this does not prevent them from wanting to make their securities portfolios profitable in other ways. For example, hedge funds and other speculators can borrow securities for a fee. These are often shorts, meaning short sales. As soon as the short seller obtains the desired stocks, they sell them immediately. They then wait for the stock price to drop to repurchase the stocks. The profit they make from the transaction is the difference, minus the lending fees. The lender, on the other hand, also benefits significantly. This additional income is particularly attractive for index funds, which are required to keep their fees low due to competition and therefore have razor-thin margins. For example, BlackRock earned approximately $170 million in the last three months of 2019 through this method. This is despite the decision made a few years ago to limit the portion of stocks that could be borrowed to 50% of the portfolio for one of its funds. "Out of consideration for the clients," as a BlackRock insider euphemistically put it. These clients likely pressured the company because securities lending is not without risks. The solvency of financial institutions acting as intermediaries in securities lending, in particular, is not guaranteed. If banks were to go bankrupt, the stocks could be dragged down with them. The 2008 financial crisis showed that this was not a purely theoretical possibility.

Did BlackRock lend the stocks needed by the CumEx fraudsters? What did New Yorkers know about these transactions? There are currently no answers to these questions.

In response to the question of whether its employees were involved or at least aware of the CumEx transactions, BlackRock responded: "As part of a comprehensive investigation involving many market participants, the German tax authorities and local prosecutors are examining the tax treatment of dividends paid on stocks held by investors between 2007 and 2011. Representatives of the German authorities visited BlackRock's offices in Munich on Tuesday, November 6, 2018, requesting access to physical as well as digital documents. BlackRock cooperated with the investigators and will continue to do so."

It is clear that this investigation does not fit well with the image of integrity and probity that Fink & Co. strive to present. Listening to interviews with Fink, one might get the impression that despite its enormous firepower, his company presents practically less risk to the financial system than the savings accounts of a local bank. BlackRock is merely a mediator of the investor's will, insists its CEO. "It's not my money," he repeats again and again when the question of systemic risk arises in interviews. And he is right: losses from investment products are borne by the investor in question, not by BlackRock as the administrator. Unlike banks, asset managers do not risk their own capital or state-guaranteed savings. And asset managers also do not use leverage from loans. Unlike Lehman and other banks that, before the financial crisis, borrowed up to $50 for every dollar they held.

But that does not mean that the money lords present no risk to the community. The dangers are simply different from those brought by banks.

In the spring of 2014, the London Business School invited Andrew Haldane for a conference. The theme was money management. At the time, Haldane was responsible for financial stability at the Bank of England, the central bank of the United Kingdom. What he had to say to the conference participants made fund operators and supervisors around the world sit up and take notice. "We live in the age of asset managers," Haldane declared. There are more and more potential savers in the world - and therefore potential clients for the sector. Since 1950, life expectancy has increased by nearly 50%, the world's population has tripled, and per capita gross domestic product has multiplied by about forty. Wealth has also increased significantly since the post-war period. Today, the total wealth collected by managers is estimated at nearly $74 trillion. By 2025, PwC, the new name for PricewaterhouseCoopers, predicts that asset managers will have $145 trillion in their funds. If previous trends are taken as a basis, then the industry could manage the sum of $400 trillion by 2050. That's a hundred times the German gross domestic product!

According to Haldane, size in itself represents a danger. A battered asset manager might have to sell bonds, stocks, and commodities quickly in order to be able to return investors' money. A "fire sale" could then ignite. And here's what the fiery scenario could look like: the sale of a struggling industry giant causes prices to collapse in the market. This then triggers a cascade of sales by other market players and leads more and more investors to also demand their capital, which in turn leads to further sales - and, in the worst case, to a collapse of the entire market. A study by the Chicago Booth School of Business wondered whether non-banks could trigger a crash even if they did not use credit leverage. The authors' answer: yes. Fund managers vie for client favor and therefore always want to outperform their competitors. No one wants to be the last one out of a losing position and sell. In the worst case, this can trigger a self-feeding selling wave that becomes uncontrollable. Conversely, there is a risk that all funds rush in the same direction, in the perpetual quest for maximum profit. In its 2013 report, the Office of

Financial Research warned that asset managers could succumb to a herd instinct, pushing them all in the same direction, which can trigger bubbles and other vulnerabilities. Competitive pressure could lead investment managers to take higher risks.

Since the first edition of this book, warnings have multiplied. In July 2019, the Bank of England stated in its financial stability report that the gap between investors' short-term payment demands and the lack of liquidity in a fund's assets could "potentially become a systemic problem." In a November 2019 report, ECB risk assessors wrote: "Abrupt adjustments in the prices of financial assets as well as increasing credit and liquidity risks in certain parts of the non-bank sector in the euro area - with greater leverage in investment funds - could lead non-bank actors to react in a way that causes tensions in the financial system at large." The IMF's Global Financial Stability Report, published in October 2019, also addresses asset managers. It is noted that an environment of persistently low interest rates particularly contributes to risk creation, as investors invest in increasingly risky and less liquid assets to achieve their return goals. "This higher risk-taking could lead to increased vulnerability." This low interest rate environment could also lead to portfolio alignment, which could also increase the risk of market collapse.

The terrain of fund managers and shadow banks is difficult for regulators to navigate: the sector has grown and evolved so rapidly that many threats are simply unknown. "There is still not enough data to make macroeconomic assessments with a high degree of certainty," admitted Peter Breuer, one of the authors of the IMF report. "There is still a lot of uncertainty about underlying vulnerabilities."

This obviously does not mean that there is no risk. "Black swan adventures could be a real and growing threat," Haldane also warned. Black swans: this is what Nassim Nicholas Taleb, a former derivatives trader and professor at New York University, calls his theory of unforeseen events with massive consequences, such as the terrorist attacks of September 11, 2001, the invention of the internet, or the collapse of the US real estate market before the 2007 crisis. Events that exceed our way of thinking, like the discovery of black swans in Western Australia in the 17th century, which literally refuted

Europeans' preconceived notion that swans are generally white. Fortunately, this event had no serious consequences, except for the swans that were captured and locked up in zoos in the Old World. Even experts cannot - yet - exactly envision the risks potentially brought by a money colossus like BlackRock. One thing is certain: if there are pile-ups among asset managers, it will not be as harmless as the discovery of a new species of water birds.

Fink & Co. have not remained blind to regulators' concerns. One reason why the BlackRock giant prefers to stay under the radar is the fear that it will suffer the same fate as the big banks following the financial crisis: they were trapped by thousands of new regulations, like Gulliver, whom the Lilliputians tied down with ropes to the ground. In recent years, BlackRock has increasingly feared that the "Let's stay well hidden" strategy and the constantly repeated mantra "We're just a big savings group" are no longer enough. It was therefore time to tackle the problem in Washington - and Fink already had someone to take on this delicate mission: Barbara Novick.

How BlackRock's Supermom Conquered Washington

The security check, including the scanner at the entrance, enhances the feeling of entering the Holy of Holies. On this windy and rainy winter evening, about a hundred guests gather at the German House, the official representation of the Federal Republic of Germany in New York. The German Center for Research and Innovation and Women in Sovereign Entities, an association aiming to promote women in government bodies, are behind the invitation. But the event has little to do with women or German research. According to the title, it's about "the impact of innovation on the effectiveness of central banks." It quickly becomes clear that insiders are addressing insiders here. The audience includes representatives from central banks of Indonesia, Thailand, and Austria, as well as financial authorities from Singapore and Hong Kong. There's also an emissary from the United Nations pension fund and another from the People's Bank of China. In other words: VIP clients of BlackRock. And on stage sits Mervyn King, governor of the Bank of England for ten years, along with Christine Cumming, vice president of the Federal Reserve Bank of New York. A slender woman in her fifties sits next to the two central bankers. With her discreet glasses and long black hair neatly parted on either side, she could be mistaken for a teacher - of biology or sports, for example. A teacher among the strictest, in any case. This is Barbara Novick, a founding member of BlackRock. She was already part of the Fink and Kapito clique at First Boston. Online business journal Business Insider counts this mother of three among the "most powerful moms in the world." As a member of BlackRock's global executive committee, she is part of top management. She was long responsible for business development and client relations. She knows the company at least as well as Fink. In 2010, Novick took on a new role: government relations. In plain terms: she is BlackRock's chief lobbyist. Her mission: to protect BlackRock from increasingly intrusive regulators. At this event, her voice is surprisingly low (the microphone isn't working) and she speaks very fast. But during the panel discussion, she quickly gets to her main message. "We see that in the speeches of regulators and experts around the world, the term shadow banking is increasingly being replaced by market financing," she says with satisfaction. It's interesting: BlackRock apparently systematically scans speeches by supervisors and central bankers worldwide, looking for the term. What may seem like the height of language subtlety has a much deeper meaning. Because formulations and designations are very important on Wall Street. The sector has become a champion in this regard. This is how Milken's work, toxic corporate bonds, whose solvency isn't great, are called junk bonds - with refreshing honesty. However, bankers attach great importance to talking about high-yield bonds, rather than junk bonds, when it comes to investors. Corporate raiders have become beautiful "private equity" firms, which sounds more like an exclusive club than corporate raiders. "One consequence of the financial crisis was that Wall Street lost its diplomatic power. They stuttered, mumbled when they had to explain how the disaster happened," criticized the Financial Times. But with the resurgence of Anglo-Saxon financial capitalism, diplomatic power has returned. Now, shadow finance, a term that even laypeople associate with something dubious, becomes meaningless "market financing." It seems quite harmless - and it's supposed to be.

Novick has the tenacity of a good teacher. During the question time after the panel discussion that evening, she immediately corrects. "The term shadow finance has a negative connotation." Shadow suggests a threat. The goal is to finance projects useful to society, such as infrastructure measures. When asked about possible conflicts of interest among asset managers regarding the need for new rules for shadow finance, Novick gets upset. She doesn't know what they're talking about. "We are fiduciarily committed to our clients, that's BlackRock's priority," she says before turning away without greeting us and disappearing into the stairwell. Upstairs, where champagne is being served, small talk among her peers will undoubtedly be more pleasant. For BlackRock's top diplomat, it's an unexpectedly emotional moment on stage. It's also possible that questions from her interlocutors in Washington and Brussels are posed more delicately.

BlackRock was very cautious in Washington until the financial crisis. Essentially, the company relied on representation by industry associations of which BlackRock was a member. In 2008, for example, there was no entry for BlackRock at OpenSecrets, the Washington website that tracks lobbying activities of companies and associations. In 2009, OpenSecrets recorded only $545,000 in fees for two lobbying firms - an amount that doesn't even register as a rounding error in the giant's analytical accounting. This is when BlackRock appeared as an ally of the Treasury and the Federal Reserve. And then there's also the trusted relationship with Treasury Secretary Geithner. Why spend money on something that BlackRock gets virtually for free and at home?

However, shortly afterward, New Yorkers took their activities in the capital more seriously. It's now time for financial reform. After completely forgetting (or ignoring) the danger in the banking system, lawmakers and regulators were suddenly more sensitive to potential risks. And the size of BlackRock, Fidelity, and others suddenly makes them uncomfortable. The Financial Stability Oversight Council, an agency within the US Treasury Department that oversees monitoring, begins to openly consider whether large asset managers should be classified as SIFIs - Systemically Important Financial Institutions.

This would imply special requirements and monitoring - which Fink & Co. categorically reject. It is time to intervene in Washington: for 2011, OpenSecrets suddenly recorded over 2.5 million dollars in lobbying expenses for BlackRock20. The seriousness with which Fink takes the threat is demonstrated by the fact that he does not hire former members of Congress or former ministerial lobbyists - like most of his competitors - but rather sends his co-founder Novick to the capital.

There, BlackRock's diplomat visits several times, among others, Debbie Matz, the president of the National Credit Union Administration, an association that even political junkies in the American capital have rarely heard of. Officially, the NCUA, whose headquarters are not even directly in DC but in a suburb of the capital, is responsible for representing the interests of local savings associations. But Matz has another function. She is part of the Financial Stability Oversight Council - yes: the body that must decide whether BlackRock would receive the SIFI warning label in the future. The FSOC makes decisions with a two-thirds majority: Novick must convince at least four members for BlackRock not to be classified as a danger. Her visits to Matz have helped clarify the situation, according to Bloomberg citing Novick. Many supervisors have little experience with asset managers. To secure the necessary votes at the FSOC, BlackRock even allies with Allianz, the parent company of arch-rival PIMCO.

But BlackRock has gained a much more valuable ally among the members of the FSOC. Mary Jo White. If one wants to imagine Mary Jo White, one can think of Yoda, the wrinkled master with the appearance of a gnome from the Jedi Knights saga Star Wars. Like Master Yoda, it would be a mistake to underestimate White. She is one of the lawyers whom other lawyers always speak of with a hint of respect and her opponents with a hint of fear. Mary Jo White has crossed the revolving door - when one moves from public service to private in the United States - so often that simply reading her resume can cause slight dizziness. A young lawyer in the 1970s, she was already working for Debevoise & Plimpton. The famous New York-based law firm is reputed to be "the weapon of the bosses." For a long time, Debevoise & Plimpton remained primarily a point of contact between companies and US authorities. The client list reads like the Who's Who of major American companies: American Airlines, CNN, Coca-Cola, ExxonMobil, General Electric, clothing chain Gap, insurer Metlife, investment bank Goldman Sachs, Universal Music, or online portal Yahoo, the New York Times, and the world's largest toy manufacturer Hasbro. Internationally as well, troubled supervisory boards are happy to be able to contact the lawyers of this honorable firm, which has offices in Paris, Moscow, Hong Kong, Shanghai, and Frankfurt. Among its clients were Russian airline Aeroflot, French insurer Axa, DaimlerChrysler, Swiss pharmaceutical manufacturer Novartis, and Japanese entertainment giant Sony. After her first hiring at Debevoise & Plimpton, White joined the prosecutor's office. In the 1980s, she worked again for her former law firm. Then she was again chief federal prosecutor in New York for nine years, with Wall Street also part of her field of expertise. In two hundred years of judicial authority history, she was the first woman to hold this position. She investigated, among other things, the terrorists of the first attack on the World Trade Center, the mafia, and its attempts to expand its influence and activities on the stock exchange. In 2002, White changed sides again and became head of litigation at Debevoise & Plimpton. The Siemens case also fell within her area of expertise - internal investigations and defense of companies against accusations from government agencies or US stock market regulators. The Munich-based group mandated the law firm for an internal investigation into its corruption case. The purpose of such investigations, according to the harsh judgment of detractors, would ultimately only be to issue a certificate whitewashing the company. In 2013, President Obama finally appointed White head of the US securities authority. Supporters of the revolving door see an advantage in that representatives of the authorities are familiar with the other side. And that's the problem, say critics of the system.

In any case, White was on the side of the asset managers in the discussion about the warning label that was to be attached to them. She even repeated their arguments publicly. White undertook a "reverence tour" among fund managers to assure them of her sympathy, mocked even the New York Times. But something else was happening behind the scenes: a territorial war had broken out between the SEC and the Fed. If asset managers were classified as SIFI, former Fed chair Janet Yellen would be primarily responsible for oversight. White wanted to prevent this. She had taken over the SEC in a sorry state. The once feared watchdog of Wall Street had become a mere lapdog. Not only had the SEC supervisors completely ignored toxic mortgages, but they had only caught billionaire fraudster Bernie Madoff once his Ponzi scheme had collapsed on its own. In no way did White want to lose even more influence. When the FSOC, in a 2013 study, concluded that fund giants could actually pose a threat, White published the document without consulting her FSOC colleagues. When Lew, Treasury Secretary in the Obama administration, also a committee member, complained that she was going it alone, White reportedly apologized. At least that's what Washington insiders told Bloomberg News. But White's disclosure gave fund managers the opportunity to provide their lobbyists and position them.

Novick also began to act, insiders report. With representatives from Fidelity and PIMCO, she turned to members of the House of Representatives. Mostly Republicans at the time, the lawmakers were notoriously opposed to any state regulation.

And Novick & Co. achieved their goal: at a hearing before Congress, the FSOC representative responsible for the study had to hear some angry representatives, notably about the fact that the investigation had shown a lack of understanding of the sector. This discontent had consequences. After Congress expressed criticism and reluctance, the FSOC postponed the question of the SIFI classification. In the summer of 2014, the committee then announced that the focus of this classification would be changed - in the future, it would concern individual financial products, not entire companies. The question of an SIFI label for BlackRock or Fidelity was thus initially set aside.

In September 2019, the BlackRock Transparency Project, a Washington watchdog that had the giant in its sights, published a report on how BlackRock had managed to massively fend off regulators' efforts. It spoke of a "coordinated strategy of lobbying, campaign donations, and revolving doors." BlackRock has more investor capital than the entire hedge fund sector and yet the company has managed to escape the "too big to fail" warning, according to Daniel Stevens, the project's director.

In February 2020, Novick officially resigned from her high-flying lobbyist position for BlackRock. "Her farewell marks the end of a chess game for BlackRock, at the end of which the company managed not to be classified as a large bank by regulators," concludes the Wall Street Journal. Hats off, Novick!

Donald Trump's presidency did not hinder the success of BlackRock's revolving door strategy, even though it is true that Fink already saw himself in Washington as Treasury Secretary for Hillary Clinton after her election victory. When Trump, against all expectations, won the elections and became the new occupant of the White House, Fink showed flexibility. The BlackRock boss became a member of an advisory board, composed of eminent personalities from finance and industry, convened by the president21. BlackRock CEO Craig Phillips was also a supporter of Clinton. He then made a donation of $100,000 for Trump's inauguration party and became an advisor to Steve Mnuchin, a former Goldman Sachs banker and Hollywood producer whom Trump had chosen as Treasury Secretary. As such, Phillips dealt mainly with real estate financing. He had to develop a reform project for the two semi-public giants of mortgage credit, Fannie Mae and Freddy Mac, both clients of BlackRock and well known to Fink since the beginning of his career.

These ominous and discreet lords of the world

January 2009. The owner of the newsstand next to the New York Stock Exchange, more accustomed to being asked for the Wall Street Journal or the Financial Times, is surprised: "Today, everyone wants the Rolling Stones magazine, what's in it?" Bankers and traders had not suddenly developed a keen interest in rapper Snoop Dogg or the latest songs by Bob Dylan. In the magazine had appeared an article, or rather, a controversial subject, by journalist Matt Taibbi, describing investment bank Goldman Sachs as a "vampire squid [that] has wrapped itself around the face of humanity and stuck its blood funnel tentacles into anything that smells like money." Wow: that made waves. Since then, Goldman has never really shaken off its vampire reputation22. What would be the zoological equivalent of BlackRock? How about the giant squid with its ten tentacles? For a long time, sailors' stories about "deep sea monsters" were not taken seriously. For example, the story told by survivors of the British troop transport ship Britannia, sunk by the Germans during World War II. They clung to a life raft when one of them was caught by a giant squid and disappeared into the depths, the shipwrecked later reported. Clues then accumulated, proving that it was not a mythical creature but a real animal. Scar-like marks in the shape of suction cup prints were discovered on the skin of sperm whales. Big suction cups. Sharks are also likely prey for the mollusk. Then one began to find meter-long tentacles washed up on beaches. Until finally dead specimens of giant cephalopods were found. But to this day, no one knows the true size of these abyssal creatures. Estimates go up to twelve meters long, tentacles stretched. Their way of life is poorly understood.

BlackRock's financial tentacles are spread almost everywhere today. New Yorkers hold shares in companies from almost every sector, on every continent. They are also creditors of thousands of companies. Fink & Co. are the owners and clients of the largest banks in the world. They act as ghost banks, hedge funds, and big data vacuums. BlackRock representatives whisper in the ears of central bankers and authorities, those who pull the strings in Washington and Brussels, Berlin, and Paris.

The portfolio manager now enjoys influence in almost every area of our lives: jobs, housing, roads, bridges, education, health. Fifteen years ago, anyone who would have described such a giant squid of money would have been met with as much incredulity as the survivors of the Britannia. Such a monster in the financial system would have exceeded imagination.

In the era of mega-fund managers, BlackRock's influence will only increase. China and other emerging countries are aligning with the Anglo-Saxon financial system. If Fink and his successors handle it skillfully, more trillions will flow into their coffers. But, as with its animal counterpart, our understanding of its actions and the risks posed by the rise of the giant squid of the financial market is at best incomplete. This is not only true for citizens and politicians. Academics and regulators must also admit that there are still areas of darkness. While the behavior and collapse of banks have been studied for centuries, a similar analysis of the fund management sector is only just beginning, concludes Andrew Haldane, the Bank of England's expert on financial markets, in his April 2014 warning. The sector is a "green field to be carefully cultivated" to avoid pitfalls, just like banks.

When the giant squid meets the black swan

When the first reports from Wuhan, China reached the Western public in December 2019, it was initially thought that the epidemic would cause a problem in supply chains for industrialized countries, for example, for the automotive industry. This misjudgment would prove to be catastrophic.

Rarely has Wall Street staggered as it did in March 2020. Finally awakened, investors, traders, and bankers realized the true threat posed by the virus. The traders' screens turned bright red - the color of losses. The S&P 500, the stock index comprising the largest and most important American companies, lost over 4 trillion dollars in the following days. For comparison: this figure corresponds to the gross domestic product of Germany. And it was not only stocks that collapsed. Commodities such as copper, aluminum, and zinc also plummeted. The price of oil dropped to the point where its price became negative - a surreal mechanism that had never happened before. Even gold, usually considered a safe haven, was not spared. It was called a "pandemic panic." Stock market fluctuations resembled roller coasters. Suddenly, prices plummeted as violently as they did in the 1930s; then the Dow Jones, the index of heavyweights of the American economy, had its best week in decades. These huge fluctuations - and the destruction of capital they caused - frightened even the hardened veterans of Wall Street. Over the past hundred years, daily fluctuations have averaged around 1% compared to the previous day. Suddenly, spikes of 3% or even 5% became almost the rule. Wall Street's fear gauge, the VIX (Volatility Index), measures the volatility of the American financial market using the prices of call and put options. In recent years, it fluctuated between values of 12 to 20. On March 16, when the Covid-19 panic gripped market participants, it reached 82.

Covid-19 mutated into Taleb's "black swan." ETFs were particularly affected by the ups and downs. During the first week of March, when panic set in, ETF transactions accounted for about 40% of total daily transactions, much more than at the same time the previous year, according to an analysis of stock market data by the Wall Street Journal. Market participants hoped that ETFs would provide enough liquidity and also the possibility to diversify investments across sectors or entire markets via index funds. At first glance, ETFs seemed to defy skeptics and withstand the greatest crisis in decades.

However, upon closer inspection, there are worrying shadows that appear on this tableau. There were episodes, already mentioned, where fund prices deviated radically from those of the values they were supposed to reflect, showing that arbitrators were no longer performing their task of reducing these gaps in times of stress. In response, investors withdrew their money from certain funds. A massive withdrawal of funds invested in ETFs would have triggered new waves of sales. Exactly the scenario that experts from the IMF, ECB, and Bank of England had warned against in 2019.

No one knows if the situation would have worsened if Jay Powell and his central bankers had not injected trillions to calm the markets.

Not only did the collapse not occur, but financial markets, on the contrary, recovered. Their recovery was so strong that insiders even worried about it. The flood of bad news did not stop, with millions more Americans signing up for unemployment every week. "Has the market said goodbye to reality?" worried commentators on the CNBC channel, who are more accustomed to cheering any upward movement as enthusiastically as cheerleaders for their team's touchdown.

BlackRock, for its part, is very satisfied. "The true story of ETFs during fluctuations is about resilience and performance," according to a statement from the company regarding the panic related to the Covid-19 crisis. In BlackRock's version, events take on an almost heroic legendary air. Despite historic turbulence, four trading interruptions, and other unknown dangers of all kinds, ETFs and iShares have functioned effectively! Thanks to a stroke of genius from BlackRock's press service, what worries regulators and market participants, namely the very large liquidity difference between ETFs and underlying assets, becomes an unbeatable asset. BlackRock's flamboyant rhetoric managed to show how HYG stocks, the largest junk bond ETF, traded faster than the underlying securities, i.e., the original bonds. For example, during the acute phase of the crisis, HYG securities traded 168,000 times a day, while the top five bonds in HYG traded only 25 times a day. This had already been Mark Wiedman's reasoning, the prince of iShares. It's a topsy-turvy world.

By deciding to buy ETF shares for the first time in a rescue operation, the Fed is only recognizing the paramount importance of these instruments. The near-catastrophe makes it clear what BlackRock and other fund giants vehemently deny: their systemic importance. "This crisis not only shows that ETFs are widely used as a trading tool and represent a significant reserve of investor assets, but also that the State perceives them as fundamentally interconnected with corporate finance." This was written in early April 2020 by Ryan Clements in an article for the Duke Law Global Financial Markets Center's FinReg blog, which analyzes systemic risks and their regulation. This is why it was considered that ETFs were important enough to be saved with public funds. For Clements, who is now a lecturer at the University of Calgary, it would be wise to reassess the systemic importance of major ETF providers. Because they are at the heart of the financial system, "interconnected by a complex operational structure that creates countless contractual, institutional, and mutual dependencies." In other words, it would be worth scrutinizing the giant squid a little more closely.

The rescue operation undertaken by central bankers to deal with the crisis was so gigantic that the particular measures barely stand out in this flood of money. Their significance is likely to go unnoticed, both because of the complexity of the subject and the lack of clarity of the Fed's programs. However, one of its decisions is remarkable: on March 18, 2020, a Wednesday, the Fed announced that it would lend billions to financial institutions as part of a new program, so that they could buy shares of money market funds. In plain language: the Fed saved money market funds with public credit. In a pandemic panic, investors began to withdraw their deposits, endangering these funds. To borrow the words of baseball legend Yogi Berra, who was almost more famous for his quirky sayings than for his performances on the field: it was "deja vu all over again23." As previously seen, money market funds had already been at the heart of the 2008 crisis.

In September of that year, after the collapse of Lehman Brothers (also a Wednesday), then-Fed Chairman Ben Bernanke had already announced a bailout with billions for money market funds. Despite new rules, ten years later it was still necessary to rescue these same financial products, which the industry often praises as an alternative to savings accounts. And who are the largest money market fund providers, in 2008 as today? Vanguard, Fidelity, and - drumroll, please - BlackRock.

Central bankers - and therefore all of us - once again saved Wall Street. But no, that's too modest. We rewarded it!

Poor Mexico, so far from God and so close to the United States

When it comes to bonds and ETFs, possible dangers can be identified. But what about the many new varieties of ghost banks that are diversifying within the new digital financial system? Will we recognize the origin of the danger too late, as we did with mortgage-backed securities and money market funds?

And what about the characteristic ownership role of the mega-fund manager? How does "capitalism without capitalists" fit into our current world, where we increasingly demand that our companies focus on sustainable development and social responsibility? This is not just a question for academics. For Kofi Thompson, for example, it's very real. The Ghanaian journalist is concerned about the future of his country. There, large mining companies ruthlessly exploit gold and oil following what he calls a "all-gratis-for-us" model. They plunder natural reserves for gold. At the same time, there is a lack of resources to build the necessary infrastructure in this African country. Frustrated that the repeated requests from African leaders for fairer deals with companies have always fallen on deaf ears, Thompson had an idea: what if the country's leaders turned to Michelle Edkins, the corporate governance lady at BlackRock? "If multinational corporations can ignore the demands of our heads of state, they will not dare to ignore the wishes of BlackRock," he writes in his column for the Ghanaweb site. BlackRock could help countries like Ghana by ensuring that the largest shareholder in mining companies insists that they pay taxes on the profits they make from Ghana's natural resources—instead of using tax tricks to rake money out of the country. "Ghana needs this money to improve the quality of life for its people," Thompson writes in an email. "Michelle Edkins could do a lot for developing countries by insisting that the same ethical standards be upheld worldwide." The fact that Thompson sees BlackRock as more influential than the government or international organizations speaks volumes.

However, the actions of BlackRock in different countries cast doubt on whether the giant black entity is exerting a positive influence on rulers. The BlackRock Transparency Project, on the other hand, accuses the asset manager of a "new entrepreneurial colonialism." Washington activists explained what they mean by this concept in a 2018 study on Mexico. "Pobre México, tan lejos de Dios y tan cerca de los Estados Unidos," Porfirio Díaz, who was president of the country for over thirty years until 1911, is said to have sighed. Poor Mexico, so far from God and so close to the United States. Larry Fink has a very different view of the relationship with the southern neighbor: "I love Mexico, Mexico embodies an incredible growth opportunity," he enthused in 2013 on the "Money Honey" show hosted by journalist Maria Bartiromo. And he went on to list everything he liked about the country: energy—not referring to the Mexican temperament, but to oil and gas reserves—cheap labor, a convenient location close to the United States. According to the BlackRock boss, Mexico is "a great place." Transparency International, on the other hand, which ranks countries according to corruption and abuse of power, counts the country, firmly held by drug cartels, among the most corrupt nations in the world. According to a study by the U.S. Congress, 150,000 people were killed by drug gangs between 2006 and 2019. Mexican drug lords reportedly bring in between 19 and 29 billion dollars a year to the United States.

While Fink likes to talk about responsible capitalism, his company has close ties to Mexico's ruling elite. For example, Marco Antonio Slim Domit, the son of Carlos Slim, Mexico's richest man, has been on the board of BlackRock since 2011. Slim senior, the son of Lebanese immigrants, made his fortune in the early 1990s by acquiring a dominant position in the telecommunications market following its privatization. Currently, Mexicans pay more for telecommunications services than in comparable countries. According to a 2012 study by the Organization for Economic Cooperation and Development (OECD), these higher rates cost the country about $129 billion, or 2% of GDP, just for the period 2005-2009.

Fink was quite close to Enrique Peña Nieto, the former president of Mexico. They met for talks, and Fink praised Peña Nieto's economic policy. Even during his term, there were serious allegations of corruption against the president and his government. At his trial in New York, Joaquín Guzmán Loera, better known as El Chapo - the dwarf - claimed to have given Peña Nieto 100 million dollars through an intermediary. El Chapo was the feared leader of the even more feared Sinaloa cartel. The criminal organization is said to have smuggled about 200 tons of cocaine and heroin into the United States between 1990 and 2008, according to U.S. prosecutors, who sought his extradition. El Chapo's arrest by Mexican security forces in 2014 is considered Peña Nieto's greatest success. But the little man managed to escape from prison in July 2015. His escape, spectacular, took place on a motorcycle through a lit tunnel that his henchmen had dug to his cell. Six months later, he was rearrested, sentenced to life imprisonment in the United States, where he is serving his sentence in a high-security prison. Peña Nieto denied the drug lord's accusation. In the spring of 2020, the Mexican judiciary announced a preliminary investigation against the former president. In a statement about its activities in Mexico, BlackRock referred to them - as for other countries - as long-term commitments, which also required maintaining relationships with local governments. "As a trustee of its clients and spokesman for investors," BlackRock would conduct a constructive dialogue with governments around the world, regardless of their political stripe.

In 2013, BlackRock brought in Gerardo Rodriguez Regordosa, a former undersecretary of Finance and Public Credit. The revolving door, the famous revolving door that BlackRock likes to spin, worked in Mexico too. In 2016, Isaac Volin, managing director of BlackRock Mexico, became CEO of PMI Comercio Internacional, the international marketing company of the national oil company Petróleos Mexicanos. The group, commonly known as Pemex, whose white and green logo features a stylized eagle's head representing Mexico's heraldic animal, has long been a source of pride for Mexicans. The group was created on March 18, 1938, by a decree of the then president, Lázaro Cárdenas, who overnight expropriated foreign private companies that had previously extracted Mexican oil, declaring the reserves public property. This day, known in history as Expropiación petrolera, has been celebrated every year since as a public holiday.

However, over the past decades, Pemex has increasingly stood out for its mismanagement and the corruption that prevailed there. "Corruption is everywhere, in all departments, at all hierarchical levels," Adrian Lajous Vargas, himself a former head of Pemex, revealed to the daily La Jornada. With a debt of over 100 billion dollars, the company has the dubious honor of being the most indebted oil company. Peña Nieto promised to modernize Pemex, counting on foreign private investors. The reform met fierce opposition. In parliament, Antonio García, a left-wing deputy, stripped down to his underwear to protest the plan. But Peña Nieto's Institutional Revolutionary Party (PRI) held the necessary majorities in the states that needed approval, and the new law was adopted in December 2013. Seventy-five years after the Expropiación petrolera, Mexico's oil was once again open to the private sector.

Among the potential buyers was Sierra Oil and Gas, Mexico's first private and independent extraction company. In September 2014, the company announced that it had secured about $525 million in investment for development, drilling, and extraction. Among the investors was Infraestructura Institucional, better known as I Cuadrada. Eight months later, in June 2015, BlackRock acquired I Cuadrada for $71 million. "Excellent timing," commented the authors of a BlackRock Transparency Project investigation into Mexico. A month after the acquisition, Sierra, a company that had never drilled a single well, easily obtained the authorization for oil extraction granted to private companies.

I Cuadrada also financed projects for Juan Armando Hinojosa and his group, Grupo Higa. Hinojosa is very close to Peña Nieto. When the latter was still governor of the State of Mexico, Hinojosa's companies were already receiving numerous public orders. But apparently also private orders. In 2014, journalists discovered that the luxury villa La Casa Blanca located in Las Lomas, the chic district of the capital where Peña Nieto and his wife Angélica Rivera, a pop singer and telenovela actress, planned to move after the end of his term, did not belong to the couple but to Hinojosa, who had built it for the president and his family. The generous entrepreneur had also sold a villa to Finance Minister Luis Videgaray at a favorable price. Following this revelation, the government canceled a contract for the construction of an express train line between Mexico City and Querétaro. The group involved was a consortium led by Chinese companies and also included Hinojosa's Grupo Higa. Peña Nieto apologized for the La Casa Blanca scandal in 2016.

Asked about the acquisition of I Cuadrada, BlackRock stated that it had carefully checked in advance whether the agreement complied with the ethical standards that the firm applies in each country. "As a trustee of our clients, we subject all projects and transactions to thorough risk assessments," explained a spokesperson for the company. The evaluation concerned I Cuadrada and not Grupo Higa.

2015 was a busy year for BlackRock in Mexico. In March, BlackRock agreed to finance, along with Pemex and First Reserve, a private equity firm specializing in energy projects, the construction of a 450-kilometer gas pipeline crossing the Sierra Madre, named Los Ramones II. The order was placed with TAG, a Pemex subsidiary, but the company that would build the pipeline was Odebrecht Infrastructure Latin America. This Brazilian company, founded by German immigrants in the 1940s, has, among other projects, the construction of the Caracas metro, ports in Cuba, and facilities for the 2014 FIFA World Cup in Brazil. In June 2015, Marcelo Odebrecht, the CEO and descendant of the founders, was arrested. The family business became the center of one of the largest corruption scandals in Latin America - which is saying something. Investigations were opened in a dozen countries, and Odebrecht executives confessed to the US Department of Justice that they had paid around $800 million in bribes between 2001 and 2015. The total scope of the affair will probably remain unmatched. In 2016, the company finally paid $2.6 billion to US regulators and Swiss authorities to settle the matter. Odebrecht himself was sentenced to 19 years in prison.

There are also allegations of corruption against Emilio Lozoya, head of Pemex at the time of the energy agreement with BlackRock. Lozoya first went into hiding, before being arrested in February 2020 in the bourgeois enclave of Marbella, Spain, and then extradited to his native country. The accusation includes, among other things, his dealings with Odebrecht and tax evasion. Lozoya denies all allegations.

BlackRock, on the other hand, has never been investigated for corruption in Mexico.

In early 2017, New Yorkers further strengthened their position by taking back their former partner First Reserve, thus also appropriating the Los Ramones share that First Reserve held. The package also included a refinery and a wind farm. BlackRock then sold the shares of Los Ramones, an operation whose profits benefited not only BlackRock's clients, as emphasized by a company spokesperson: the project also gave the Mexican industry access to cheap natural gas from the United States and brought new capital into the country through the sale to a new investor.

Nevertheless, BlackRock also benefited somewhat by investing in I Cuadrada. Thanks to this, the New Yorkers gained access to the Mexican retirement system. Fink's leitmotif! I Cuadrada had the authorization for two "CKD24" funds, intermediary funds that allow Mexican public pension funds to invest in private equity funds. The money at stake is mainly used for infrastructure projects. For BlackRock, this was ideal: Mexico not only offered a wide range of investment opportunities, but the public sector also provided capital! BlackRock's new man, Rodríguez Regordosa, would certainly be useful. During his time at the Ministry of Finance, he was not only responsible for retirement issues but also involved in the development of infrastructure projects. One of the projects that the Peña Nieto government awarded to Grupo Higa, co-financed by I Cuadrada and now, following the takeover, by BlackRock, was the private highway Toluca-Naucalpan. The route, large parts of which had already been concreted, crosses a forest area used by the Otomis people for their sacred ceremonies. The Otomis communities are still trying to block the completion of the highway through a court and to recover their land. Contrary to Mexican law, they were neither consulted nor considered in the planning. BlackRock states that the project was already part of I Cuadrada's portfolio before the takeover and that the company is only one investor among many others, in fact with the smallest share of financing and not playing an active role in the management of the ongoing project. BlackRock also mentions another project in Mexico, the La Bufa wind farm, which is said to be a good example of an operation involving the local population. Furthermore, the GRESB25, the global benchmark for environmental labeling for real estate and infrastructure investments, is said to have praised BlackRock for other projects in Mexico.

But Enrique Peña Nieto's term was coming to an end, and BlackRock apparently feared that the friendly environment in Mexico that Fink had been so fond of would also disappear. A fear not without foundation. The scandals of the EPN government, as Mexicans called it, had made it difficult for candidates from his party. Corruption was not the only issue; the brutal violence of drug cartels had also intensified under his term, contrary to his promises. In December 2017, Andrés Manuel Lopéz Obrador, known as AMLO, declared his candidacy for the presidency. The leader of the Morena party, a left-wing populist movement, had strongly criticized the opening of the energy sector to private investors. He announced his intention to hold a referendum on the matter. For Fink & Co., this measure resembled an expulsion from paradise. A few weeks before the summer 2018 elections, BlackRock addressed the wealthy private clients of the Santander bank with a presentation entitled "Dive into the 2018 Mexican Election," warning that the Mexican economy would deteriorate if AMLO won.

A warning that must have offended the candidate, whom Fink had already met in a conversation that future Finance Minister Carlos Urzúa Macías described as "friendly." Urzúa Macías later emphasized to Reuters that AMLO was by no means a radical. "We are not extreme left, we are center-left," he told journalists. Consequently, the referendum was no longer on the agenda. But AMLO's promise to end corruption and his criticism of politicians close to American interests, whom he called the "power mafia," appealed to the electorate. In July 2018, he won the election by a landslide.

The alarm bells that had sounded on 52nd Street in New York quickly quieted down. Once in office, AMLO proved to be more than accommodating. In March 2020, he met with Fink again for another "friendly" conversation. The head of BlackRock expressed interest in investing in the Tren Maya, an $8 billion railway project to link the tourist centers of the Yucatán Peninsula. A month later, the two men met again, but this time by video conference due to the pandemic. This time, it was AMLO who had a proposal, asking for Fink's help in creating a Marshall Plan for developing countries severely affected by the pandemic to help revive their economies.

The Mexican president did not call the World Bank or the International Monetary Fund. He turned to a major private investor. The world now belongs to BlackRock. We are only tenants there.

A Frozen Digital Universe

Aladdin's algorithms are part of this world. There is obviously the issue of security and data protection. But it's the less tangible aspects that create discomfort. Adam Curtis, a British documentary filmmaker, has identified a more subtle threat posed by BlackRock. In his work, Curtis mainly deals with power and how it is exercised in society. In July 2014, he published a text on his BBC blog entitled "The Hidden Systems That Freeze Time and Prevent Us from Changing the World." It discusses the combination of constant surveillance and digitization. One of his examples: recommendations, like those that the online retail company Amazon suggests to its customers. An algorithm analyzes previous orders based on patterns, creates a buyer profile based on them, and then makes offers for products that match the customer's tastes as sifted through. What bothers Curtis about this: we are defined by our past decisions.

Those called digital trackers, which American politicians are increasingly confronted with, are less harmless. Trackers work for the opponent's election campaign and store speeches, interviews with the press, and citizens of the targeted politician. They look for contradictions with his previous statements. Changing one's mind becomes a risk to avoid for politicians. It also makes it more difficult to seek compromise, which could partly explain the polarization of American politics. But Curtis continues to hammer home: "Throughout the West, new systems have been created whose task is to constantly record the present and compare it with the past, which has been recorded. The aim is to recognize patterns - coincidences and correlations - in order to find ways to prevent changes," writes Curtis. Ultimately, the effect of all these systems is to lock us into a giant refrigerator. One of these freezing systems, discovered by Curtis: Aladdin. BlackRock's superbrain, which analyzes $20 trillion. Curtis believes that in some respects BlackRock is more powerful than traditional politics. What scares Curtis about Aladdin is not the possibility for BlackRock to change the world with it but, on the contrary, the attempt to delay change via a system like Aladdin.

A system that prevents risks does not want change. And there is no change without risk.

In this sense, BlackRock's rise is a change that harbors new risks. Risks we must face. And at the same time, there is great irony in this: avoiding risk is precisely BlackRock's mission. But when Fink and his troops seek to fulfill this mission diligently, they themselves create new dangers.

CHAPTER 11

Larry Fink Hasn't Said His Last Word

No one has transformed the financial markets as enduringly since J.P. Morgan. But unlike the latter, Fink is not an American Medici prince, enveloped in velvet and silk. Fink knows how dangerous it would be for BlackRock if his clients, namely pension fund managers, were to learn that he leads a lavish lifestyle in the headlines of the infamous "page six," full of gossip, of the New York Post. In interviews, he prefers to talk about his preference for train travel. For a long time, he took regular flights instead of using the Gulfstream private jet, a common practice among billionaires and Wall Street elite (BlackRock holds a stake in General Dynamics, the parent company of the luxury aircraft manufacturer). This corresponds to the image that Fink wants to convey: that of a frugal asset manager, the foremost servant of his investors. But Fink does indulge in the privileges that come with his ascent.

Shaded dirt paths wind through forests and gently rising meadows, passing by crystalline streams. Behind dense hedges and discreet fences, four kilometers long, one occasionally catches a glimpse of shining roofs, but they are too far away to distinguish the buildings. In front of them, horse parks, cows sometimes. At the crossroads, centuries-old oaks stretch their gnarled branches above the weathered stone walls. Silence. This is how one imagines the universe of the English aristocracy before industrialization. But we are in North Salem, a good hour by train and 20 minutes by car from the office towers and skyscrapers of Manhattan.

North Salem is so discreet that it is known only to insiders. "We don't want publicity," declared a resident interviewed by the New York Times. "We don't want people to learn about this place, to come here and ruin everything with their big feet." If you drive around in a small car, you quickly attract suspicious looks. A lady on horseback, followed by her dog, waves to the disruptive driver with a vigorous movement of her gloved hand to ask him to slow down. At Farmer and the Fish, a café located in a whitewashed colonial house dating back to before the War of Independence, a fire crackles in the fireplace and men in camouflage attire sit at the bar, baseball caps pulled down over their heads. But to mistake them for simple farmers would be a mistake. The sports watches look as casual as they are expensive, and they gulp down a dozen oysters with their beer. Not far away, after a tangle of streets, alleys, and finally, driveways, you arrive at a farm worthy of a children's book, which the American artist Grandma Moses could not have painted more beautifully. This is Fink's farm. Here he is, the gentleman farmer, here he is. A kind of Disneyland farm, as his own brother, a Silicon Valley investor, mockingly called it. There, on 18 hectares of land, Fink raises horses.

And he collects works of art—not French impressionists or American minimalists like those bought for hundreds of millions at Sotheby's or Christie's by his hedge fund colleagues. Fink collects American folk art. For example, old weather vanes. "Suitable for those whose activity must react to the unpredictable market changes," wrote the British magazine The Economist, lightly mocking Fink's down-to-earth pastime. His investment in the record label Octone is also out of the ordinary. One of the label's early signings was Maroon 5, a pop rock band from California, just like Fink, created by a few high school friends in the early 2000s—the first album, Songs About Jane, was a success—and Maroon 5 even played at BlackRock's Christmas party. However, Octone no longer exists in this form.

Larry and his wife Lori also bought a house in Aspen. Thanks to its fine powder, the old mining town in the Colorado Rocky Mountains has become a ski resort that the American elite invades just in time for the winter season, like migratory birds. In the past, adventurers came here to make their fortune by digging in the mines, but today, it is people who have already made their fortune elsewhere. And it is not surprising that real estate in Aspen is one of the most expensive in the country. However, at the Aspen land registry office, their names cannot be found. The owners of "chalets" or "mountain retreats," which easily cost tens of millions, are usually "camouflaged" in the administration, registered under the names of trust companies through which celebrities manage their properties. Depending on their temperament, they are either uninspired, like "Trust Company II," boastful, like "Goldader Investments," or playful, like "Welpe Smith." American oligarchs do not want their address published.

And the new offices, where BlackRock plans to move by 2023, also suggest that the former outsiders are ultimately not so different from the rest of the financial sector. It will be one of the skyscrapers rising in the Hudson Yards district, like steel and glass stalagmites. The redevelopment of the former railway site cost $25 billion. It is the largest private real estate project in American history. The four thousand luxury apartments, upscale restaurants, and shopping center, which includes stores like Cartier, Gucci, Chanel, and Fendi, are de facto a gated community for billionaires, as an architectural critic summarized in the New York Times. In the office towers, which are not yet all finished, L'Oréal USA, the German software publisher SAP, the Californian financial group Wells Fargo, and the private equity firms of KKR will move in. And BlackRock. For another reason, this location does not really fit with the image of a trustee for the little people that Fink likes to portray: New York taxpayers, most of whom cannot even afford an aperitif in the establishments of this complex, subsidized the Hudson Yards project with over $4 billion. Critics doubt that this public financial assistance will be offset in the near future by job creation and increased tax revenue.

Thus, Fink exhibits almost all the outward signs of success characteristic of a Wall Street tycoon. Almost all. His work still lacks one final stone that would be its crowning glory.

At the end of their careers, one of the customs of these envied finance men is to go "serve the community," as it is nicely put in official speeches. In other words, to hold as prestigious positions as possible in Washington: executive positions in various ministries and authorities, or, like two former Goldman bosses, Treasury Secretary. Robert Rubin was Bill Clinton's Treasury Secretary, as was Hank Paulson in the George W. Bush administration. Larry Fink, a Democrat, was one of Obama's early supporters, and rumors have long claimed that he could be called to Washington. This did not happen. According to some rumors, he would have had his chances under Hillary Clinton's presidency. The Clintons have never made a secret of their relaxed relationship with the moneyed class. Their daughter Chelsea married in 2010, not far from Fink's farm, a former Goldman banker who now runs a hedge fund. But Donald Trump put an end to these ambitions by choosing former Goldman Sachs banker and Hollywood producer Steve Mnuchin, a second or even third-tier choice on Wall Street.

Larry thus had no choice but to bravely remain at the top of his financial kingdom.

But his position is becoming increasingly uncomfortable. Take Fink's commitment to climate change. As described earlier, BlackRock cannot simply sell shares of oil companies or coal mining companies if they are part of an index and, therefore, an ETF that BlackRock offers corresponding to that index. The Covid-19 crisis exposed Fink's insoluble problem like never before. As soon as the Federal Reserve announced in March 2020 that BlackRock would develop the criteria for purchasing corporate bonds, Republican senators spoke up: those billions had to also buy bonds from oil companies and coal mining companies. A necessity that does not quite align with Fink's call, claiming the opportunity offered by the crisis to make the economy more climate-friendly. Environmental activists promptly accused the head of BlackRock of not keeping his green promises, which were probably made half-heartedly. In front of the company's headquarters in New York, they released a balloon symbolizing BlackRock's climate protection policy: hot air.

Fink has also strained his relationships with the primarily conservative investor class by, for example, asking companies to no longer exclusively aim for shareholder value maximization. "Perhaps he will now realize that the left will never forgive him for making a fortune as a capitalist, even if he now refuses to defend capitalism," angrily commented the Wall Street Journal.

The Covid-19 crisis was not the only thing shaking the world in the first months of 2020. After the murder of George Floyd, an African American, by a white police officer in Minneapolis, protests erupted not only in the United States but around the world. One of the demands of protesters in the United States was to "Defund the police," cut its funding. After the terrorist attacks of September 11, law enforcement received military equipment and their budgets were increased. According to activists, these funds should be redirected to programs that help disadvantaged people. Instead of reacting to the consequences of social inequality with oppression and police violence, the causes must be addressed.

Like many business leaders, Fink also apparently felt compelled to speak out following Floyd's death. In a letter to his "colleagues," he said he was "horrified" by this act, reassuring all employees who "suffer from these tragedies" that the company's management was on their side and listening to them. However, the Color of Change association did not really appreciate Fink's warm words. For three consecutive years, Fink attended the annual gala of the New York Police Foundation, the last time in April 2019. Thanks to this event, the New York Police Department, which at the time had an annual budget of six billion dollars, raised additional private funds, which, according to the foundation's statutes, were used to train, equip, and reward citizens who anonymously provided information leading to the arrest of violent criminals. BlackRock's CEO was not the only donor from Wall Street. Representatives from Goldman Sachs, Morgan Stanley, the Thyssen Investor Foundation, and hedge fund manager Paul Singer were also present. The amount of Fink's donations to the police foundation is not known. For Jade Magnus Ogunnaike, however, this is not the decisive factor. The deputy director of Color of Change explained to the specialized magazine Institutional Investors that Fink was a driver for the financial sector: "BlackRock is an extremely important organization." Even if Fink only donated $1,000 a year to the police foundation, the symbolic meaning would still be there. His support is problematic in light of the behavior of the New York police toward protesters. During the mainly peaceful protests of June 2020, a police officer violently pushed back a crowd with his patrol car, another hit a protester with the door of his car. Other officers hit passersby with batons. Ogunnaike told journalists that Color of Change, following Fink's letter regarding George Floyd's death, had reached out to BlackRock to propose a private conversation. "No reaction." Hence her conclusion: "They just want to continue as before."

BlackRock's rise also outlines a society that is becoming less and less cohesive. Provision—for retirement, illness, unemployment—is increasingly the responsibility of the individual. Everyone fights to save their skin. Those who do not earn enough to save and do not inherit are out of luck. We are thus creating ever greater distance between those who have and those who have nothing. Of course, Larry Fink is not responsible for this development, but he has benefited from it, and so has BlackRock.

It is equally true that Larry personally campaigned for more social justice. In his annual letter to the CEOs of companies in BlackRock's portfolios in 2018, he was categorical: "Society demands that companies serve a social purpose. Every company must not only deliver financial performance, but also show how it makes a positive contribution to society."

Fink has turned the small branch that BlackRock was at its inception into a global player, unique in its gigantic size and unprecedented firepower. But this is precisely what makes it almost impossible for him and his colleagues to realize these noble intentions in terms of climate protection or social justice. Despite their individual good intentions. BlackRock, one could say, has emancipated itself from its founders.

New York, June 2020. After weeks, the first stores are allowed to reopen; soon, it will be the turn of hairdressers and fitness studios. Restaurants will soon be able to welcome a limited number of customers indoors. Andrew Cuomo, the governor of New York State, promised this. However, for many New York institutions, it is already too late. They have closed their doors forever. Like the Paris Café, which was located in the old fishing port of South Street Seaport and did not serve coffee, contrary to what its name indicated, but beer and fish & chips. Since 1873. "Without it being anyone else's fault other than this epidemic, we are unable to find an economically reasonable way out," wrote the last managers on their Facebook page. One restaurant owner predicted that up to 40% of pubs and restaurants in New York would eventually disappear. The crisis not only affects gastronomy. The situation was already bleak before the crisis for retailers who were not Amazon or Walmart. In May 2020, Mark Zandi, chief economist at Moody's Analytics (an investment consulting firm), wrote in a report to his clients that he would not be surprised if more than a million microenterprises with fewer than ten employees were to close in the United States alone.

Large companies are also suffering from the crisis. But thanks to their size, they have access to liquidity. The flood of money from central banks has made debts cheaper than ever for companies. And they can invest in new distribution channels while the virus sweeps away the competition.

Still, the concentration movement began well before the pandemic. Covid-19 has only accelerated the monopolistic trend. Amazon was already an overwhelming competitor for traditional retailers. The crisis has made Jeff Bezos's online giant (who originally wanted to call his company "Relentless") an indispensable auxiliary in our lives. Even those who do not directly order from Amazon cannot escape the group. In their distress, small suppliers have started selling on Amazon to reach customers. And competition authorities? "Bezos, who compared his warehouse workers and couriers to medical personnel fighting Covid-19, is betting that Amazon's stronger position will not provoke a new reaction from competition authorities, even though they are already targeting the company," Bloomberg wrote during the crisis.

Larry Fink's BlackRock will also emerge stronger from the crisis. It is true that investors initially withdrew their money—by June, assets under management were down to $6.5 trillion—but, like Amazon, Walmart, and Google, the top asset manager will benefit from the market upheaval. Soon, Fink's giant squid will tighten its tentacles even more around our economy.

Unless antitrust regulators and financial controllers finally launch a fight against its stranglehold. This is only possible if we make this fight our political cause. The future of BlackRock also depends on us.

In 1988, no one would have believed that Larry Fink would build a global colossus from a back office, making him the most influential financier of his time. No one can match BlackRock in size, influence, and reach. No one knows what consequences such a financial system will have for all of us. It is time for that to change. And for light to be shed on the black giant.

Don't miss out!

Visit the website below and you can sign up to receive emails whenever Edward Branson publishes a new book. There's no charge and no obligation.

https://books2read.com/r/B-A-KPLMC-TBHDF

BOOKS 2 READ

Connecting independent readers to independent writers.

Also by Edward Branson

The Emergence of BlackRock
El surgimiento del Black Rock
The Secret Empire BlackRock

www.ingramcontent.com/pod-product-compliance
Lightning Source LLC
Chambersburg PA
CBHW070744160726
48004CB00001B/49